ENCHANTMENT

The Life of Audrey Hepburn

Donald Spoto

THREE RIVERS PRESS • NEW YORK

Originally published in hardcover in the United States by Harmony Books,
an imprint of the Crown Publishing Group, a division of Random House Inc.,
New York, in 2006.

Library of Congress Cataloging-in-Publication Data
Spoto, Donald.
Enchantment : the life of Audrey Hepburn / Donald Spoto.—1st ed.
Includes bibliographical references and index.
1. Hepburn, Audrey, 1929–1993.   2. Motion picture actors and actresses—
United States—Biography.   I. Title.
PN2287.H43S66   2006
791.4302'8092—dc22   2006000584

ISBN: 978-0-307-23759-0

Printed in the United States of America

Design by Lauren Dong

Title page photograph: Paramount/The Kobal Collection/Fraker, Bud

10 9 8 7

First Paperback Edition

for
Ole Flemming Larsen

~

"...right next to the right one..."

Tim Christensen,
Danish composer and lyricist

Contents

*"It was the coming true
that was the proof of the enchantment."*

HENRY JAMES, *The Sacred Fount* (1901)

Acknowledgments

DURING THE COURSE of my research, many people who knew, worked with and had professional and personal connections to Audrey Hepburn shared their memories and impressions with me. Among them, I am grateful most of all to Jacqueline Bisset, Patricia Bosworth, Karen Cadle, Christa Roth, Marian Seldes, Michael Tilson Thomas, Frederica von Stade, Robert Wagner, Martha Hyer Wallis, John Waxman, Arthur Wilde, Audrey Wilder and Roger Young.

Andrew Lownie kindly put me in contact with Adrian Weale, one of England's experts in the field of military intelligence, who enabled me to clarify important details about Audrey's father.

Not for the first time in my career, the personnel at the Margaret Herrick Library of the Academy of Motion Picture Arts and Sciences, Beverly Hills, provided me with expert help and guidance. Stacey Behlmer, Coordinator of Special Projects and Research Assistance, pointed me to many items I might otherwise have overlooked; at every stage of this project, she offered the most generous, enthusiastic and friendly support. Her colleagues were similarly gracious, each offering particular contributions: Barbara Hall, Research Archivist; Sandra Archer, Head of Reference Services; Faye Thompson, Photograph Department Coordinator; Kristine Krueger, of the National Film Information Service at the Herrick; Jonathan Wahl, Library Page Supervisor; and staff members Matthew Severson and Kevin Wilkerson.

At the University of Southern California, Los Angeles, I was fortunate once again to have the invaluable aid of Ned Comstock, Archivist in the Doheny Memorial Library; and of Haden Guest, Curator of the Warner Bros. Archives.

In the last years of her life, Audrey Hepburn gave herself tirelessly to the causes of UNICEF, the United Nations International Children's Fund. In Denmark, Anne Tennant helped me to contact the right colleagues at UNICEF's New York offices. There, I met a remarkable team of dedicated people who made available to me documents of singular significance detailing Audrey's years of service to UNICEF. I offer deep thanks to Adhiratha Keefe, John Manfredi, Fran Silverberg and Upasana Young. UNICEF also granted me permission to publish important photos; in this regard, I received very kind assistance from Ellen Tolmie and Nicole Toutounji. Also in the New York office, I must acknowledge Gloria Adwutum, Margaret Majuk, Patricia Moccia, Edwin Ramirez, Sharad Sapra, Veronica Theodoro and Maria Zanca.

Thanks to the kindness of Library Supervisor Gary Browning at the Museum of Television and Radio in Beverly Hills, I was able to view Audrey Hepburn's early television performances.

Simone Potter, Senior Picture Researcher at the British Film Institute, cleared my way to finding some of the telling photos in the book.

Rose Puntillo, Business Center Representative at the Beverly Wilshire Hotel, Beverly Hills, provided helpful and generous office assistance.

⁓

THOMAS SMITH was my research assistant in London; I acknowledge him with my thanks and admiration. He tracked down obscure texts, scoured archives and libraries for rare articles and essays and applied his first-rate scholarship at every stage. In the United States, I was fortunate to have the help of Destiny Leake, who helped me locate important letters in the Beinecke Rare Book and Manuscript Library at Yale University. Frank Turner, Library Director of the Beinecke, supervises an admirable staff—among them Naomi Saito, Public Services Assistant.

Debra Campbell, chair of the Department of Religious Studies at Colby College in Waterville, Maine, graciously provided me with a copy of her elegantly written and scholarly paper, "The Nun and the Crocodile," which clarified several fine points in the life of the novelist Kathryn Hulme, one of Audrey's closest friends.

Bernard Dick, author and scholar, pointed out to me important aspects of Lillian Hellman's play *The Children's Hour* and its film version.

The esteemed playwright and screenwriter Robert Anderson has been a devoted friend and an advocate of my writing for more than thirty years. During many long conversations, he confided his relationship with Audrey, entrusting the details without restriction. I am grateful for his trust.

My brother-in-law, John Møller, is a talented graphic designer and a superb technician with a fund of creative ideas: he performed miracles as he transferred dozens of Audrey Hepburn photographs onto disks. This painstaking task, requiring an artist's eye and many arduous days, John dispatched with a cheerful, generous dedication of his time.

For various kindnesses extended to me during the course of my work, I express my warm thanks to Mary-Kelly Busch; Mart Crowley; Mary Evans; Lewis Falb and Gerald Pinciss; Mike Farrell and Shelley Fabares; Joshua Robison; and Erica Wagner. As always, Mona and Karl Malden have a special claim on my gratitude for their loving endorsement of me and my work.

For almost thirty years, I have been represented by my incomparable friend, Elaine Markson, who has guided my career so judiciously and with such wise affection. She and her colleagues—Gary Johnson, Geri Thoma and Julia Kenny—are, each and all, very dear to me indeed.

From day one of this project, I was fortunate to have the enthusiastic and warm support of Shaye Areheart, a generous, discerning and perceptive publisher. To my editor, Julia Pastore, I offer very many thanks for her constant friendliness, her alacrity, her astute comments on the manuscript, and her shrewd suggestions where improvement was indicated. In Julia's office, Kate Kennedy dispatched numerous tasks cheerfully and efficiently, and Janet Biehl was my meticulous and attentive copy editor.

AUDREY HEPBURN would have admired and loved Ole Flemming Larsen, whose name appears on the dedication page. A respected academic and a gifted artist, he spent many evenings watching and discussing her films with me. All during the course of my research, he contributed valuable ideas, and then he listened patiently as I read aloud parts of the manuscript. Most of all, Ole has blessed my life with very great serenity and happiness, the consequence of devotion deep and true. For that and for so much, I am grateful every day, far beyond my ability to express. I share this book with him, as I do my life.

Part One

FIRST STEPS
[1929–1950]

At school in England, 1938.

Chapter One

~

1929 – 1939

THERE HAD BEEN bright sunshine when they left the English shore, but midway across the Channel, dark clouds swept overhead, and the wind had shifted from breezy to almost gale force. Now, as the ship headed for the Continent, they were suddenly caught in a late-winter storm. Cold rain whipped across the deck and stung their faces as the ferry rolled and pitched. Years later, the baroness could not recall feeling any anxiety during the crossing, and therefore she had not communicated any fear to her two small boys as they steadied themselves against her.

This squall was far less threatening than the typhoon she had once endured in the South China Sea; nor was it as threatening as the violent conditions that routinely battered the ships that had taken her from Asia to South America or from the Netherlands to the East Indies. Thanks to the composure of the Dutch baroness, her eight- and four-year-old sons could face the heavy weather cheerfully. But if she did not hold their hands tightly, the wind might easily sweep the children overboard. Better to take them inside for hot chocolate.

On her way to the ferry's café, the baroness passed her husband in the small, smoky lounge bar. Warming himself with Irish whiskey, he glanced toward her but did not interrupt his conversation with a fellow passenger. Her husband was not the boys' father—they were sons from her first marriage. And from his diffidence, no one in the room would have guessed that he had any connection to this handsome, patrician woman and her two docile children. She heard him tell his drinking partner that he had left England to take up a new position in Belgium with great prospects. Indeed, she hoped for the best, for him as for herself and the boys: if at last he could hold a job longer than a month or two without succumbing to indolence—well, that might help secure the marriage, too. He was her second husband, and they had been married for three years; during that entire time, she reckoned that he had not worked a total of three months.

Her first husband had jumped from the matrimonial ship five years after their wedding, which was just four years ago, and she was left with two small boys when she was twenty-five; now, domestic storm clouds were once again on the horizon. And she was seven months pregnant.

She had some financial resources and a share of ancestral property, for her family was of old European aristocracy. And she had a title: she was the Dutch Baroness Ella van Heemstra, now also Mrs. Ruston. Dutch baronesses were not a rare breed even in 1929; most democratic Netherlanders did not mind the last of the noble gentry using venerable titles—but only if their holders adopted no airs and graces and imitated the Dutch royal family, an amiably down-to-earth clan.

The four travelers reached Brussels safely and proceeded to a rented house. There, with the help of a relative who arrived from Holland, the baroness prepared for the child's birth while her husband went off to his job with a British insurance company as a minor clerk with no confidential duties. He was bored from the first day.

On the morning of Saturday, May 4, the baroness went into labor, and by mid-afternoon she was nursing her newborn daughter. "Saturday's child works hard for a living," according to Mother Goose.

ELLA, THE BARONESS van Heemstra, was born in the fashionable Dutch suburb of Velp, near Arnhem, on June 12, 1900. One of nine children, she was the daughter of Baron Arnoud Jan Adolf van Heemstra (once the governor of Dutch Guiana in South America—later Surinam) and his wife, the Baroness Elbrig Wilhelmine Henrietta van Asbeck; both families were titled aristocrats. The precise reasons for the baronetcies remain unclear, but in each case both sets of Ella's grandparents were respected jurists or judges with a long history of service to Crown and country. Their children, Ella's parents, inherited the titles according to the custom of the time.

Ella's childhood was not underprivileged: her parents owned a country mansion, a city house and a summer cottage, and they employed a small platoon of servants who attended them everywhere. Photos taken of Ella in her mid-twenties show a strikingly attractive woman with fine features, dark hair, a clear, translucent complexion and a certain dignified smile, neither girlish, coy nor seductive. She was, in other words, every bit the image of a somewhat Germanic-Victorian aristocrat, and it was, of course, the Germanic-Victorian style (overstuffed in furniture and formal in demeanor) that was the standard all over Europe—if not among the royal families, certainly among their social rivals, the landed gentry.

At the age of nineteen, Ella concluded a respectable but undemanding upper-class education, at which she excelled mostly in singing and amateur theatricals, to the point where she expressed a desire to become an opera singer. Her parents thought little of that and instead purchased her a first-class ticket on a long steamship journey to visit relatives who worked for Dutch colonial companies in Batavia—the Latin name in the Netherlands for what was later called Jakarta—in the Dutch East Indies (later Indonesia).

There Ella blossomed and flourished. Much in demand for her fine voice, which she put to good use entertaining at parties; for her clever repartee and her air of sophistication; and for her genteel flirtatiousness, Ella impressed many eligible young men and their parents in the colonies. On March 11, 1920—five months after her arrival and three months before her twentieth birthday—Ella's parents traveled to Batavia for her marriage to Hendrik Gustaaf Adolf Quarles van Ufford, who was six years her senior and held a respectable job. Business was thriving that year in the Indies, at least partly because at home the Netherlands began to experience a severe depression and relied on the colonies more than ever.

Van Ufford's mother was a baroness with a respected Dutch and French pedigree, and everything augured well for a happy and profitable union. On December 5 of that same year, Ella bore a son they named Arnoud Robert Alexander Quarles van Ufford (always known as Alex); and on August 27, 1924, they welcomed Ian Edgar Bruce Quarles van Ufford. But things soon went very wrong. When Hendrik returned to the Netherlands at Christmas 1924 to discuss a transfer from Batavia, Ella and the toddlers accompanied him. Early in 1925, she and her husband registered their divorce in Arnhem, for reasons that may forever remain unclear.

At once, van Ufford took ship for San Francisco, where (he said) he had a good offer of work; there, he soon met and married a German immigrant named Marie Caroline Rohde. With that, Hendrik Quarles van Ufford removed himself from the lives of Ella and their two sons; the public record shows only that he returned to the Netherlands years later, where he died on July 14, 1955, at the age of sixty.

And so, that spring of 1925, the twenty-four-year-old Baroness Ella van Heemstra van Ufford was left with two babies and no husband. Her friends in Holland noted that she had become somewhat imperious, perhaps from defensiveness about the dissolution of her marriage, but she had a title, a Dutch home with her parents and a nanny for her sons.

These benefits notwithstanding, Ella surprised her parents by returning to Batavia, and there she renewed a friendship she had earlier formed with a dashing, courtly Englishman she had met even while her marriage was foundering. Joseph Victor Anthony Ruston, eleven years older than Ella, was born November 21, 1889, in Onzic, Bohemia, where his London-born father, Victor John Ruston, had worked and where he had married a local girl named Anna Catherina Wels. Joseph's maternal grandmother's maiden name was Kathleen Hepburn.

When Joseph and Ella were reunited that spring of 1926, he was still married to Cornelia Wilhelmina Bisschop, a Dutch woman he had married in the East Indies. They were living entirely on her family inheritance, which was certainly helpful, for Ruston never really had any sort of career—nor much of a desire for one. Later identified by Hepburn biographers as an Anglo-Irish banker, he was neither Irish nor a banker; "the sad truth is, he never really hung on to any job," according to one of his grandsons. But he had a calm manner, a handsome expression, dark eyes like velvet (according to Ella's description) and, thanks to Cornelia, a fine wardrobe. He sported a little moustache like an artist's brush, and he photographed well; it was not difficult to understand his appeal to Ella, who in any case was eager to find a new father for her boys.

She had every reason to expect that a man with a good job could be found. The direct rule by the Netherlands over the Dutch

East Indies had greatly expanded since 1900, and Dutch strategies to control both the economy and tax revenues meant that virtually every exported item was shipped through Batavia.

Joseph found Ella cultivated, elegant and as enamored of the good life as he, and they enjoyed attending cotillions, military parades, fine restaurants and sporting events. But Ella's greatest appeal was her title—about which he joked so often that she recognized how seriously he took it. Never mind that the title was a centuries-old honorific used by other ladies in Batavia—and never mind that Ella took an office job to support herself and her boys. Joseph, besotted with all things that had a trace of the upper classes, took to introducing her as his friend, the baroness. He understood quite clearly that marriage would not promote him to a baronetcy, yet he greatly valued her background and breeding, and perhaps most of all, he saw her family's affluence as a very comfortable cushion in life—indeed, as a plush settee on which he could, when so inclined, rest and relax.

Cornelia, meanwhile, apparently complaisant and much on her own, luxuriated in the rarefied precincts of colonial life, with a home lavishly appointed in ivory and gold (common for the white Europeans), and there was no shortage of natives to look after their needs. Daily life among the wealthy could neatly be described in terms of a Somerset Maugham novel: the setting was not a dreary backwater outpost but a rather chic preserve for the few advantaged foreigners who controlled the economy.

When Joseph said he could obtain a speedy divorce from his wife, Ella accepted his proposal. Fortunately, Cornelia Bisschop Ruston made no objections, for she had romantic interests elsewhere. Papers were drawn up, signed and countersigned on all sides, there was a quick divorce, and on September 7, 1926, Ella and Joseph were married.

For a brief time, the baroness was flattered by her handsome husband, who was at least a presentable escort in society. But she was also alert, and soon she became impatient with his idle and morose comportment. Alas, Joseph Ruston was revealing himself as a common adventurer who had married her for access to her money and the chance to live in the capacious light of her aristocratic family. He made no effort to work for a living, and he seemed to have an excuse when, in November, a Communist revolt caused massive rioting and was put down only with great difficulty. How, he protested, could he go out to work in so unstable a colony? From this time, Joseph Ruston's conversations were peppered with fervent anti-Communist declamations.

But languor, political tirades and the trivialities of social life were not in Ella's character, and she had no appreciation of those qualities in others, the general public discord notwithstanding. Within a year of the marriage, there were heated arguments about money, Joseph's idleness and his alarming emotional indifference to her two sons. In muted desperation, Ella wrote to her parents, who suggested that Joseph might do well to meet some of their business associates in London. This he agreed to do; he very much missed England in any case, and he considered London far more agreeable than Batavia. Hence, in late 1928, Joseph, Ella, Ian and Alexander took the long journey from the East Indies to Britain.

They arrived on Christmas Eve and leased a flat in fashionable Mayfair, a few steps from Hyde Park. The holiday season, Joseph insisted, was no time to hunt for employment, and so he waited until February. A colleague of his father-in-law then made Joseph an offer of employment at a British insurance company in Belgium, and in mid-March the baroness and her husband again packed their luggage, boarded the storm-swept ferry for France and then proceeded to Brussels by train.

AT THE END of May, the newborn baby nearly succumbed to whooping cough. She stopped breathing and began to turn blue, and the nanny froze with panic and called out to Ella, who did not know panic. Adding audible prayers to her procedure of turning, spanking and warming the infant, Ella effectively saved her life.

On July 18, ten weeks after their daughter was born, Ella and Joseph Ruston registered the birth with the British vice consulate in Brussels, for the law considered the child English by descent from her father. According to the document, she was born at 48 rue Keyenveld, also called Keienveldstraat, in the Ixelles district, southeast of the center of Brussels. The child's full legal name was Audrey Kathleen Ruston; throughout her life, Audrey carried a British passport.

After World War II and the death of the last Hepburn relative in Joseph's maternal ancestry, he legally changed his surname to Hepburn-Ruston, which he thought very posh. The Hepburn clan, which may be traced centuries back in Scots-Irish history, had dozens of various orthographies, among them Hebburne, Hyburn and Hopbourn. Among his most notable forebears—or so Joseph said—was James Hepburn, Earl of Bothwell and third husband of Mary, Queen of Scots. But the multiple branches on the Hepburn tree and the doubtful genealogies at several critical junctures render difficult any positive verification of this grand assertion.

THE VAN HEEMSTRA–RUSTON house in Brussels was but one of Audrey's childhood residences. She often spent time with her grandparents at their estates in Arnhem, Holland, and outside Arnhem, at Velp. Ella also often took her to visit cousins, most of all when Joseph was absent. He was frequently dispatched to the finance management company's London office, and when he was at home with the family, he often attended political meetings in the city center.

Whenever he returned home from a day's or a week's business,

Joseph was welcomed excitedly by his adoring daughter. But by all accounts, he doted on her no more than he did on Ian and Alex. Ella taught Audrey to read and draw, to enjoy the standard children's classics and good music, and the child longed to show her father what she was learning. But he showed little interest in her, and Audrey's response to his coolness was typical of any child: she redoubled her efforts to win his love and approval—alas, to no avail.

Audrey could always rely on her mother's care, protection and instruction, but (like her husband) Ella was not given to overt displays of affection. A Victorian baroness to her fingertips, she was now more than ever restrained, having lost the spontaneity and gaiety of her youth. She was a serious mother who always had her daughter's best interests at heart, but the warmth in that heart was cooled by her conviction that dignity forestalled cuddling, and that anything more effusive than a perfunctory good-night kiss was indecorous. Much later, Audrey considered that her mother had been greatly hurt by the failure of her first marriage and the obvious emotional bankruptcy of her second.

Photos taken during childhood show an alert, bright-eyed, smiling and poised girl, and if her mother or half-brothers were in the picture, there was usually an impish grin on Audrey's face. She always treated household servants as if they were family friends; she loved to be outdoors and to play the usual games and pranks. Ian and Alex recalled that Audrey accompanied them on country walks and hikes, and they enjoyed playing charades. "And we were sometimes very naughty," according to Ian. "Against Mother's wishes, we did a lot of tree-climbing." But when Audrey was five, her half-brothers were fourteen and eleven, and they were dispatched to boarding school; henceforth, their times together were only occasional.

In time, the clever, resourceful and cheerful child became aware of her parents' increasing arguments and was confused by the cold war that prevailed when they sat down to dinner. The atmosphere became so strained that Audrey often wept in secret, for if she did so in the presence of others, she was scolded. "As a child, I was taught that it was bad manners to bring attention to yourself, and to never, *ever* make a spectacle of yourself . . . I always hear my mother's voice, saying, 'Be on time,' and 'Remember to think of others first,' and 'Don't talk a lot about yourself. You are not interesting. It's the others who matter.' " And of course the marital problems were never discussed in front of the child.

One of the issues was certainly Joseph's right-wing political perspective, which Ella found increasingly bizarre.

Belgium was a stable society, but the collapse of the American economy in the autumn of 1929 triggered a worldwide depression. In Brussels, where the electorate was essentially conservative, the government was granted emergency powers to regulate all trade and commerce at home and abroad—in the Congo, for example, which brought vast revenues from mining. Extremists, revolutionary socialists and German-influenced National Socialists were officially barred from holding office, but their number increased alarmingly.

By 1934, fascists could be found in virtually every government agency in Belgium—not in control, but certainly influential. At the time, Audrey had no idea that her father's political sympathies were so right-wing, that fascist ideology more and more appealed to him, and that he made frequent forays to political assemblies that were comprised of apprentice Nazis.

In fact, both Joseph and Ella had prejudices that embarrassed Audrey Hepburn for the rest of her life.

In the spring of 1935, her parents were collecting funds and recruiting for the British Union of Fascists, under the leadership of the notorious Oswald Mosley. The April 26 issue of *The Blackshirt,* Mosley's fuming weekly, featured a photo of Ella and a ringing endorsement in English so flawless it suggests her husband's hand: "We who have heard the call of Fascism, and have followed the light on the upward road to victory, have been taught to understand what dimly we knew and now fully realize. At last we are breaking the bondage and are on the road to salvation. We who follow Sir Oswald Mosley know that in him we have found a leader whose eyes are not riveted on earthly things, whose inspiration is of a higher plane, and whose idealism will carry Britain along to the bright light of the new dawn of spiritual rebirth."

Eleven days later, Ella and Joseph were lunching with Hitler in Munich, accompanied by several of Mosley's closest allies and three of the Mitford sisters. They returned to Brussels in mid-May, having missed Audrey's birthday.

Soon there was a deep alienation of Joseph from his wife and daughter. Disconsolate, inarticulate, disinclined to work, dependent on his wife and contemptuous of Jewish, Catholic and "colored" people, he seemed never to have anything to say to Ella and Audrey, and this naturally affected his daughter's spirit. "I became a rather moody child, quiet and reticent, and I liked to be by myself a great deal. I seemed to need a great deal of understanding." As for her private playtime: "I didn't care for dolls. They never seemed real to me"; she preferred the companionship of dogs, cats, rabbits and birds, which she drew in chalk and ink with remarkable virtuosity. On the live animals, she lavished the sentiments for which she longed and which her parents were unable to provide. "I myself was born with an enormous need for affection and a terrible need to give it," she said more than once in adulthood.

"When I was little, I embarrassed my mother by trying to pick babies out of prams on the streets and at markets. The one thing I dreamed of in my life was to have children of my own. It always boils down to the same thing [in my life]—not only receiving love but wanting desperately to give it."

Small animals and the children of passersby always received her embraces—such were her attempts "to give it." As for "receiving love," even the semblance of it under the guise of basic domestic security: that was forever shattered when, at the end of May 1935—with no prior threats or warnings—Joseph Ruston packed his clothes and, apparently without a word to anyone, walked out the door into rue Keyenveld, never to return.

According to some third-hand sources, Joseph had squandered much of Ella's living trust and a great deal of the money his father-in-law had settled on him at the time of the marriage. Others claim that he had become an abusive alcoholic. But because the principals remained silent, it is impossible to know for certain the catalyzing events for the separation. Both Ella and Joseph were stern, aloof, critical characters, although in Ella's favor it must be said that her sacrifices on Audrey's behalf, her work to support her daughter's lessons and interests, betokened a real devotion of which Audrey was always convinced. "My mother had great love, but she was not always able to show it . . . Of necessity, my mother became a father, too."

Neither Joseph nor Ella ever wrote or spoke publicly about their marriage or its finale, and Audrey, who was just six at the time, rarely alluded to it in later life, and then only in a few words: "I worshiped my father. Having him cut off from me was terribly awful . . . Leaving us, my father left us insecure—perhaps for life." The departure of her father was, she added in 1989, "the most traumatic event in my life. I remember my mother's reaction . . . [her] face, covered with tears . . . [I was] terrified. What was going to happen to me? The ground had gone out from under me."

According to Audrey's elder son, this abandonment "was a wound that never truly healed," and he claimed that his mother for the rest of her life "never really trusted that love would stay." She once alluded to this when she said that she felt "very insecure about affection—and terribly grateful for it." The abandonment of 1935, she added, "has stayed with me through my own relationships. When I fell in love and got married, I lived in constant fear of being left."

That day made Audrey withdraw from the few friends her mother allowed—a withdrawal that must have been partly from shame; partly from a mixture of sorrow and confusion for which she had no words; and partly from the cloud of guilt that darkens the soul of every child when a parent walks out. Did she do something to cause it? Was she in some way unlovable? Her mother assured her that was not the case. Would her father return? Ella doubted that very much. Would she never again have a father? On this matter, Ella was silent.

"Other kids had a father, but I didn't. I just couldn't bear the idea that I wouldn't see him again. And my mother went through sheer agony when my father left. Because he really left. I think he just went out and never came back. I was destroyed at the time. I cried for days and days. But my mother never, ever put him down." (Yet according to one of Audrey's sons, Ella "spent the war spewing poison about [Ruston], about his disappearance, about his lack of support of any type.")

There was some consolation, however. Audrey's maternal grandparents arrived from Holland and took the girl and her mother to the family home in Arnhem, about fifty miles southeast of Amsterdam, where the old baron had been mayor from 1920 to 1921.

By the time lawyers drew up the terms of a legal separation, Joseph had relocated to London. To the astonishment of Ella's family, he asked for visitation rights with Audrey—and to everyone's shock, Ella granted him those rights. This may have had less to do with compassion for his outcast state than with the fact that Ella had decided to place Audrey in a completely new setting—an English boarding school.

At the time, the notion of sending a well-born six-year-old

child abroad to school was not considered anything but proper, generous and, for the child, an important maturing experience. In addition, Dutch unemployment was at record levels, and some of those without work were offered low-paying jobs in Germany; if they refused to go, their unemployment benefits ceased. There was also public rioting from 1934 over several measures: when women married, for example, they were dismissed from jobs in public administration so that unemployed men with families could take those positions. And in early 1936, severe economic austerity measures were put in place by Prime Minister Hendrik Colijn. Surely, Ella reasoned, things would be calmer in the English countryside than in Holland, where suddenly there was chaos.

Despite her aristocratic bearing and sense of noblesse oblige, Ella was essentially a pragmatist, capable of adapting to life's circumstances and demands; this trait she passed on to her daughter, who was taught that home was where you made it.

If Joseph would see Audrey at school from time to time and bring her to London for a day's outing, Ella believed, things could be better for the child—and the baroness herself would be a frequent visitor. Once again, however, she miscalculated. During the time Audrey attended a small private academy for girls in Kent, she saw her father only four times in as many years. "If I could just have seen him regularly, I would have felt he loved me. I would have felt I had a father."

But something meant more to Ruston than visits with his daughter: he was indeed often in Kent, but he usually dodged the school. (Once, he fetched his daughter and took her for a short trip over southeast England in a small biplane—but such excursions were the exception to his habitual neglect.) The reason for his frequent presence near the school came to light years later. Ruston had for some time been an advocate of Mosley's British Union of Fascists. Now, he was meeting with an old friend who had relocated from Brussels—the notorious Englishman Arthur

Tester, who channeled Nazi propaganda from Germany to the Mosley headquarters in England. According to the British historian David Turner, Tester's partner was Joseph Ruston.

In light of Joseph and Ella's earlier involvement with Mosley and with Hitler, this development is not surprising—and may in fact have been the major reason for Ruston's return to Britain. In any case, it must be added that Ella's connections to the BUF ceased in 1937, and as Nazism became ever more malevolent and murderous, the baroness came to regret her contact with Hitler, her affirmation of Mosley and her endorsement of a cause she had completely misapprehended.

Of her school terms in England, from 1936 to 1939, Audrey later said that at first she was "terrified, but it turned out to be a good lesson in independence . . . I liked the children and the teachers, but I never liked the process of learning in a classroom. I was very restless and could never sit for hours on end. I liked history and mythology and astronomy—but I hated anything to do with arithmetic. School itself I found very dull, and I was happy when I was finished."

But there was one session each week that Audrey very much loved and anticipated: the hours when a London ballet master led the girls in dance classes. Ella visited the school on Audrey's tenth birthday—May 4, 1939. She arrived just in time for a dance recital that featured her daughter. The teacher and her classmates were enthusiastic in their applause, and Audrey was glowing.

Chapter Two

1939–1946

ELLA AND AUDREY spent the summer of 1939 with a family friend near the seaside town of Folkestone, England, where they toured the colorful gardens, admired the Georgian stone houses, lunched at the harbor promenade, strolled along sandy beaches, swam in a protected inlet of the Channel and enjoyed the outdoor band concerts.

Their summer idyll ended suddenly and anxiously during the first four days of September, when Nazi troops invaded Poland; Britain, France, Australia and New Zealand declared war on Germany; and the British Royal Air Force attacked Hitler's navy. With England now at war, Ella—convinced that Germany would never attack neutral Holland—at once took her daughter and headed for her father's estate in peaceful Arnhem. The old baron was delighted to welcome them, not least because a terrible depression had overcome him on the death of his wife five months earlier. Before the end of September, Ella and Audrey were comfortably and securely settled in the sprawling white family mansion. That same month, Ella received the final legal documents confirming the dissolution of her marriage to Joseph Ruston.

At the same time, Joseph was among hundreds of English fascists who were—without indictment or trial—summarily shipped off to house arrest on the Isle of Man. There was not a shred of evidence that Ruston ever acted in support of the Nazi regime during wartime. And if every Englishman who lunched with Hitler and was photographed smiling and shaking his hand could be reasonably accused of high treason, then the Duke of Windsor himself—once the (uncrowned) King of England—would have also been a candidate for arrest and internment. According to one of Joseph's grandsons, "In no way did [Ruston], or my grandmother [Ella] for that matter, ever support either the war or the Holocaust. They may have supported certain Fascist ideologies and belonged to the appropriate parties, but they never hurt anyone or knowingly support any system that did."

ARNHEM SEEMED FAR from the dangers of war. With large parks, appealing fountains and waterfalls, undulating forest paths and venues for theater, music and dance, the town was a genteel sanctuary for wealthy city residents and for tourists.

The van Heemstras celebrated a traditional Christmastide. There were parties, visits from Ian and Alex and from relatives far and near. Audrey welcomed her uncle (her mother's only brother), a much-respected and well-liked judge who hated all forms of intolerance and was dedicated to peace; and there was also a cousin to whom she was close in her childhood. Holiday gatherings and reunions with loving relatives always took the sting out of her fatherless situation.

That autumn and winter, many people saw not much cause for concern, despite the situations in Czechoslovakia and Poland, which had already come completely under Nazi hegemony. War had been declared, but it was called a phony war. Thus, at the beginning of 1940, very few Dutch people feared for their future—until the Nazis invaded Denmark and Norway on April 9. Even then, a kind of narcotized calm prevailed. The Sadler's Wells Ballet, the great English troupe, was performing in Arnhem on May 9, and Ella took Audrey as a birthday celebration.

"For the occasion, my mother had our little dressmaker make me a long taffeta dress. I remember it so well. I'd never had a long dress in my life, obviously . . . It went all the way to the ground, and it rustled. The reason she got me this, at great expense, was that I was to present a bouquet of flowers at the end of the performance to Ninette de Valois, the director of the company." She did just that, offering the spray of tulips and roses that were hurriedly accepted, for the dancers had been ordered by the British vice consul to leave Arnhem that very night.

The next day, Friday, May 10, German armies invaded the Netherlands, Belgium and Luxembourg without warning; three days later, Rotterdam fell to the Germans after the city had been blasted by an air attack that killed almost thirty thousand Dutch civilians: the Germans had issued a surrender ultimatum but then launched their attack before the Dutch could reply. The same day, Queen Wilhelmina, her family and her government fled Holland for London, where they directed the war effort of the Dutch navy, the colonies and the growing resistance. Then, incendiary bombs were dropped on The Hague. Dutch soldiers, heirs to a century-long legacy of peace in their country, were trained and equipped for defense rather than attack, and as the minimal supplies and all the aircraft were swiftly lost, the Dutch army capitulated and Holland surrendered.

Nazi troops and artillery then tore through Arnhem, exploiting local facilities and despoiling where they could to support the German war machine. "I saw German trucks coming in, and in five days Holland fell," Audrey remembered. "The occupation—that's such a small word to cover the eternity of every day after the Germans came to our country, looted it, and stayed on to make slaves of us." For the present, Audrey's family was permitted to remain in the ancestral home; word had come down from Nazi headquarters that an occupation achieved with citizens' cooperation would facilitate a total German conquest of the Low Countries.

Over the next ten months, the van Heemstra bank accounts, securities and personal jewelry were confiscated. Secure in their wealth for centuries, they now saw almost everything taken away.

The German occupiers were eager to rouse anti-English sentiment—a prejudice that took such extreme forms as banning the import of biscuits and preserves from Britain. For Ella and her family, this raised a major concern: Audrey Ruston was a British citizen with a British name and was fluent in English—a combination that might easily subject her to arrest and even deportation. Her daughter would have to learn the Dutch language and pass for Dutch. With remarkable shrewdness, Ella enrolled her daughter in the local school as Edda van Heemstra, not as Audrey Kathleen Ruston. The newly minted identity was successful for as long as the girl needed it (that is, for the duration of the war), and then it was promptly discarded.

"My real name was never Edda van Heemstra. That was a name I assumed in school, because my mother thought it wiser during the German occupation, as mine sounded too English." Ella also cautioned Audrey not to speak English in public, as German soldiers were everywhere.

"For eight formative years [1939 to 1947], I spoke Dutch. My mother is Dutch, my father English, but I was born in Belgium. So I had heard English and Dutch inside our house and French outside." Following that, she had spoken only English at school in Kent, and then only Dutch in Holland. "There is no speech I can relax into when I'm tired, because my ear has never been accustomed to one intonation. It's because I have no mother tongue that the critics accuse me of curious speech."

It was precisely these polyglot early years that accounted for her unique vocal patterns—the elegantly clipped tones, the almost musical undulation of her phrasing and the prolongation of internal vowels that characterized the mature Audrey Hepburn's spoken English. Her speech was wholly sui generis, and it always defied comparison with any known dialect. No other voice could be mistaken for hers.

DAILY LIFE IN Nazi-occupied Holland, from 1940 to 1945, began badly and became a living nightmare. There was an almost constant state of anxiety as aircraft flew low overhead. Was that a British airplane on a reconnaissance mission, or was it a German attack? Like their parents, children took cover in cellars, closets and cupboards—and when they emerged unharmed, they were scarcely reassured, for the Nazis broadcast threats daily.

Strict rationing was soon applied. Because the Germans needed oil, gasoline, tires, coffee, tea and all textiles for their military, the population had limited access to them. Barges were requisitioned; bicycles, shoes and even iron destined for church bells were commandeered. Under Nazi control, Dutch radio constantly advised people on how to economize—by reusing tea leaves several times, for example, and by encouraging families to crowd into one room, the better to save fuel.

And so a country that had enjoyed an enviably high standard of living was soon sinking into poverty and disease; as the war dragged on, very few people were able to cling to property of any value, and tuberculosis struck the citizens in epidemic numbers by 1943. During wartime winters, some citizens—who would never have considered such actions before the war—chopped down trees in public parks for use as firewood and plundered abandoned homes for whatever was marketable.

Before long, the rights of Dutch Jews were limited, Jewish teachers and professors were dismissed from their posts and Jewish students could no longer attend schools. Doctors were forbidden to treat Jewish patients, who were also turned away from hospitals. Jewish women married to Gentiles had to endure forced sterilization. The deportation of Dutch Jews occurred in 1942, a development that led to public denunciations from the Roman Catholic and Dutch Reformed churches. The first punishment for such insubordination was to deport Jews who had converted to Christianity, such as the brilliant Jewish philosopher Edith Stein, who had become a Catholic and a Carmelite nun; she was executed at Auschwitz.

"Families with babies, little children being hauled into meat wagons, wooden vans with just a slat at the top, and all those faces staring out at you," Audrey recalled later, listing snapshot-memories of those deported from Holland to concentration camps. "I knew the cold clutch of human terror all through my early teens: I saw it, felt it, heard it—and it never goes away. You see, it wasn't just a nightmare: I was there, and it all happened."

In 1941, Ella's older son, Alex, vanished. Fighting for the hapless Dutch army at the beginning of the war, he was captured when the forces surrendered. Somehow, he escaped and went into hiding until the end of the war. But at the time, Ella and Audrey had no idea what had become of him, and in their worst moments, they presumed Alex was dead. For days, Audrey wept inconsolably, asking again and again if all of them were to be sent to prison or condemned to death. "I didn't know if I would just disappear as had so many young girls and women, into the houses established for the 'entertainment' of German officers and enlisted men. And I didn't know if I would be taken for a week or a day, to help clean a building or serve at a military kitchen. All I knew was that I was twelve, and terrified."

But as E. N. van Kleffens, then the Dutch minister of foreign affairs, wrote in 1940, "The Dutch have a gift of shrewd perspicacity which no propaganda can obliterate, [and] outward resignation should not be taken for inward submission" to the Nazis.

Precisely this spirit was evident in the remarkable story of the spirited and heroic members of the Dutch resistance to the German invasion. The resistance was first concerned with maintaining calm until the end of the war. Later, when it was clear that the restoration of peace was not a proximate reality, the Council of Resistance in the Kingdom of the Netherlands was founded, and its members were armed.

A robust eighteen-year-old in 1942, Ella's younger son Ian was an early and intrepid member of the resistance during his student days in Utrecht. He began his anti-German efforts by distributing pamphlets that encouraged his countrymen and were therefore subversive to the demoralizing tactics of the occupiers. He then worked in secret with the so-called Radio Orange network, which from time to time broadcast a quarter-hour speech by Queen Wilhelmina from London; she promoted the Dutch people's identification with the Allies.

Ian was also remarkable for organizing student strikes in Delft and Leiden when Jewish professors were dismissed—and he helped obtain false identification papers and food coupons for some Jews who would otherwise have been loaded into boxcars heading for German concentration camps. Despite death threats from the Nazis, resistance workers urged labor strikes among Dutch railway personnel, so that the arrival of German matériel was interrupted whenever possible. And when the battle lines came to Holland, the resistance evoked heroic exploits from ordinary Dutch citizens, who assisted Allied solders during parachute landings, providing both first aid and hideaways for the wounded.

Unfortunately, Ian's increasingly bold activities were discovered by the Germans. He was stopped one day in Arnhem and immediately deported to Germany, where he was one of four hundred thousand Dutchmen put to forced labor in munitions factories until the war was over. His whereabouts, too, were unknown to the family until his return in 1945.

Around the same time (June 1942), Audrey and her family experienced firsthand the savagery of the Nazi regime.

The Dutch Underground had attempted to demolish a German train bringing military supplies into Holland, and reprisals were enacted at once in Arnhem. Audrey's beloved uncle, the judge; her cousin, an adjutant at court; another cousin; and four neighbors were all rounded up. The scene was forever burned into the memory of thirteen-year-old Audrey:

"Don't discount anything you hear or read about the Nazis. It was worse than you could ever imagine. We saw my relatives put against the wall and shot." With that, and to her everlasting credit, the Baroness Ella van Heemstra began to work actively with the Dutch resistance, even to the point of hiding Underground workers in their home.

IN 1941, HER MOTHER supplemented Audrey's Dutch lessons with enrollment in afternoon music and dance classes at the Arnhem Conservatory, which waived most fees during the occupation and asked only what parents could manage to pay. "Once I started [dance lessons] in Holland," she said years later, "all I wanted was to be a ballerina." In November and December that year, at the Arnhem Stadsschouwburg, or city theater, there were programs marking the one hundred and fiftieth anniversary of Mozart's death. On November 11, Ella directed a set of *levende tafeleren*, or tableaux vivants, with five players seated silently and motionless in full eighteenth-century costume—Audrey among them—while the Arnhem String Quartet played selections from Mozart.

But Audrey preferred more active performances, and soon she had her chance. At the Conservatory, she demonstrated such talent and dedication that she was chosen to study under Winja Marova, whose star pupil she quickly became. Soon Audrey was not only performing at school: she and a few other students were risking their safety by presenting private dance recitals to collect money for resistance workers. These were called "black performances," for they had to be offered with blackout curtains and little lighting.

"I designed the dances myself," Audrey recalled. "I had a friend who played the piano, and my mother made the costumes. They were very amateurish attempts—but when there was very little entertainment, it amused people and gave them an opportunity to spend an afternoon or evening listening to music. The recitals were given in houses with windows and doors closed, and no one outside knew what was going on. Afterward, money was collected and turned over to the Dutch Underground." For fear of being discovered, the little audiences could not applaud or in any way register their approval. "The best audience I ever had made not a single sound at the end of my performance." From scraps of felt, Ella herself made Audrey's ballet slippers: "They didn't give the support that ballet shoes did, but they satisfied my eager young toes."

Often at these events, some people came up to Audrey and the other young performers and, along with some small sums, gave them pieces of folded paper—messages to be stuffed into the children's shoes and transported the next day to resistance workers. By prearrangement, the apparently uninvolved girls and boys would then meet their defiant countrymen (on a crowded streetcar, for example, or along a pathway in a park) and covertly pass on important information and some cash to support the cause.

There was nothing romantic, exciting or self-important about these missions, despite their superficial resemblance to stereotypical scenes from a Hollywood thriller. Real danger was as ubiquitous as Nazi soldiers and policemen, and the children who dared defy the occupiers knew that they had no chance of survival if caught. But her ballet lessons contributed to Audrey's sense of discipline and her ability to ignore her own discomfort. She needed the same self-control when food rationing became so severe that meat, eggs, tea and coffee were not available by any means. By the end of 1942, fuel was so scarce that only one room per home was allowed to be heated. "But there is probably nothing in the world as determined as a child with a dream," Audrey said fifteen years later, "and I wanted to dance more than I feared the Germans." Although she never said so, she was just as much a fervent operative on behalf of the Dutch resistance as she was an apprentice ballerina. Later, she did not consider that she often acted heroically: "It was quite ordinary for Dutch children to risk death to save the lives of resistance workers."

One winter day in Arnhem, a small platoon of German soldiers, rifles slung over their shoulders, ordered all the girls and women within their sight into a line. They were then herded into three military trucks that bumped and lurched through the city streets, their passengers mute with terror. "The only thing I remember for certain is that, over and over and over, I kept saying to myself in Dutch, 'Our Father Who art in heaven . . . Our Father Who art in heaven . . .' "

The convoy abruptly stopped. The soldiers jumped out and began abusing some Jews, recognizable by the mandatory yellow star on their clothing. "I remember hearing the dull sound of a rifle butt hitting a man's face. And I jumped down, dropped to my knees and rolled under the truck. I then skittered out, hoping the driver would not notice me—and he didn't."

Another time, a resistance worker told Audrey that, unknown to the Germans, an English paratrooper was hiding in the Arnhem forest. But he could not remain there for long, since the Germans were about to take over the woods on maneuvering exercises. The Englishman had to be warned—and helped to find friends and shelter. Would the English-speaking Audrey be willing to approach the paratrooper with instructions from the resistance—and then report to the resistance collaborator in the village who would provide a hideaway?

She volunteered at once and entered the forest, calmly and innocently picking wildflowers as she went—a ruse in case she was stopped suddenly by a German soldier. Audrey found the paratrooper just where she was told, gave him the information, answered his questions and headed back for the village. As she did so, she was met by two of the enemy, who addressed her in German, pointing to the path from which she had emerged and asking the reason for her presence in the area. Acting as if she had no idea what they wanted, she smiled brightly and handed them the bunch of flowers. To Audrey's astonishment, the soldiers accepted the bouquet, patted her shoulder and sent her on her way.

An hour later, she located a particular street-sweeper, and as he glanced toward her, she nodded almost imperceptibly: that was the signal, and the sweeper–resistance worker knew that he might expect to be approached by a friendly English-speaker that evening. Audrey had fulfilled her task.

As AUTUMN 1944 approached, one of the most daring exploits of the war was launched by Allied forces. Operation Market Garden, as it was called, was a bold attempt by British and American airborne and ground troops to capture and control eight Dutch bridges and thus open a route for their advance into Germany.

General Bernard Montgomery, commander of British forces in Europe, conceived the plan, which was endorsed by America's General Dwight D. Eisenhower. Following the liberation of Paris on August 25 and of Brussels on September 4, an Allied victory seemed closer than ever. Operation Market Garden, it was anticipated, would secure just that. Thirty-two thousand airborne troops were to be flown behind enemy lines to break the German defenses; by gliders and parachutes, one British and two American divisions would drop near the Dutch towns of Eindhoven, Nijmegen and, most important, Arnhem (the "Market" element), and by taking the bridges, the forces would create a path straight through to Germany (the "Garden").

Two heavily armed SS Panzer divisions were stationed around Arnhem—nevertheless, the Allies went ahead with their plan. But the Allies had too few planes to deliver all the airborne troops in one mission, and so the drop would be spread over three days. And because of German antiaircraft defenses near the center of Arnhem, it was decided to drop the troops almost ten kilometers away, which dissipated any element of surprise that might have weakened the German response.

The operation was launched on Sunday, September 17—a bright and cloudless day in the Dutch countryside. Allied soldiers were flush with excitement and optimism as 1,500 planes and 500 gliders flew toward enemy lines. The first drop—16,500 paratroopers and 3,500 glider troops—was completed with astonishing accuracy. But as the British approached Eindhoven, they quickly came under violent attack. The American airborne divisions reached their targets in Nijmegen, but most of the bridges there were blown up by the Germans before they could be captured. By the time the Allies headed for Arnhem, German tanks had moved in, destroying much of the city and ordering the entire population to evacuate within hours.

The situation quickly became desperate for the Allies, as British Major Tony Hibbert recalled:

"We really had nothing we could do to them [the Germans], and they drove up and down the street, firing high explosives into the sides of buildings, then firing smoke shells through that. The phosphorus from the smoke shells burned us out. By eight o'clock on Wednesday evening (September 20), the fires got out of control."

German artillery quickly controlled the area, and thousands of

Allied soldiers died and almost seven thousand were captured—many of them badly wounded. The largest airborne operation of World War II was thus also the costliest—in fact, it was a dismal failure. Victory was no longer within sight; the war dragged on, taking the lives of thousands more civilians and servicemen.

According to the British military chronicler Richard Holmes, "Veterans and historians alike agree on the extraordinary kindness of the Dutch population, so many of whose members helped the Allies at the risk, and so often at the cost, of their own lives." But for Dutch families, at first so hopeful of their liberation, there was worse misery to come. Arnhem and the surrounding areas were in ruins, more than 450 civilians died in one day and the Nazis put the rest of the populace to flight. As an early winter fell over Holland, German soldiers looted almost everything.

That winter was one of the coldest in European history, and the Nazis calmly watched the Dutch people starve to death as all available food was diverted to German soldiers.

"After the battle of Arnhem, the Germans ordered the city to be evacuated," Audrey remembered. "We were among the ninety thousand people forced to leave, and my mother and I went to my grandfather's country house in Velp. But it was no holiday. We went for days at a time without anything to eat, and we sat and shivered in a house without heat or light . . . We lived in a vacuum—no life, no news, no books, no soap. Yet all of that was nothing by comparison with the day-to-day horror . . . For a long time, we had nothing to eat but tulip bulbs.

"An endless stream of evacuees, thrown out of the city by the Nazis, came to our door begging for food and shelter. It was human misery at its worst—masses of refugees on the move, hundreds collapsing from starvation. We took in forty people for a while, but there was literally nothing to eat, and so they had to move on.

"Then, on the morning of December 24, my mother's widowed sister told us there wasn't a scrap of food left. I had heard that one could forget hunger by sleeping. Perhaps, then, I could sleep through Christmas—I would try—but first there were the stairs to my room. I tried, but I couldn't make it—I was too weak. My legs had begun to swell from edema, I was dangerously malnourished, and I was turning a frightful color from jaundice—my mother actually feared I would die from hepatitis." Audrey's weight had dropped to ninety pounds, which was insufficient for her five-foot-seven-inch height. "Then there was a knock at the door. A man came from the Dutch Underground, with some tinned food for us. We found out later that boxes of food were left at each house from which hostages had once been taken to be shot."

When that ration was gone, they were desperate. "We kept going with one slice of bread a day per person, made from grass, and with a cup of watery broth made from one potato . . . If you went on, you might live—and if you lived, you weren't dead . . . We lost everything, of course—our houses, our possessions, our money. But we didn't give a hoot. If we got through with our lives, that was the only thing that mattered."

For months before the disaster in Arnhem, Audrey had been too frail and ill to attend ballet classes; nor could she continue her task of giving dance lessons to a few younger girls at the Conservatory—which brought at least a few coins to her needy family. Her last appearance at Arnhem's municipal theater gained Audrey her first review; as a magazine critic noted: "She seems obsessed by a real dance rage and already has a respectable technical proficiency." But that was before her health collapsed.

On May 4, 1945, Audrey's sixteenth birthday, she heard a shuffling sound outside the cellar rooms at Velp. "I ran to the window and saw the first contingent of English soldiers. Freedom has a special smell to me—the smell of English petrol and English cigarettes. When I ran out to welcome the soldiers, I inhaled their petrol as if it were a priceless perfume and I demanded a cigarette, even though it made me choke." She also asked for chocolate, and a kindly soldier, seeing her jaundice and swollen feet, gave her five bars of it; she devoured them at once and was of course violently ill. But Audrey never again lost her appetite for tobacco or chocolate candy.

Before month's end, Alex emerged from hiding, and soon after, Ian returned from Berlin, having walked almost the entire way. But there were no resources for a family celebration; there was only the deeply felt silence of gratitude. For perhaps the only time in her life, Audrey saw tears on the face of her mother.

In June, international aid slowly began to arrive, and the people of Arnhem and Velp were among the first recipients. The United Nations Relief and Rehabilitation Administration (UNRRA) brought cartons of food, powdered milk, instant coffee, blankets and basic medical supplies. "All the schools were turned into relief centers," Audrey recalled later. "I was one of the beneficiaries." Audrey joined the entire van Heemstra family in the distribution. "It was that wonderful old-fashioned idea, that others come first and you come second. This was the whole ethic by which I was brought up. Others matter more than you do, so [as her mother said] 'Don't fuss, dear—just get on with it.' " Soon after, UNRRA became UNICEF, the United Nations Children's Fund.

BUT WHERE WOULD they live? The answer came through a radio plea from Queen Wilhelmina, who had returned to the Netherlands on the eve of liberation and at once asked for volunteers to staff nursing homes for wounded veterans. One in every fifty Dutch citizens was killed or died during the war, and there were countless maimed or ill. Before the end of that summer, Audrey and her mother had decamped to two rooms of a clinic in Amsterdam, where they undertook every kind of routine duty—not only attending to the physical needs of the battered but also reading to them and writing letters for them.

One of Audrey's patients was a bedridden thirty-year-old British paratrooper named Terence Young, who had participated in the Battle of Arnhem. After his recovery a year later, he and several of his former comrades in arms returned to Arnhem, where they made a film about the events of September 1944. The result, *Men of Arnhem*, was part documentary, part dramatic re-creation and the first of many films directed by Young.

Audrey and Ella completed their nursing duties in early 1946. At once, Ella took a job as a cook to pay for their rent in a small Amsterdam apartment and to underwrite Audrey's return to the ballet classroom. Her teacher was the great pioneer Sonia Gaskell, who had studied and worked with Diaghilev and would later form the Netherlands National Ballet. Gaskell admired her new student's vitality, charm and ambition, but she was alarmed at the effects of the war on Audrey's slender form: the girl's lack of energy and her poor muscle tone did not augur well for a career. Nor did her age: careers in ballet ordinarily begin when the student is much younger than seventeen.

THAT SUMMER, the long chain of difficulties in Audrey's life finally overtook her, and she suffered the first in a lifelong series of profound emotional depressions. The manifestations were classic: apart from a few hours of class each day, she slept constantly; she was melancholy and taciturn; and she began to overeat.

Since Audrey was six, she had endured an astonishing array of challenges. Abandoned by her father, she then had to accustom herself to loneliness abroad at school; trained by her mother never to complain, she put a brave face on everything, so constant was her desire to be loved and accepted. Although she relished it, ballet gave her more to be disciplined about, and into her exercises she poured all the ambition and dedication a sensitive girl can muster. But artistic apprenticeship, however rewarding at the moment, has an uncertain future, and her teachers were too honest to promise anything to anyone.

Fear had been her constant companion, and since 1940, the progressive deprivation of life's necessities had very nearly ruined her health forever. At the same time, the war had an odd but widespread corollary: like many others, Audrey found solidarity of purpose in working with her family and friends for the resistance. Everyone underwent the same tribulations; everyone was carried along by the same stubborn hope. And there had at last been an end to that long night of suffering. Her brothers had come home, aid had come from the Allies and she and her mother found something valuable to do in attending the injured.

Now everything had changed. Alex and Ian were off pursuing their own lives and careers. The tense drama of daily survival, which heightens and pinpoints life itself and renders meaningless so much that is less, gave way to the quotidian reality of remaking one's own world. Governments were attempting the reconstruction of Europe, but Audrey had to renew, rediscover and advance her own young life. No sense of teamwork or international program was there to help her. At seventeen, she was no longer a child but not yet a mature woman. She had her mother's courage for an example, but there was no emotional component of affection in Audrey's life.

As so often with people in crisis, Audrey directed her confusion toward dissatisfaction with herself, as she later confided: "I've often been depressed and deeply disappointed in myself. You can even say that I hated myself at certain periods. I was too fat, or maybe too tall, or just plain too ugly. I couldn't seem to handle any of my problems or cope with people I met." Just then, on April 3, the Amsterdam newspaper *Het Parool* reported an extraordinary discovery. "I read the diary of Anne Frank when it came out," Audrey said years later, "and it just destroyed me. I identified so strongly with this little girl, who was exactly my own age."

In fact, it would have been remarkable if Audrey were not depressed in 1946; it might even be alarming if we could say that she had sailed valiantly through every storm and had arrived calmly at the shores of young adulthood. Indeed, had she moved from episode to episode without feeling events deeply and attempting to integrate those negative experiences into her subsequent life, she would have been forever wounded—perhaps even psychologically blocked. Without the depression and the core of strength to move beyond it, she might have become a rather chilly woman with a loss of emotional health. And she certainly would not have become a film actress who often conveyed uncommon interiority.

"I had gone through the war years deprived of food, money, books, music and clothing," she said of this time. "Now I began to overcompensate by eating everything in sight, particularly chocolates. I became as swollen and unattractive as a balloon." Her self-assessment was more inflated than her body, but by autumn, Audrey's weight was 68 kilograms, or 150 pounds. By no standard was she fat (as she later claimed); her face, neck, arms and upper torso remained thin, but now there was more to her thighs and hips. If she really intended a career in ballet, she would have to lose weight. Audrey soon achieved her goal of 110 pounds, which she maintained her entire life.

The reason for the successful and rapid weight reduction in late 1946 was simple. Sonia Gaskell told Ella that Audrey might have a chance for advanced study abroad with a famous colleague in London. If she intended to be serious about dance, Ella said, weight loss was vital.

In London, they found a very different atmosphere from Folkestone in 1939. Postwar England still suffered serious deprivations.

For most people, the cessation of bombings removed the constant dread of sudden death but did not otherwise improve the quality of life.

But the indomitable Ella van Heemstra was thoroughly dedicated to her daughter's career. She gamely took a job as concierge in a Mayfair apartment building, very close to Hyde Park and Grosvenor Square. There the titled lady, now forty-seven, could be seen putting out the trash and washing the staircase at 65 South Audley Street. The modest building, just opposite the Grosvenor Chapel, was of red brick with marble pilasters; it had half a dozen flats and one room for the concierge and her daughter. Each morning, as Ella dispatched her charwoman's tasks, Audrey rushed past on her way to dance class.

Chapter Three

~

1947–1951

Sonia Gaskell's contact in London was none other than the brilliant, formidable Marie Rambert, then at the height of her influence in the world of British classical dance. Born Cyvia Rambam in Warsaw in 1888, she had collaborated with Diaghilev, Nijinsky, Stravinsky and Isadora Duncan, among others. In 1920, she opened a London school that trained some of the great dancers and choreographers of the century—Frederick Ashton, Antony Tudor and Agnes de Mille, for example—and by 1936, her company and school comprised Ballet Rambert. Worldwide recognition followed, and in early 1947 she was fielding several offers for international tours.

Audrey arrived at Rambert's newly rented but poorly heated rehearsal rooms in Cambridge Circus in early 1948, armed with a recommendation from Gaskell, her own prodigious energy and little else. Her weight was 110 pounds, she stood five feet seven inches tall and had a twenty-inch waistline. At sixty, Madame Rambert weighed (so her students estimated) about seventy pounds and was just five feet tall. Everyone seemed impossibly big to her, and she routinely invited others to sit opposite her, the better to avoid straining her neck. Petite, feathery ballerinas were not merely easier for her male dancers to partner: Madame found them more to her liking for instruction and choreography, too.

Cultivated, dynamic, fluent in many languages and graced with an impeccable sense of theater, Rambert was inspiring as a mentor, but she could also be indiscreet and even rude. Agnes de Mille, who had been a student of Rambert in the 1930s, called her "Madame Wasp," and students often ran from her studio in tears. There was no doubt, however, that she could evoke from good dancers an extraordinary range of styles and remarkable effects.

Stern but generous with young talent, Rambert watched Audrey's brief audition and listened to her describe her previous studies. She then told Audrey to come back in the spring, when she expected to have the financial resources to offer a scholarship; at that time, there would also be a room for her at the home Rambert shared with her family in Kensington, which invariably housed a small flock of her impecunious dance students. At these prospects, optimism crowded out Audrey's depression. And at this point, she dropped the Ruston in her father's surname but kept the Hepburn (her great-grandmother's maiden name). Henceforth, she was known as Audrey Hepburn.

But this was late January: what to do until April? The answer came in a letter from cousins in Amsterdam. Two of their friends, C. H. van der Linden and H. M. Josephson, were hiring cast and crew for an independent short film comedy, and the men needed attractive young extras. There would be a few days' employment if Audrey could return briefly to Holland. In February, she did just that—not because movies held any interest for her, but because she needed the money over the next several months.

Despite its title, *Nederlands in 7 lessen (Dutch in 7 Lessons)* was not an educational tool for learning a language. Audrey Hepburn's first screen appearance, filmed in one day on a quiet street in Amsterdam, was, on the contrary, a feeble little comedy about a movie cameraman who is assigned to make a travelogue of the Netherlands but is more interested in pursuing local young women. The scatterbrained narrative ("dull and conventional," according to a British critic) relied heavily on documentary footage of the city seen from aerial shots. In two scenes filmed on the ground, Audrey made her movie debut—at the beginning, when the bumbling cinematographer accidentally collides with her on a street corner; and at the finale, when (dressed as a KLM flight attendant) she waves goodbye to him. Her total footage was clocked at less than a minute; she was uncredited, and the few reviews made no mention of her.

Returning to London, Audrey was, as she later said, "always short of money, although I modeled and clerked and did all sorts of little odd jobs." When her classes began with Rambert, Audrey continued to accept evening work as a secretary or a photographer's model; she appeared, for example, in magazine advertisements for soap and shampoo. Ella, meanwhile, worked variously as a hotel clerk, a florist, a decorator and a nanny for wealthy tourists; she and her daughter shared their incomes and frequently their lodgings.

For much of 1948, Audrey was pitched into a demanding schedule of ballet study by day and part-time employment in the evenings. "My first class was at ten a.m. and my last at six p.m., so it was work, work, work all day and into the night." As for dance lessons, they became "the most completely exhausting thing I have ever done," and there was constant, sometimes nerve-wracking attendance to detail. If Madame caught her students "folding our arms or slouching our shoulders, she'd give us a good rap across the knuckles with a stick." The new student may not have anticipated this antique form of corporal punishment, but she bore it because "my dream was to wear a tutu and dance at Covent Garden."

Despite her keen ambition and estimable energy, Audrey's dream remained just that. At the end of summer, Ballet Rambert was preparing to depart for a fifteen-month tour of Australia and New Zealand, and Madame announced her choice of dancers. Audrey asked why her name was not on the list, and her teacher explained the reasons: Audrey was too tall; she had begun serious training too late; she might be employed in the corps de ballet or as a chorine in musical theater, and Rambert thought she could have a fine career as a ballet instructor—but Audrey would never be a prima ballerina.

"My technique," she said a few years later, "didn't compare with that of the girls who had had five years of Sadler's Wells teaching, paid for by their families, and who had always had good food and bomb shelters. Reason made me see that I just couldn't be so square as to go on studying ballet. Still, I thought it was way below my dignity to go into a musical."

Whatever her momentary reaction to Madame Rambert's pronouncement, there was no time for melancholy. In October 1948, Audrey left the house in Kensington, moved back with her mother and, with a few other students who had been left out of the Rambert tour, made the rounds of producers' and agents' offices in search of theater work.

SHE WAS NOT unemployed for long, but the job was not to her taste. In late October, auditions were announced for the London production of *High Button Shoes*, a popular American musical comedy then in its second year on Broadway. With music and lyrics by Jule Styne and Sammy Cahn and choreography by Jerome Robbins, the show—a series of zany sketches about a confidence man in the early part of the century—called for a dancing/singing chorus of girls as bathing beauties, dashing about in fast and funny dance numbers that recalled silent-film farces. Audrey was one of the last of forty to be selected from three thousand candidates. She signed a one-page contract and received eight pounds weekly, then about thirty-two dollars.

"When I was chosen for *High Button Shoes,*" she remembered a few years later, "I didn't know one syncopated beat from another, so I had to work much harder than the other girls." Throughout the weeks of rehearsal, she stayed late to work with dance assistants, and she rose early to practice on her own before the next day's call.

High Button Shoes opened at the Hippodrome on December 22, 1948, and had a successful run of 291 performances. It was "one of the maddest pieces of hurly-burly dancing . . . that London has seen for a long time," according to the London *Daily Telegraph*, "and the high spot . . . is the ballet in the manner of the early Mack Sennett films." But this was only temporizing for Audrey; once again, no reviews mentioned her, and the show seemed to lead her nowhere. When it closed on May 5, 1949, she was invited to join its touring company—but the producer Cecil Landeau had spotted the third girl from the left in the second row onstage and offered her a job in his new musical revue, set to open on May 18 at the Cambridge Theatre.

Still a chorine, she was to have walk-on bits with a line or two in some of the twenty-seven short sketches, and she would be one of only five dancers. Audrey knew that she was fortunate to be working at all during those difficult times. And work she did: her schedule of six evening and two matinee performances allowed her to accept more modeling assignments for magazine and newspaper ads.

Landeau staged genial and entertaining shows, and *Sauce Tartare* was but the latest and most successful assembly of those songs and satiric sketches so beloved by English audiences. The cast was composed of talent from a dozen countries, among them the comedic South African singer Zoë Gail, who stopped the show with "A Hick in Piccadilly." *Tartare* was reviewed positively, although only one or two principal players were mentioned. Critics hailed the show's freshness, wit and style; the accomplished cast ("Everyone in the company can do something and has the chance to do it"); and the inventive sets and costumes ("tropical forests, skyscrapers painted in sepia, the South America of sheet music, mysterious lamp lit avenues in Paris—the exotic [is] all in far better taste than the exotic in fact ever is").

Audrey portrayed something called a Boogie Woogie Yoga Follower in one sketch, a shopgirl in another and a classical dancer in a third. According to a spectator who attended several times, she "stood out, with an eager freshness, a Peter Pan–like litheness to her dancing and a quality of always being alive and alert, although the spotlight was invariably on someone else."

Her colleagues in the show had mixed reactions to her. "We all noticed Audrey's potential," said Jessie Matthews, a renowned British musical star. "She had a lovely, indefinable quality, and when Cecil Landeau asked me to take her through some of my numbers, I was very happy to do so. She just had to be a star, given the right breaks."

Aud Johanssen, a Scandinavian dancer, was blunt: "I have the biggest tits onstage, but everyone looks at the girl who has none at all!" Fashion photographer Anthony Beauchamp, who documented the production of *Sauce Tartare*, said that he had photographed stars like Vivien Leigh and Greta Garbo, but with Audrey he "had the feeling of making a true discovery when I found her. She had such freshness and a kind of spiritual beauty." That was an estimation often repeated over the decades: many people claimed to have "discovered" Audrey, but it was actually Cecil Landeau (not Beauchamp) who first recognized her talent for theater and encouraged it.

Bob Monkhouse, later a famous comedian, was another performer with Audrey in both *Sauce Tartare* and its sequel; his recollection was of a somewhat controversial performer. "As far as the dancing was concerned, Audrey was on the lowest rank," he recalled. "If she had been a good dancer, the other girls [in the show] wouldn't have disliked her so much. You see, they liked her off stage but not on: they saw that if Audrey so much as jumped in place, the audience was captivated. Her appearance was so adorable that you held your breath while she smiled and batted her eyes. Later, she learned to do less of all this." Her little antics may have been from nervousness, or the desire to cover for what she perceived as awkwardness and poor technique. "I felt I was really ugly compared to those other girls," Audrey said later; what others regarded as scene-stealing may have been mere compensation. In any case, audiences loved her and Cecil Landeau could count on her for unexpected turns of comic vivacity.

However, the producer was anxious. He always reminded his casts that relations among them must remain strictly professional, that he was managing an upright and proper company. But Audrey had quite obviously fallen in love with fellow player Marcel Le Bon. A handsome French singer and lyricist, Le Bon had the kind of casual Gallic charm that some women find irresistible, and he became Audrey Hepburn's first suitor. Landeau hoped the affair would quickly run its course before the couple became an official item, stealing newspaper space and the attention of audiences for the wrong reasons and besmirching the good name of his organization.

Established and ascendant luminaries did not—at that time—trumpet the details of their personal lives to press and public. Promoters, producers, agents and managers worked zealously to envelop the trade in the best image, and so only the most generous, the most flattering, the most exemplary impressions were set forth. And the press, for the most part, collaborated, since the public (once upon a time) demanded that those in show business lead blameless lives.

The making and unmaking of marriages among celebrities were noted, but there was never any allusion to the personal lives of those not legally united. An unmarried couple was "dating" or "engaged"—with the inference of propriety, which meant chastity. Anything but traditional wedlock could scarcely be mentioned in public without fear of legal action.

A consequence of this was a regrettable double standard of which Audrey had to be aware. Men who had an adulterous relationship, serial affairs or multiple mistresses, and even those who were almost pathologically promiscuous, were regarded as charming rakes and roués—or as puerile chaps in need of taming. A woman with a lover or two in her past or present, on the other hand, could be forever branded as an unprincipled tart. A young woman hoping to make a career—especially so public a career—had to be exceedingly vigilant for the way she was regarded. A woman of easy virtue, as it was once called, was not desirable.

In addition, Audrey had been raised and trained with a certain decorum about sex—not prudery, but a kind of reserve or restraint. She never rehearsed her private life and never confided her affairs to a journalist. Remarkably, she managed to sustain the image throughout her life, despite her healthy sexual appetite and several more or less protracted romances. After two broken marriages, she finally lived quite openly with a man for almost a dozen years: by that time, such was her persona and the standard of a new era that she almost seemed to hallow the unmarried state.

This is not to suggest that Audrey Hepburn was deceitful or sanctimonious, much less that she simply inhabited gentility as if it were a role. Her public demeanor was never Victorian, her private manner never tainted with false or expedient convention. She was apparently in all situations entirely herself, and that self—while not revealed to everyone—was neither inhibited nor intemperate. It amused her to know that many regarded her as without desire or passion, just as some people wrongly believed that so slim a woman must have had an eating disorder.

And so l'affaire Le Bon simmered pleasurably in 1949 and 1950. Sealed envelopes were passed through discreet friends at the Cambridge Theatre; Audrey received flowers "from an anonymous admirer" backstage; sometimes she did not return home until the small hours (or not at all); and she politely but insistently avoided the topic with her mother, who somehow learned about Le Bon and was alarmed that Audrey might marry a cabaret singer whose model was that Gallic boulevardier, Maurice Chevalier.

THERE WERE 433 performances of *Sauce Tartare*, which lasted for one year. During its Christmas season, Audrey supplemented her twelve-pound-a-week salary by also appearing in a play for children, which meant that she did twenty-one shows a week for four weeks.

The success of *Tartare* inspired Landeau to extend his franchise and stage a sequel of sorts. He called it *Sauce Piquante*, an uneven blend of comic sketches and musical numbers that satirized the movies and plays of the time ("A Tramcar Called Culture," for example, spoofed the prize-winning Tennessee Williams play). In one scene, Audrey posed as the spirit of champagne, wearing gold lamé and the ears of a leprechaun, or were they a pixie's? Landeau also gave her a solo dance. The revue opened on April 27, 1950, to less enthusiastic notices than its predecessor; it sank into oblivion after eight weeks. By that time, however, the shrewd Landeau had gone one step further, shuttling his favorite players over to the club known as Ciro's, where he presented *Summer Nights*, an abbreviated version of *Sauce Piquante*, twice more each evening after the cast had completed *Piquante*. "I worked like an idiot!" Audrey recalled. Ciro's was more intimate than a theater, and for the first time audiences could see her at closer range.

Landeau did not choose Marcel Le Bon for Ciro's, and his strategy worked. With Audrey working until almost three in the morning, Le Bon's attention turned elsewhere, and soon he was off to other adventures. Audrey may indeed have lamented his absence, but she was too busy to languish in fond memories. One habit became more pronounced at this time, however: Audrey began to smoke more heavily, preferring Golden Flake cigarettes.

"Audrey communicated something in *Sauce Piquante* that served her well all during her career," according to Bob Monkhouse. "It was an impression she gave—'I am alone and defenseless in the world, and I need you to save me.' Maybe without even knowing it, people seemed to react at once: 'I'll take this poor little creature under my wing.' " Monkhouse was neither mean-spirited nor critical: he merely identified an authentic part of Audrey Hepburn's character that was eventually emphasized by certain kinds of roles and performances, by the way she stood or glanced or spoke, and by the appeal she made to her audience. She often did feel alone and defenseless in the world—but not always. Her habit of getting on with it (as her mother always urged) had created a core of strength, and from that core she drew reserves to battle the occasional fears and depressions that occurred like sudden summer squalls.

On different occasions, two spectators were particularly impressed with Audrey's performance in *Sauce Piquante*. Writer and director Thorold Dickinson was planning to film an espionage thriller with an international cast. He went to meet her after a performance and promised her a screen test for an important role that, he said, would put both her dance skills and her youthful beauty to good use. But the project was not scheduled until later that year. In addition, moviemaker Mario Zampi thought Audrey would be an attractive addition to the opening sequence of a comedy to be filmed that autumn.

Meanwhile, she continued to gain favorable publicity from modeling and from movie magazines. Her dignified sense of repose, her long legs and her slightly aloof (but not haughty) air were a fashion photographer's dream, and from this time a favorable symbiosis occurred. On the one hand, her looks and her manner made Audrey the ideal fashion model; on the other, her work as a fashion model made her more conscious of clothes and eventually contributed significantly to her success as a movie actress. Now, the glossier periodicals like *Film Review* and *Picturegoer*, which celebrated rising stars, or at least attractive newcomers whose face and figure sold copies, began regularly to feature her on their covers.

AFTER THE VISITS from Dickinson and Zampi, Audrey correctly reasoned that she ought to know something about the art and craft of acting. With their casual and improvisatory style, cabaret sketches and musical revues were one thing. But the camera's merciless close-ups would betray any halting awkwardness or insecure hesitation: a performance on film had to appear natural, even after multiple takes. Accepted as a drama student by Felix Aylmer, Audrey undertook her first serious study since she began to dance. "He taught me to concentrate intelligently on what I was doing," Audrey said later.

Aylmer, born in 1889, had one of the longest careers in British theater and film. A renowned interpreter of Shakespeare and Shaw, he also excelled in modern plays and popular movies; and he was a dedicated mentor to young talent. "What's most important is poise and motion," according to Aylmer. "She had that naturally." Audrey's sessions with Aylmer and several of his other students continued for several months: they read and discussed scenes from classic and modern plays, she learned how to project her normally quiet voice, and she practiced proper stress within lines of dialogue.

His professional connections enabled Aylmer to send likely candidates to read for movie roles, and during the early summer of 1950, Audrey was costumed and screen-tested for the Hollywood religious epic *Quo Vadis*. "For three months, we tested hundreds of girls," said director Mervyn LeRoy, recalling the casting of Lygia, a Christian heroine in that story. "In London, I thought I had found her when we tested a young actress named Audrey Hepburn. I thought she was sensational, but the studio [Metro-Goldwyn-Mayer] took one look at the test and turned her down. Eventually, we decided we couldn't use an unknown after all." The role went to Deborah Kerr.

At about the same time, Audrey had the good luck to meet Robert Lennard, casting director at Associated British Pictures Corporation (ABPC), which then co-owned Elstree Studios. Despite all the claims and counterclaims as to who facilitated Audrey's entrance into films, it was Robert Lennard to whom the credit must be assigned. His efforts were not without difficulty, for although she was only twenty-one, Audrey was hesitant to bind herself to a studio and thus, she thought, restrict her opportunities.

ABPC, a company founded by John Maxwell in 1927, was bankrupt at the time of his death. By 1950, the rescuing co-owner of the company—and effectively the power behind it—was none other than Jack Warner, of Warner Bros. This co-ownership gave Warner major influence over the entire ABPC combine, including its Elstree Studios in Hertfordshire, its worldwide distribution deal through the British arm of Pathé and its circuit of ABC cinemas, then the largest movie theater chain in Britain.

At first reluctant to sign the studio contract Lennard proposed, Audrey at last agreed to his offer of a three-picture deal with

ABPC. She was to receive £500 for her first picture, with pay raises to £1,500 for her third. These sums must have seemed royal indeed to a performer who had received only £12 a week for her most recent job and was now essentially unemployed.

Audrey's first assignment for ABPC was not that company's production at all. They sold her to an independent corporation for a minuscule role in a woefully tedious movie called *One Wild Oat*, in which she was seen for less than twenty seconds. In her moment of screen time, Audrey portrays a rather too stylishly outfitted hotel receptionist who takes a call from her married older boyfriend (Stanley Holloway): "Good morning, Regency Hotel . . . Who? . . . Mr. Gilbey? . . . Oh, *hello*, Alfred!" And before you know it, Audrey has vanished from the movie; that it was never released outside England did no harm to her career. Still, during her one day of work at Elstree Studios, in Hertfordshire, she made an impression on Holloway, who pointed her out to co-star Robertson Hare: "There's a girl who seems to me to have what it takes to get on in pictures."

After that, Mario Zampi was ready for Audrey in his film *Laughter in Paradise*. After the opening credits for the established actors, ABCP then trumpeted her first film for them (and that of another new contract player): "And Introducing Veronica Hurst and Audrey Hepburn." Audrey's bit part, a cigarette girl in a nightclub, required little more than a few moments of rehearsal and shooting. Then, in the Alec Guinness comedy *The Lavender Hill Mob* (for which she was again loaned out, this time to Ealing Studios), Audrey played a girl named Chiquita, apparently a paramour of the Guinness character. "Oh, you *are* sweet—thank you!" she purrs, accepting a handful of cash from him and wandering elegantly off among the crowd at a South American restaurant.

Audrey's inchoate career in ballet, such as it had been, was finished, and now her future in films was doubtful. She was making movies only to pay her bills and to contribute to the support of Ella, who was temporarily unemployed that year. More to the point, there was very little else in her life at this time—not even the choice of the films in which she would appear. "If you add them all up," she said later of the six pictures in which she appeared during 1950 and 1951, "they made [a total of] one quick appearance." But a paycheck was better than none, and so, hopeful for better roles, she renewed her contract with ABPC for three more films, with remuneration escalating to £2,500. A secondary clause gave the company the right to use her in one picture a year thereafter.

Although Audrey had seven scenes in her next picture, she hated every day of work on it. *Young Wives' Tale* was to be a witty and slightly risqué farce about people forced to share lodgings during the postwar housing shortage in England. Added to the community of young married couples is a single, professional typist (Audrey), a pretty but obviously neurotic woman convinced that every man is out to do her harm. She thinks that a pedestrian is a mad stalker and that a diner at a restaurant is a potential attacker—not the best plot idea for a comedy.

Nor was the director, Henry Cass, much help: he found fault with everything Audrey did. His major complaint was her absurdly exaggerated, faux-upper-class English accent, which bore no resemblance to her normal speech and sounded merely affected instead of amusing. The other players in this *Tale* were established stage and screen actors—among them Joan Greenwood, Guy Middleton, Athene Seyler and Irene Handl—and they spoke in a similarly idiosyncratic manner, mostly for comic effect, which was a fairly common, if curious, tradition in some British comedies of the period. Cass said nothing to them.

"He had it in for me," Audrey recalled. "It was the only unhappy experience I ever had making a picture." Cast members came to her defense when they could, but the atmosphere on the set remained tense and uncongenial—rather like the finished picture. One American critic took favorable if brief notice: the players tried hard, wrote Bosley Crowther in *The New York Times*, "including that pretty Audrey Hepburn as the unwed boarder."

DURING PRODUCTION OF *Young Wives' Tale* in November 1950, Thorold Dickinson was finally able to test Audrey for the part of Nora Brentano in his forthcoming political thriller, *Secret People* (not, as it is usually misidentified, *The Secret People*). This was to be the most important part she had undertaken so far, for it would provide an opportunity to work with established European stars and to dance in two ballet sequences. Weeks before filming began, however, she learned that there might be a problem: because neither of the two leading players was tall, "the rest of the cast must be scaled to them," as production notes indicated. "This of course applies particularly to Nora—a slight discouragement to Audrey Hepburn." As late as the end of 1950, just when *Young Wives' Tale* was concluding, Audrey's participation in *Secret People* was uncertain.

On the morning of February 23, 1951, a professional dancer auditioned for the role—the eleventh candidate to be seriously considered. Then, that afternoon, the director ushered in "our first choice, Audrey Hepburn," as the production notes document. "After the first run-through, people start eyeing each other meaningfully; she has the quality, all right. After another rehearsal, it seems almost a waste of time to shoot the test." Audrey won the part of Nora.

The film was planned as a serious drama with a political-moral subtext in the tradition of Joseph Conrad and Graham Greene. The story concerns two young sisters, Maria and Nora Brentano, who flee to London from an unnamed central-European dictatorship when their father is killed by a dictator. As adults, played by

Audrey Hepburn and Valentina Cortese,* they are drawn into various aspects of an assassination plot against their father's killer—but the attempt misfires, and an innocent waitress is killed when a bomb is planted at a dance recital. Maria (Cortese), who had been pressed into collaboration by her lover (Serge Reggiani), is accused and arrested, but the police know she will be a valuable informer. Her identity is changed, she undergoes plastic surgery, and Nora believes her dead. The sisters are finally reunited, but there is a tragic finale.

That year in *Secret People*, "the quality" was seen for the first time on film, and it was in fact an amalgam of traits and talents rooted in Hepburn's ingenuousness, her directness, her credible and unstudied artlessness. She seemed to have "an endless fund of vitality to expend," as the production notes added (especially in the sequence for the ballet performance, filmed on March 19, 1951), and an ability to convey grief or shock, dismay or apprehension, anxiety or astonishment precisely by underplaying those emotions—by just a slight turn of the head when that was right; by a slight opening of the mouth and an enigmatic darkening of her glance when that was natural; by a moment's hesitation that made listeners believe she was not reciting a line of dialogue but coming upon the unexpected depths and challenges of life.

Her technique, in other words, was a complete lack of technique, and so the feelings of her characters were not something deliberated, labored or contrived. We cannot know if or how much Audrey thought of her own wartime past in Arnhem during the scene in which a bomb explodes while she is dancing. That sequence took several days, many retakes and some arduous camera

---

* The admirable Italian actress Valentina Cortese worked in Britain and America for a time in the late 1940s and early 1950s, when she was sometimes billed as Valentina Cortesa, as she was in this film. But her true name, which she much preferred, is used here.

setups, and there were numerous attempts to find the right sound for the studio bombing; it was not a pleasant time for her.

But whatever cloud of memories may momentarily have returned, Audrey was not overcome by them. She seemed to know instinctively how subtle gradations of feeling had to be communicated for the camera. None of her directors had thus far donated more than a moment or two of explanation about eye-line or key lighting; before Dickinson, she had more than a line of dialogue only in the picture directed by Henry Cass. Now, Dickinson found that indeed he had to tell her very little. "The quality" was there at once. He and his cameraman had only to capture it.

Working with gifted and seasoned veterans like Serge Reggiani (then appearing in his twenty-first film) and Valentina Cortese (in her thirty-second) made the production of *Secret People* especially gratifying for Audrey because she learned so much from them—that publicity must be always subordinated to the limits of professionalism, for example. When an interviewer visiting the set referred to acting as Reggiani's life, he replied, "No, it's my job." Always happy to answer questions (but not to initiate discussion) about his work, he politely but firmly refused to discuss his personal life or his family. This impressed Audrey.

Cortese, with some experience of Hollywood behind her, was even more emphatic: "If an actress is popular . . . people want to know about her, to feel they know her. And sometimes that can be very touching. But we must be allowed to have our own lives. In Hollywood, it is terrible—they expect you to be their slave; you have to be ready to do anything for them, at any time, not just when you're making a picture." And then Cortese turned to Audrey: "Think hard before you sign a long-term contract, dear. Liberty is the most wonderful thing of all."

The problem, and Audrey knew it, was that she had to decide what sort of publicity was necessary and what was not—what to say and what to withhold. If she gave too many interviews, she knew, the public would "get sick of [me]. I'd much rather wait until I have something to show, instead of risking a tremendous anti-climax when people finally do start seeing the first little bits I've done in films." This was highly problematic, of course: her contract for ABPC stipulated—the very week after this little publicity seminar with Reggiani and Cortese—that Audrey had to be photographed feeding ducks on the South Downs and paddling in a village pond, all for the benefit of *Illustrated* magazine.

Without question, *Secret People* was Audrey's most important film so far, and the critics in Britain and America said so. "Audrey Hepburn combines beauty with skill, shining particularly in two short dance sequences," according to a typical notice.

THAT SEASON THERE were the usual parties to which stars, directors, producers, contract players and those anointed for celebrity were invited—in fact, studio moguls commanded them to attend. Often hosted by those with financial stakes in the British film industry, these events were held in fashionable Mayfair or Belgravia reception rooms, in posh clubs and even in consular chambers. At such events, business chatter could be heard along with the gossip of the day—and sometimes the rituals of courtship and seduction, too.

Early one evening during the spring of 1951, Audrey attended a cocktail party sponsored by ABPC, where she was introduced to a man of ferocious charm, not to say considerable sex appeal. At six foot four, with wavy, dark blond hair and a two-hundred-watt smile, James Hanson could not go unnoticed at any gathering. Then twenty-eight, he was seven years older than Audrey and heir to an enormous family fortune made in long-distance trucking— first in England, then in Canada; eventually, oil and shipping were added to the family interests. By the time Hanson met Hepburn, his net worth was in the tens of millions of pounds sterling. But as it was later noted, in the early 1950s he was "more interested in being a playboy than a businessman."

James Hanson had no professional connection to the world of movie stars, but in that firmament he had a definite personal interest. An industrious partygoer and a diligent pursuer of attractive women, he counted among his girlfriends Ava Gardner, Jean Simmons and Joan Collins. In 1951, he added Audrey Hepburn's name to his list of favorites. Very soon, this became a serious love affair that could not be kept from the press. As for the baroness, she heartily approved of the match and confidently predicted an auspicious union that would provide her daughter with stability and security.

Part Two

CELEBRITY

[1951–1956]

Chapter Four

1951

"WITLESS . . . FRENETIC . . . CONTRIVED . . . pointless."
These were some of the gentler terms used by critics to describe Audrey Hepburn's seventh film; happily, she was not mentioned in reviews.

Producer and band director Ray Ventura had borrowed her from ABPC to join the cast of a comedy with music called *Monte Carlo Baby*, filmed hurriedly on the Riviera in the spring of 1951. Actually, there were two films of the story made on the spot: immediately after each scene was shot in English, it was repeated in French. In the latter version (released as *Nous irons à Monte Carlo*), because of her fine command of the language, Audrey was the only player to repeat her role. Both films were dismal failures, for the weak narrative was merely a pretext for Ventura's musical numbers. In a few poorly written scenes, Audrey played a famous actress whose toddler is mistakenly given to a traveling musician; farcical excursions ensue before the obligatory happy finale. She was not the leading lady: that doubtful distinction went to Michele Farmer, Gloria Swanson's daughter, whose first and last performances were in *Monte Carlo Baby*. With two directors, two sets of colleagues and two scripts, Audrey was kept busy, but not happily so.

For one thing, she missed James Hanson. For another, she had not wanted to do the picture, for she feared that if she left London for this meager assignment, she might miss better opportunities at home. She discussed the matter with Valentina Cortese, who advised that Audrey should indeed go to Monaco—who knew what good contacts were to be made in that warm and sunny spot?

As if on cue, things happened quickly. And the catalyzing event for the dramatic shift in her life and career was almost fanciful, with just the right touch of serendipitous whimsy.

One afternoon in May, the *Monte Carlo Baby* company was filming outside the sumptuous Hôtel de Paris. Audrey was gamely leaping about, appearing in a silly sequence that was, as usual, being twice directed, twice shot. As the filming continued, an elderly woman in a wheelchair, with a crown of frizzy hair, was returning to the hotel from the seaside. She raised an imperious hand, a signal to the man who was carefully guiding her contraption through the small gathering. He bent over in attendance, she whispered to him, they glanced toward the scene, and then the old lady was rolled majestically onward, into the hotel lobby.

The eccentric figure in the wheelchair was none other than the popular and distinguished French writer Sidonie-Gabrielle Colette, who used only her surname; her caregiver was her husband, Maurice Goudeket. For her highly sensual and often controversial short stories and novels, Colette drew quite directly on her own lively and checkered history—three times a wife; a prodigious lover of men and women; a former actress, a sometime poet, once a painter, always a rebel and a relentless critic of social hypocrisies.

In May 1951, Colette was seventy-eight years old and permanently confined to her wheelchair or her bed, virtually immobilized with arthritis and requiring constant assistance. But her mind was as agile as ever, her perceptions clear and her eyesight unimpaired. Celebrated as a bemused realist who punctured moralistic stereotypes and constantly asked disconcerting questions about the role of women in society, she kept on adding to her long list of popular achievements even in advanced age. Her novella *Gigi* had been published in 1945 and was transformed into a French film three years later. (An American musical movie version would follow in 1958, and a Broadway version of that in 1973.) Now, in 1951, the American novelist, playwright and screenwriter Anita Loos was completing her stage adaptation of *Gigi* and had mildly piqued the interest of the producer Gilbert Miller. At the same time, Miller got George Cukor to sign on as director; this would mark his return to Broadway after almost a quarter century in Hollywood.

Miller always insisted that he had been zealously committed to producing a play of *Gigi* since its publication as a book. When he learned that Loos was working on a dramatization, he was, so he later claimed, "delighted and told her as much. A week later we agreed on its production and I flew to Spain on vacation."

The reality was not quite as Miller recorded.

In fact, the general manager of his production company, the clever Morton Gottlieb, had initiated conversations about *Gigi* with Anita Loos and had unilaterally and publicly announced it during one of Miller's many absences from New York. As Loos recalled, Miller was a man who much preferred "losing himself in the pursuits of a Park Avenue playboy, [and so he] turned the job of producing the play over to Mortie. But the production had hit one snag . . . After auditioning all the ingénues on Broadway, [we] couldn't find a Gigi." There was a concomitant problem: according to the terms of Colette's contract, any actress who was to portray Gigi had to have her approval—just as she had the right to approve Loos's adaptation.

Why she indeed authorized the Loos adaptation may forever remain obscure. Colette's original two-hundred-and-fifty page novella was written with her Gallic tongue firmly planted in her cheek. Gigi, a delightful adolescent Parisian girl at the turn of the twentieth century, is being raised by her grandmother, aunt and mother to follow in their privileged footsteps and to become a fashionable courtesan—the mistress to a wealthy gentleman. This is considered to be the most expeditious route to an easy and luxurious life, and so the older women undertake to train her in all the arts necessary to succeed. Gigi hates the idea, even when the gentleman in question is handsome, loving and attentive. To the horror of her family, the man then decides to marry Gigi, and she accepts his proposal.

From Colette's novella, Anita Loos had fashioned a rather flat and literal English adaptation of what is essentially a very French social satire: until the play was finally staged, no one (apparently not even Colette) recognized that the adaptation was a serious attenuation of the novella. Everything allusive in the French had become candid in the English, everything subtle overstated.

PRECISELY WHEN ANITA LOOS, Morton Gottlieb and Gilbert Miller were temporizing with the press and theater owners and abandoning hope of finding the right talent, Maurice Goudeket, on orders from his wife, sent a telegram to Miller:

DO NOT CAST YOUR GIGI UNTIL YOU READ MY LETTER.

The letter followed a few days later:

Colette and I have just seen a young English actress playing in a film now being made in Monte Carlo. On seeing her, Colette said, "This would be a very good Gigi." I should like you not to decide definitely on any Gigi without seeing her . . . I believe she has had little experi-

ence on the stage, [but] she is very pretty and has that piquant quality necessary for the part.

As it happened, Colette and Goudeket had invited Audrey to their suite the very day they saw her at work, "and asked me if I would like to do the play. I said, 'I can't! I've never acted—I'm a dancer and have never spoken on stage!' Colette said that as a hard-working dancer, I could do it." Audrey read a few lines with the lady, but for most of their meeting, they discussed travel, food, music, romance. At the end of the evening, Colette handed her an autographed photo: "To Audrey Hepburn—the treasure I found on the beach."

On the morning of July 7, the treasure went by train from the Riviera to London's Victoria Station and there transferred to the waiting arms of James Hanson, who swept her off for a weekend in the country. The following week, she went to the Savoy Hotel to meet Gilbert Miller and Anita Loos, who had come from New York to consider her. "After a brief chat with Miss Hepburn, we named her for our Gigi," was all Miller had to say. "She didn't do it very well, but Audrey was engaged," according to Loos. Colette's blessing had in fact won Audrey the role so many had sought.

"I started walking on a cloud," Audrey said of that summer day, "a very worried cloud . . . I tried to explain to all of them that I wasn't ready to do a lead, but they didn't agree—and I was not going to try to change their minds."

Now Miller and company had a leading lady—but the delay had cost them Cukor, who was by this time busy working on another film. The producer settled on the French stage director Raymond Rouleau, who spoke no English. No problem there, said Miller: Audrey Hepburn spoke French fluently, and Loos would translate her adaptation into French for Rouleau's benefit. For the moment, everyone was euphoric—even James Hanson, whose proposal of marriage Audrey accepted. They announced the engagement in September, and the marriage was to follow the following June. Neither of them saw any reason why their professional schedules could not be made congruent; in any case, Audrey longed to subordinate her work to marriage and children.

Gilbert Miller paid a few thousand pounds to ABPC in consideration of Audrey's time out of her studio contract. Otherwise, the men there were somewhat diffident: after all, she was nothing like an English film star whose absence would mean a considerable loss to them. They reasoned that if *Gigi* failed, she would return to them eager to work; if it succeeded, she would return to them a star and would much improve their fortunes. And so, with a comprehensible blend of elation and anxiety, Audrey prepared to leave for America as soon as possible.

But the best-laid plans had to be briefly postponed. One morning in September, she took a call from Robert Lennard at Associated British Pictures, who had just spoken with Richard Mealand, a story editor and casting director at the London office of Paramount Pictures. Mealand told Lennard that he had been instructed by his Hollywood superiors to be on the lookout for an actress to star in a movie to be made in Rome the following summer. He had in hand a list of British studios and contract players, and on his desk, he said, was a magazine cover with a photo of—what was her name?

IT HAD TAKEN more than five years to shape the screenplay of *Roman Holiday* into something that could be filmed, and although a team of writers was still tinkering with a few sequences, William Wyler had read enough that he agreed to direct, and Gregory Peck (who was longing to break out of mold and do a comedy) had signed on as the male lead. Peck's agents had obtained for him a powerful prerogative in that deal: as a major Hollywood star then appearing in his twentieth film, he had the right of approval when it came to the choice of the female lead.

The story concerned a bored young princess who escapes from her gilded cage, explores Rome like a tourist for twenty-four hours, falls in love with an American journalist and finally, dutifully, returns to her royal obligations. Peck and Wyler knew that the ultimate success of the film would depend on adroit direction, a blend of comedy, romance and restrained sentimentality, and most of all on the credible and unpretentious appeal of the two principal players.

Wyler's previous three films—*The Heiress, Detective Story* and *Carrie*—had been critical and popular successes for Paramount. Meticulous, professional, incisive and sometimes ruthless with his actors, he had a completely European sensibility, although he had left his Alsatian home for America when he was eighteen and had, since 1920, directed fifty-nine pictures in Hollywood. In the business, he was known for wearing down even seasoned actors like Bette Davis and Laurence Olivier with his demands for repeated takes until, despite Wyler's inability to explain precisely what he wanted, they somehow gave him memorable and often award-winning performances.

By 1951, Wyler had two Oscars on his shelf (for *Mrs. Miniver* and *The Best Years of Our Lives*), fourteen of his actors had won statuettes and thirty-six of them had been nominated. It is doubtful that anyone in Hollywood ever knowingly turned down the opportunity to work on a William Wyler picture.

ROBERT LENNARD AGREED to send Audrey to meet the director. Apart from any potential financial benefits to ABPC from a deal to loan her to Paramount, Lennard sincerely liked Audrey and was pleased to advance her career if at all possible. She introduced herself to Wyler at Claridge's Hotel; after only five minutes, he had an impression that she was "very alert, very smart, very talented, very ambitious." And her lack of an American accent would make her more credible as a European princess. For her part, she recalled simply, "I didn't know what was expected of me." More to the point, she had no knowledge of William Wyler or his films, and so she did not feel nervous or intimidated in the presence of a great Hollywood director.

Wyler ordered a screen test, which was made on September 18 and was directed by Thorold Dickinson, her mentor on *Secret People*. Dressed in a full-length white nightgown, she enacted a portion of the script of *Roman Holiday* in which, bored with the prim formalities and stifling protocol of her royal station, the princess is put to bed by her lady-in-waiting; that role was read off-camera by an assistant.

But Wyler, a savvy veteran, had arranged for more. He asked Dickinson to conspire with the crew to keep the camera rolling at the end of the scene. At that point, she sat up, clasped her knees, smiled broadly and asked with complete abandon, "Well—how was I? Was I any good?" For several moments, she bantered with Dickinson and the crew, the camera capturing both her gaiety and her craving for approval. Her evident ambition was not something that came from a conniving, manipulative or seductive instinct: it simply betokened the determination of a young woman both vulnerable and strong who, despite her ignorance of the fine points of acting, was resolved to achieve the best she could.

Dickinson took the project further still. He asked Audrey to put off the costume, put her street clothes back on and return to a chair on the set to chat with him—while unknown to her, the film was still rolling in the camera. "I came back and sat down and talked to him," she recalled, long after she knew of the ruse. "He asked me a lot of questions about myself, about my work, and even about my past during the war in Holland . . . [and] that's what made the test. He had me on film being as natural as possible, not trying to act."

The film of Audrey was rushed to Wyler, who was by this time back in Hollywood. "The Hepburn test was very good," he wrote to Richard Mealand on October 12. "Everyone at the studio was enthused about the girl, and I am delighted. Please tell Dickinson that he did an excellent job." Paramount executive Don Hartman added, "We were fascinated. It's no credit to anyone here that we signed her immediately."

A contract was hurriedly composed and sent to her, and on October 15, at the flat she shared with her mother, Audrey signed with Paramount to appear in seven pictures in as many years. She was allowed a year off between each film and was permitted to do stage and television work during that year, but Paramount had the right to loan her out to another studio for one of her seven pictures. With that, Audrey Hepburn was perhaps the first inexperienced actor in history to be contracted simultaneously for leading roles on Broadway and in film. That evening, James took her and her mother to dine at the Café Royal in Regent Street, where the champagne flowed like champagne.

To settle the matter of Audrey's legal commitment to Associated British Pictures, Paramount wanted to buy out her contract for £100,000. Instead, ABPC executives realized that it would be preferable to receive a handsome fee for each film Audrey made for Paramount and also to acquire rights to distribute them in Britain. The unprecedented deal was made that autumn, and the principal beneficiary of it was none other than ABPC's chief stockholder and most active official—Jack L. Warner, who bided his time, secure in the conviction that one day Audrey Hepburn would work at his studio.

As for Paramount and Wyler, they were convinced that *Gigi* would run for a month, maybe two at the most, and that Audrey would be theirs early in 1952 so they could complete *Roman*

Holiday before the stifling heat of the Italian summer. The director showed the test to a warmly responsive Gregory Peck, and the matter of Audrey's participation was settled.

BEFORE THE END of October, Audrey boarded ship for New York. She traveled without her mother, who had a job in London as an interior decorator and would visit for the Broadway premiere; James would follow soon, too.

From sheer pleasure or anxiety or loneliness—or, most likely, a combination of causes—Audrey indulged in a kind of caloric abandon during the crossing, and by the time she was met at the West Side pier in Manhattan, she had managed to put on almost fifteen pounds. "When Gilbert saw her, he was appalled," according to Anita Loos. "He had engaged a sprite who had suddenly turned into a dumpling."

The dumpling's first task was to find a home. She had limited funds, but she presumed that she could lease comfortable quarters in a good New York hotel for a reasonable rate. Actors frequently booked at the Blackstone Hotel on 58th Street, and so Audrey asked to see the manager. He showed her a bright and cheerful suite—but she was astonished to learn that the rate was fifteen dollars per day. She could not spend more than nine, Audrey protested to the manager. He was sympathetic, but fifteen it had to be. A few minutes later, the manager shook Audrey's hand and escorted her to the door with her receipt for the room, which she had booked for nine dollars per day.

"I can't say just how she got me to change my mind," the manager said later. "She certainly didn't bargain with me—good Lord, you couldn't conceive of this elegant young woman lowering herself to haggle about money! She just talked and smiled and laughed, and somehow I found myself bewitched into the notion that I had no right in the world to charge her fifteen dollars." Audrey's charm was invariably persuasive, and few could resist.

The cast gathered all day for readings of the play, and then rehearsals began at the Fulton Theatre, where the opening was scheduled for November 24. At the same time, the dumpling was taken firmly in hand and the sprite was restored to form by Morton Gottlieb's strategy of a crash diet: he escorted Audrey twice daily to Dinty Moore's restaurant, next door to the theater, where a large portion of steak tartare was her only daily meal. This was a classic European dish composed of prime raw chopped sirloin with raw eggs, mustard, Worcestershire sauce, onions, capers and spices. After a month, Audrey was back in trim, and Dinty Moore's remained a place she liked—a colorful, sometimes raucous Irish tavern that served pub food, draft beers and generous drinks. After the opening of *Gigi*, she frequently returned with friends to Dinty Moore's, where she especially liked the poached eggs on corned beef hash, washed down with a good Belgian beer.

AUDREY ARRIVED AT a favorable time in Broadway history, and there were grand hopes for Colette's play. While the theaters were sold out for months with successful musicals (*Guys and Dolls*, *Call Me Madam*, *A Tree Grows in Brooklyn*, *The King and I* and Anita Loos's own *Gentlemen Prefer Blondes*), there were not many long-running plays; the exceptions were *The Rose Tattoo*, *The Four-poster*, *Saint Joan* and *The Moon Is Blue*. Julie Harris was about to have a great triumph in *I Am a Camera*, but the arrival of *Gigi* was more than any show trumpeted about town, thanks to Gilbert Miller's hyperactive publicity machine.

Rehearsals proceeded mostly in French, which caused no problem for Audrey. Cathleen Nesbitt was also fluent in French, and she acted as occasional interpreter for the other players. Nesbitt portrayed Gigi's Aunt Alicia and offstage became a kind of surrogate mother as well as both counselor and drama coach to Audrey.

Born in England in 1888, Cathleen Nesbitt made her London and New York theater debuts in 1910 and 1911. Among her stage and film credits in Britain and America, she is perhaps best known as Mrs. Higgins in the original 1956 New York production of *My Fair Lady*. One of the great beauties of her day, she had a historic romance with the poet Rupert Brooke in 1912, three years before his death at twenty-seven.

Cathleen's help was much appreciated, for the truth was that, apart from her fluency in French, Audrey needed all the assistance she could get. "I'm frightened," she blurted out to a journalist one day after rehearsal. "I have no stage training whatever. Others spend their lives at it before they get anywhere. I guess I'll have to act by intuition—until I learn." Her humility, based in reality, served her well. Later in the decade, the deep impression her performances made was due at least partly to the fact that she always considered herself an apprentice, acting by intuition as she learned, studied, read and worked her way meticulously through the rigors of filmmaking. She also developed a shrewd ability to choose the right characters for herself—even in comedies, these were mostly women challenged by life's circumstances who triumphed by courage, perseverance, wit and ingenuity.

"The role of Gigi required the technique of a seasoned actress," as Anita Loos recalled about the rehearsal period. "And in rehearsing Gigi's passionate blowup at the climax of the last act, Audrey remained much more the petulant teenager than a young woman suffering the sharp anguish of a first tragic love affair."

Cathleen Nesbitt came to the rescue. "Audrey was terribly frightened," she recalled. "She didn't have much idea of phrasing. She had no idea how to project, and she came bounding onto the stage like a gazelle. But she had that rare thing—audience authority, and that makes everybody look at you when you are on stage."

Until the show opened, however, only the cast, director and producer were looking at her on stage, and what they saw made them anxious indeed. Early each morning and late each evening, Cathleen and Audrey met, read lines, worked on diction and projection—and slowly, their efforts began to yield results.

Besides her constant trepidation about her debut (and the fact that the success of the play depended entirely on her), Audrey missed her mother and longed for her fiancé—especially after she witnessed a terrible scene. One evening after she returned to the hotel from a full dress rehearsal and a late supper at Dinty Moore's, she was preparing for bed when a guest on the eighteenth floor jumped from his window and bounced off her windowsill as he fell to his death. Shaking with sobs, Audrey fled her room and pounded on the next door, which was opened by the actor David Niven; he and his wife got Audrey through an upsetting experience and became lifelong friends.

FROM NOVEMBER 8 through 22, *Gigi* had an out-of-town preview at the Walnut Street Theatre in Philadelphia, America's oldest playhouse. Audiences were polite but not zealous, and the critics were mostly indifferent. Miller, Loos, Gottlieb, Rouleau, Hepburn and Nesbitt had no idea how to interpret the response. They decided against last-minute changes.

On the morning of Saturday, November 24, 1951, Audrey rose early. She put through a call to the wedding celebration of her half-brother Ian, who had just been married and would name his first child Audrey.

She then ate a light breakfast, took a walk on Fifth Avenue along Central Park, read *Gigi* again, sent a telegram to Colette in Paris—and met Cathleen Nesbitt for the ride to the Fulton Theatre and the opening night. Neither of them ever forgot that Audrey was white and cold with terror.

She need not have been.

Most critics had tepid reactions to the play—but not to Audrey Hepburn, who in two hours leaped from obscurity to celebrity. Brooks Atkinson, in *The New York Times*, wrote that she was "a young actress of charm, honesty and talent who ought to be interned in America and trapped into appearing in a fine play . . . [She] is the one fresh element in the performance. She is an actress; and as Gigi, she develops a full-length character from artless gaucheries in the first act to a stirring climax in the last scene. It is a fine piece of sustained acting that is spontaneous, lucid and captivating." Another critic noted "a candid innocence and a tomboy intelligence . . . and her performance comes like a breath of fresh air in a stifling season." And a third praised her "unquestionable beauty and talent. She acts with grace and authority—if, in this case, without much relaxation." There were a few dissenting voices, among them that of Noël Coward, who attended the following spring. As quick to praise as not, he nevertheless confided to his diary that *Gigi* offered "an orgy of overacting and a vulgar script. Cathleen Nesbitt good and dignified, and the sets lovely. Audrey Hepburn inexperienced and rather too noisy, and the whole thing badly directed."

By all accounts, the critical approbation did not diminish Audrey's stage fright, which seems to have made her quite ill every evening; nor did it diminish her conviction that she was doing very badly indeed. Her insecurity endured throughout her lifetime, as her elder son confirmed years later: "She was basically a very insecure person whose very insecurity made everyone fall in love with her . . . [She was] a star who couldn't see her own light." Her insecurity and concomitant inability to appreciate her best gifts perhaps derived, at least in part, from a lack of parental endorsement, from the deeply rooted effects of the war, and from the realization that there could be something perilously selfish in the life of an actor—something she did not, on the other hand, see in the disciplined life of a dancer.

After the first week of performances, Gilbert Miller ordered Audrey's name placed above the title outside the theater. Audrey was commanded to pose for the press, turning the last lightbulb in the last letter of her last name, so that when AUDREY HEPBURN finally illuminated the marquee, it seemed—but only in the photos—as if she might be electrocuted by sheer vanity. "Oh, dear," she told reporters huddling around her as she climbed down from the ladder, "I still have to learn how to act!"

She was twenty-two years old and, literally overnight, had become a Broadway luminary the way a naïve vedette becomes a star in a sentimental movie about a chorus girl leaping to stage center. Amid all the clinking of glasses in the week following the premiere, and despite the massive bouquets sent to her dressing room, Audrey was resentful that Cathleen Nesbitt and the other cast members were virtually ignored by the press and the public. Autograph hounds clamored only for Audrey outside the stage door every night and after every matinee.

Perhaps it was precisely the shock and the extreme nature of it all that led her to distrust that what was happening would endure. Certainly she had no conviction that she had earned it. But not many people had any idea of the real Audrey, a considerate and unpretentious young woman with impeccable manners and un-stuffy refinement, who could also be a clown, an irrepressible mimic, a spontaneous turner of cartwheels and, as Milton wrote of Nature, a lusty paramour.

THE BARONESS ARRIVED on December 19, attended a performance of the play, went backstage, smiled and hugged her daughter for the cameras—and, typically, offered no praise. Indeed, her remark can hardly have been what Audrey expected or needed at the moment: "You've done very well, my dear, considering that you have no talent."

On December 21, Ella stood just off-camera when a television crew visited Audrey's dressing room at the Fulton. Appearing on a live program called *We, the People,* Audrey spoke of Christmas 1944 in Arnhem, when she and her family were saved from the brink of starvation by a gift of ten potatoes.

In time for Christmas, the ardent James Hanson flew to New York from his Canadian office. Proud of his fiancée, he squired her around town and, for the holidays, transferred her from the Blackstone to a suite at the far more opulent Waldorf Towers; there he also installed Ella in luxury, on the same floor. On Christmas Eve, James gave Audrey an emerald and diamond floral ring in white gold.

But it was Cathleen Nesbitt whose presence in Audrey's life that season was more precious to her than anything. She was in every way the kind of woman and mentor Audrey respected and loved, and her affection was returned. Madame Rambert had certainly been encouraging—but only to a point, and finally she had bad news for her young dancer. With Cathleen it was very different: a patient and tireless teacher, she was the champion of Audrey's cause and the endorser of her talent. And when it was appropriate, she also offered the forthright praise that any young person needs in order to continue in a difficult and demanding craft with so many public judges waiting to pronounce their critical opinion. Playing Audrey's aunt onstage, she was so much more in life, and to far greater effect.

Cathleen was an example to Audrey of a successful, highly respected actress with consummate dignity but without an atom of affectation or arrogance; by sheer example, she enhanced those same qualities in Audrey. Fulfilling a professional function as a tutor and an emotional one as an encouraging older woman, she offset both Ella's incompetence and her incapability.

Cathleen Nesbitt had a long and troubled marriage to an alcoholic actor named Cecil Ramage, a burden she bore in discreet privacy; their daughter Jennifer, exactly Audrey's age, was working successfully in England in 1951. The devoted rapport between Cathleen Nesbitt and Audrey Hepburn is easy to understand on both sides. A cherished friendship, it endured without interruption until Cathleen died in 1982, at the age of ninety-three.

Chapter Five

∽

1952

"MY CAREER IS a complete mystery to me," said Audrey Hepburn, reflecting later on her success. "It's been a total surprise since the first day. I never thought I was going to be an actress, I never thought I was going to be in movies, I never thought it would all happen the way it did."

The fame certainly happened literally overnight. As the new year began, her face appeared glossily on the pages of magazines all over America. *Life* offered a full-page spread and five photos, proclaiming "Audrey Is a Hit—Young Miss Hepburn Becomes Star on First U.S. Try." *Look* agreed: "Audrey Hepburn—Her Star Is Rising." In these and countless articles over the next decades, journalists frequently stumbled and fell into a thicket of empty clichés in the race to their typewriters.

She was, for example, routinely termed "elfin," although an elf is (according to the *Oxford English Dictionary*) a mischievous, spiteful male creature; she was regularly called "gazelle-like," despite the fact that gazelles are spotted antelopes; she was often described as "coltish," even if colts are male horses . . . and so it went. "Gamine" was the usual designation—but the primary meaning of the word is a street urchin or homeless waif. The misapplication of words did, however, reveal that for Audrey Hepburn the press needed a new vocabulary.

Whatever terms were used in print or conversation, people were certainly enchanted with the real thing in person. Even among Manhattan's cool socialites, there were reports of audible intakes of breath when this twenty-two-year-old appeared at the wave of luncheons and prizes in her honor. A group called the Twelfth Night Club gave a breakfast in Audrey's honor (at one o'clock in the afternoon) on February 18, and a Westchester County hunt club hosted an event for her at the 21 Club on May 13, to raise money for cancer research.

Between those dates, and until *Gigi* closed in May after 219 performances, the leading lady had few weekdays to herself, for her diary was quickly crowded with events. Gilbert Miller and his team of publicists were busy every day, fielding calls for interviews—"and would Miss Hepburn be available for photographs with her charming fiancé?" No, she would not. That part of her life was off limits, she insisted. Newsmen did not know that Audrey traveled by airplane to visit James in Toronto every Sunday morning when weather permitted, returning just in time for her Monday evening performance.

On February 10, she made her dramatic debut on television, appearing live on the Sunday evening variety show *Toast of the Town*. She portrayed Lady Jane Grey in a few moments from the play *Nine Days a Queen*. Following that scene, Gilbert Miller joined Audrey for a chat with the show's host, Ed Sullivan. Thus the publicity for *Gigi* rolled along.

On April 13, she was first seen on television in a complete, live half-hour dramatic role. Written especially for her by Meade

Roberts and directed by David Rich, "Rainy Day in Paradise Junction" depended on Audrey herself for much of the character of Virginia Forsyte.

"My father was English," she says, explaining her accent to a group of people waiting for a train in a small American town. As a lame sixteen-year-old girl, she captivates the attention of the lost souls in the café with her improbable longing to be a dancer in Hollywood movies. "But most of all, I want to dance in ballet," she says, with wistful earnestness. "You're all thinking, 'How in the world is a cripple going to be a dancer?' " And with that, she tries to waltz with one of the café patrons. She knows this is only a momentary fantasy, and at the conclusion—as a close-up reveals both her melancholy and her dignity—she boards a train to return to her sister in Wichita. This was a fully realized performance with a remarkable mixture of humor and pathos, all the more important for Audrey because, despite its brevity, it allowed her to attempt something more serious than the youthful antics of a Parisian adolescent.

AFTER *GIGI*'S ASTONISHING success, Paramount had agreed to postpone *Roman Holiday*—but only so long. By springtime, they could wait no longer, and so in consideration of a $50,000 fee, Gilbert Miller posted a closing notice for May: Audrey would leave Broadway and arrive in Rome the following month. Miller also got a guarantee that *Roman Holiday* would be completed by the end of September, in time for Audrey's return for a national tour of *Gigi*.

This required an intense preproduction schedule for the movie: the fine points of every character's wardrobe, the details of makeup, the logistics of an enormous international crew working in Rome, the necessary legal clearances for filming at great monu-

ments and palazzos, the strategy of finalizing actors' schedules—
everything had to be firmly in place so that Wyler, his cast and the
technical team would have to deal only with the usual unforeseen
daily circumstances, personal situations and delays that routinely
attend moviemaking.

In February, Audrey read the latest script version of *Roman
Holiday,* which was not the last; in fact, it would not be finalized
until the actual shooting was completed.

The development of this movie had already been long and
complicated. First, Dalton Trumbo wrote a story that remained
unpublished.* Then his prose narrative was turned into a script by
Ian McLellan Hunter, with additions by John Dighton. They were
not the first screenwriters on the project. A team had worked with
Frank Capra when he had hoped to do the picture in 1946, and
then, during the early Wyler tenure, Valentine Davies and Preston
Sturges signed on briefly to deal with some thorny scenes. Much of
the final script, however, must be credited to the great Ben Hecht,
who took over after Hunter and Dighton were off the project and
who, as usual, cared not at all about credit as long as he was paid:
Hecht actually wrote or rewrote more than two hundred movies
but was credited with about sixty—his name appears nowhere on
the film of *Gone With the Wind,* but the final script is mostly his.
Later, even while *Roman Holiday* was in production, the eminent

---

* When the film was released in 1953, Trumbo's name was omitted: he had been blacklisted
in the notorious anti-Communist hysteria of the time. Ian McLellan Hunter "fronted" for
Trumbo as creator of the story and secretly shared a portion of the screenwriting income
with him. When the picture won Academy Awards for best story and for best screenplay,
the statuettes were presented to Hunter (for story) and to Hunter and John Dighton (for
screenplay), which is how the screen credit then appeared. The Academy of Motion Picture Arts and Sciences rectified the matter forty years later, and the Oscar was posthu-
mously presented to Trumbo in 1993. Since then the rerelease prints of *Roman Holiday*
carry the credit: "Screenplay by Ian McLellan Hunter and John Dighton . . . Story by Dalton Trumbo."

Italian writers Suso Cecchi d'Amico and Ennio Flaiano rewrote scenes for Wyler. "The picture was kind of put together as it went along," according to the film's editor, Robert Swink.

What seems like a messy and inefficient way of writing a screenplay is often standard operating procedure in the business; indeed, some of the most admired movies were in fact masterpieces of improvisation. Producer David O. Selznick hoped that the script prepared by Sidney Howard and revised by others would be "locked" when filming began on *Gone With the Wind*, but major changes had to be made during filming, and that is when Ben Hecht's expeditious brilliance was required.

As the laborious process of constructing the script and the shooting schedule proceeded without Audrey, some things required her attention even during the run of the play. In February, for example, Edith Head swept into Manhattan from Paramount's California offices with her portfolio of ideas for Audrey's costumes. A native Californian of keen intelligence, educated at Stanford and always intensely ambitious for her hegemony, Edith, then fifty-five, suffered no fools gladly, in or out of her studio. Always seen and photographed wearing dark glasses (the better to camouflage certain age lines), she forced her black hair into severe bangs over her forehead, à la Louise Brooks in the 1920s, and her voice had an oddly strident pitch. Neither especially feminine nor particularly graceful, she nevertheless designed some of the most glorious costumes for Hollywood women. Either directly or through her staff at the studios, she was involved in more than seven hundred films and was awarded the Oscar eight times, more than any other individual.

During her sixty-year career (first at Paramount, then at Universal), Edith seemed to have no enemies in the business—perhaps because she refused to discuss the stars whose forms and figures she knew so well and who confided in her. Edith was diplomatic as few in the business were, and although she had a kind of stiffness many found off-putting, she refused to malign anyone. That discretion restricted her usefulness for gossip at parties, but it also gained her the loyalty she prized. For her first two movies, Audrey worked genially with Edith, who always claimed that no actress ever made her task easier.

Audrey arrived at Edith's hotel room wearing a dark suit with white collar and cuffs, a sprig of white lily-of-the-valley in her buttonhole and white gloves. "This was a girl way ahead of high fashion," according to Edith. "She deliberately looked different from other women and dramatized her own slenderness into her chief asset."

Edith appreciated Audrey's intelligence and directness and quickly had the impression that this young actress knew more about fashion than any actress except Marlene Dietrich. "But what impressed me most was her body. I knew she would be the perfect mannequin for anything I would make. I knew it would be a great temptation to design clothes that would overpower her. I could have used her to show off my talents and detract from hers, but I didn't. I considered doing it, believe me." That she did not was a testimony to Edith Head's cool professionalism—and to Audrey's polite but firm insistence on her own ideas.

With a height of five feet seven inches and a waist of just twenty inches, Audrey had the perfect model figure. Unusual for her time, she wore no shoulder pads and refused to pad her brassiere. To Edith's sketches, Audrey made significant additions, especially the style of simpler necklines, wider belts and flatter shoes for the movie spree around Rome. She always considered her wardrobe for films as personal as her outfits for everyday use, and in her gently resolute way, Audrey Hepburn would teach every designer that she never wore anything she had not approved or to which she had not made some significant alteration. Only rarely was she off the mark.

Very soon after Edith departed New York, two men arrived

from Paramount's makeup department. In 1952, cosmetics for black-and-white films were exceptionally complex and detailed; the ingredients and procedures for each sequence depended not only on skin type but also on the personality of the character, the interior or exterior lighting required, the clothing worn—and of course the extent of the actor's vanity. The on-set supervision for Audrey in Rome was done by the great Italian cosmetician Alberto De Rossi, but Paramount's Wally Westmore sent ahead the materials for testing on Audrey, with specific instructions on their use:

> First apply #12 Hi Light to the dark circles under the eyes, then powder. Apply 626-C Panstick all over the face, then rub gently to spread it evenly. Then pat the face all over to remove any finger marks. Use 626-C Panstick and #12 Hi Light mixed, and apply lightly under the eyes in the same dark area as before. Apply blue-grey eye shadow to the eyelids and smooth down gently. Powder under the eyes first and then the rest of the face and eyelids. IMPORTANT: Don't use too much powder. She should have a nice skin sheen and not the dull flat look. Then brush off excess powder. Line the upper eyelid with brown pencil, NOT BLACK, close to the eye-lashes to make the lashes appear heavier. Add brown mascara only to the upper lashes. Apply lip rouge. Cover the exposed parts of the body with 626-C Pancake.*

Audrey's contract with Paramount had been in place since the previous autumn, but the details for her participation in *Roman Holiday* had to be fixed. Finally, on March 20, the deal was countersigned. Audrey was to start work in Rome on June 1; her salary was a total

---

* In Rome, Alberto De Rossi eventually made strategic makeup changes due to the circumstances of lighting, weather and other contingencies. He so pleased Audrey that she asked for him on five of her subsequent European films; his wife, Grazia De Rossi, styled Audrey's hair for four of them.

of $7,000 for twelve weeks of work (payable in weekly installments of $583.33), with an additional $250 per week to cover living expenses. That year, Twentieth Century–Fox was paying Marilyn Monroe (then twenty-six) slightly less than Audrey received, and with no expense allowance; Elizabeth Taylor (age twenty) commanded $5,000 a week and virtually whatever trinkets she desired from Metro-Goldwyn-Mayer. Appearing in his twentieth picture, Gregory Peck received $100,000 and $1,000 weekly living expenses.

"I went to work for the money, because I had to," Audrey said of this time. "But I was one of the lucky ones. I chose a profession I liked, and I was terribly fortunate in being discovered by William Wyler—and from then on, I went into such quality movies that I was able to accept them for the joy of doing them. And I would have been crazy if I hadn't!"

THE LAST PERFORMANCE of *Gigi* was presented on May 31; a few days later, Audrey left with James for a Paris holiday. Because of the late closing of the play, they decided to postpone their wedding from June until late September, after *Roman Holiday* concluded. From Paris, she proceeded to Rome on June 12, and he returned to work in London and Toronto. Everyone presumed that the marriage would go forward in the autumn, before Audrey returned for the American road tour of *Gigi*.

She had not so much as visited Hollywood yet, although the film was officially Audrey's first American picture—but it was so only in the sense that it was made under contract to and financed by an American company. Paramount had previously earned the money in Italy, but the funds had been frozen by the Italian government, the better to ensure employment for Italian workers after the war. *Roman Holiday* was made entirely on location in and around the city, and the interior scenes were shot at the Cinecittà studios.

Apart from record heat and humidity in Rome that summer, the moviemaking experience was an exceptionally gratifying time for everyone involved, and the common feeling was that the newcomer was largely responsible. "She is that almost extinct type—a serious student of acting," said Wyler, who was not easily impressed with young stars. More to the point, there was, according to Peck, "nothing mean or petty about [about Audrey]. She had a good character, so I think people picked up on that. She didn't have any of the backstabbing, grasping, petty, gossipy personality that you see in this business. I liked her a lot; in fact, I loved Audrey. It was easy to love her."

Most people took his last statement for what it meant—an assertion of loving friendship—and interpreted nothing more. But the question of an affair was whispered for decades by those who dine on rumors or cook them up for others. Without an atom of evidence and despite silence on the matter from the principals, tales of a romance flew wildly from Rome to Hollywood; even today, there are those who swear it was a reality, although no one has come forth to assert that he held the lamp. Peck had, in fact, recently met and was ardently courting his inamorata, Véronique Passani, a French journalist who was to be his second wife. In addition, James Hanson rushed to spend every weekend with Audrey—and was often present during the week, too. They spent their free time in an air-conditioned suite at the Hotel Hassler, planning their wedding.

The high spirits of Hepburn and Peck and their relaxed, genial collaboration certainly contributed to their remarkable onscreen performances that summer. Peck "always put me at ease before starting a scene," she recalled. "It was a happy company, without anybody going temperamental or putting up emotional barriers. I soon learned to relax, to look for guidance from Peck and Wyler. I trusted them, and they never let me down." As for her co-star, he regretted that so many people primarily thought of Audrey "as regal—but I like to think of her as spunky."

For decades, Peck delighted in telling interviewers that early in the shooting, he realized that Audrey was delivering a first-rate performance, and that the film was certainly as much (if not more) her story than his. And so, he said, he contacted his agent in Hollywood. His contract stipulated that only his name was to appear above the title of the film, but he wanted that changed: Audrey was magnificent, she would very likely win an Oscar, and her name belonged above the title with his. The agent demurred, but Peck pressed him—and so, thanks to his generosity, Audrey's name was indeed moved above the title to accompany his.

There is no doubt that, in his career as in his personal life, Gregory Peck was an enormously considerate and generous man; that many people benefited from his kindness and support; and that the circle of his friends and admirers was wide and inclusive. But in the matter of Audrey's credit, his memory was imprecise. In fact, as the production files for *Roman Holiday* reveal, it was Wyler and the studio personnel in Hollywood who had the idea to bill Audrey Hepburn above the title with Peck, but they realized this was a delicate matter because of the actor's contract.

After filming was completed, Wyler returned to Hollywood for the editing process. When he saw the first cut and had his high estimate of Audrey's performance confirmed by the images on screen, Wyler made the recommendation to Paramount that they reconsider the credits. His assistant received a swift reply on January 20, 1953: "The Audrey Hepburn credit [you recommend] is not strictly in accordance with the contractual agreement with Gregory Peck, although we do not see any problem in getting him to agree to this setup—but we do need his consent. Therefore, please explain this to William Wyler and have him get Gregory Peck to initial the attached billing opposite the Audrey Hepburn credit."

On or about January 25, Wyler met Peck for lunch and made
the request, with which Peck agreed; he may well have regretted
not suggesting the idea in the first place—hence his revised account. Still, his agent, the scrupulous George Chasin, had to work
out the exact language in a codicil to the Peck/Paramount contract: the credit must not be "Gregory Peck and Audrey Hepburn
in . . ." and there had to be no indication of star parity. The result
of the legal sparring, even with Peck's agreement to share credit
above the title, may be seen in the finished picture. There is no
doubt about the identity of the primary star, and no doubt about
the presentation of a neophyte:

A Paramount Picture
presenting Gregory Peck
and introducing
Audrey Hepburn
in
William Wyler's production
ROMAN HOLIDAY

"She's a very funny lady," Peck said later, "and I have always
thought that she should have played more comedy. They seized
upon her with this image in mind, and they practically put a halo
on her head. In fact, they wanted to do [variations on] the *Roman
Holiday* story over and over again. It's not that she hasn't had a
great career . . . but I wish that she had been allowed to do a few
broad comedies along the way." Later, part of the problem was the
sheer vulgarity of the so-called comic roles offered to Audrey;
these she would not do.

But everyone enjoyed Audrey's earthy humor that summer.
The cast remembered her account of the tomcat adopted when
Audrey was in the chorus of *High Button Shoes*. When he became
too amorous with some female cats belonging to the players and

orchestra members, the tomcat was sterilized. The chorus then discussed a name for him. "That's easy—we shall have to name him Tomorrow," said Audrey innocently. Asked why, she replied with perfect poise, "Because Tomorrow never comes."

Audrey never found acting easy. Moviemaking is usually a chaotic business, and she was enormously sensitive to noisy commotion. She needed time to prepare; to concentrate and keep her focus, she required some quiet distance and some solitude on the set. Audrey was, in other words, not an actress who could swiftly move from casual chatter or idle joking to the task of acting for the camera.

Usually, however, she could be a clown, and she seemed to enjoy everything that summer—all the hard work; the necessary retakes during the long, scorching afternoons; even the distractions of acting while surrounded by a crowd of gaping Romans and tourists. Nor did she object to Wyler's habit of multiple takes. After the director had called for more than fifty takes on a single shot, Eddie Albert, also in the cast, recalled that the director announced earnestly, "That was fine—but we seem to have lost the spontaneity!"

Audrey was animated and exuberant, perhaps as only a young woman could be who was having sudden, unexpected success in what she loved to do; and it could not have diminished her exhilaration that she was engaged to an adoring and attractive man who flew to her side every day he could.

DECADES LATER, *Roman Holiday* has lost none of its bright appeal, its restrained sentiment and its incisive wit. The venerable conventions of the fairy tale, here put into clever reverse, are combined with elements of classic screwball comedy, delicate social satire and (thanks to the performers) the story of a tender but brief affection that cannot become an enduring romance.

Princess Ann (Hepburn), daughter of the king and queen of an unnamed country, travels on a goodwill tour of Europe. By the time she comes to Rome, she is bored and angry with the stifling protocols, the endless reception lines, the tedious schedule of royal engagements and the total lack of anything casual, informal, spontaneous or merely enjoyable: "Everything we do is so *wholesome!*" She longs to know something of ordinary people and common life, and in the presence of her lady-in-waiting, she sobs uncontrollably. A doctor is summoned and an injection given, but before it takes effect, she changes into a simple blouse and skirt and steals out of the embassy. As she freewheels among crowds in the Roman night, she is at last overcome by the force of the sedation.

Joe Bradley (Peck), an American journalist returning from a late-night card game, finds the princess sleeping near the Colosseum and, unaware of her identity and believing her to be drunk, reluctantly allows her to spend the night in his apartment. Next morning, he recognizes her and also a potentially lucrative newspaper story. She, on the other hand, is unaware that she is to be the subject when Joe and his photographer colleague Irving (Eddie Albert) show Ann the sights of Rome and oblige her whims for a day. She eats ice cream, has her hair fashionably cut, buys a new pair of shoes, smokes her first cigarette, is arrested by the police for causing mayhem on a Vespa and goes dancing at a riverside nightclub.

By the time Joe and Ann reveal their identities to each other, they are in love, and he cannot betray her by turning in the story. Then reality intervenes; they realize they have lives separated by a complex of differing obligations and professional duties; and after a last nighttime ride, she returns to her royal life. At a reception for the press next day, Joe and Irving signal to Ann that her Roman holiday will remain their shared secret.

IT HAS OFTEN been claimed that the story of Princess Ann was modeled on Britain's Princess Margaret, who fell in love with an older, divorced man named Peter Townsend and was discouraged (by her family and the government) from marrying him. However, the Townsend affair was unknown until 1953, after *Roman Holiday* was completed, and the unhappy end of Princess Margaret's relationship did not occur until 1955. "We are not drawing any parallel" between Ann and Margaret, Wyler wrote in a 1951 studio memorandum, but the articles and stories on Margaret that they used for research did, at the time, "give us good insight into the life of a modern princess." It was, in other words, not Margaret's personal life they studied (for they knew nothing of it in 1952), but rather her official activities and her well-documented sense of fun. When the film was made, Margaret was twenty-two.

IT IS NO EXAGGERATION to say that *Roman Holiday* would very likely have failed if Audrey's performance had not been so natural, credible, textured, witty and poignant. She moves with stately poise in her scenes as a princess on duty, while elsewhere, she cavorts, dances, falls in the river and tears around the city with the abandon of a teenager. In no sequence is she coy or fey, and there is no indication that she was wearied by Wyler's habit of demanding multiple takes of a scene.

It is this completely balanced, highly nuanced portrait, without a false move or intonation, that ought to be taken into account when assessing this stage of Audrey's career, for in a way Princess Ann *is* Audrey. The daughter of the baroness, properly raised with all the refinements of European etiquette, trained in the discipline of ballet and schooled in the deprivations of war, Audrey found a counterpart in Ann's personality—the character as a spontaneous, giggling, frisky girl who knows how to frolic when she has the chance. Ann/Audrey does more than let her hair down, she has it cut off: when the barber shears Ann's long, luxuriant tresses and leaves only the short pixie cut we forever associate with the young Audrey, her face and the scene are incandescent.

In this regard, *Roman Holiday* has some elements of screwball comedy—of Depression-era films like *It Happened One Night* and *Holiday*, in which audiences were told that the rich are not as happy as we commoners. Screwball comedy depended on a certain folksiness that is a staple of the comic tradition—the notion, for example, that royals and the rich can truly enjoy life only when they doff their finery, deny their privileges and come down to earth, joining the masses and perhaps never returning to their gilded cages. But *Roman Holiday* scores its final emotional point—the poignancy of personal happiness sacrificed to public duty—and thus is too honest to stop with the last convention of screwball comedy. Joe and Ann simply do not live happily ever after, at least not together.

Supporting this bittersweetness is the canny and comic use of the reverse fairy tale. We first see the princess in a series of shots, clothed magnificently. Then there is a reception in which, coolly dignified, she makes a grand entrance, wearing a tiara and a spectacular ball gown; she maintains her composure during an interminable presentation line of international dignitaries. But her feet are aching, and we see beneath her floor-length gown: she has slipped off one shoe and cannot retrieve it—Cinderella-as-princess has lost her slipper. Soon we move to the scene in which Sleeping Beauty/Snow White is approached by the handsome prince, but he cannot awaken her. At the final fadeout, she rushes back to the palace—not with the prince, but alone, to the embassy and her duties.

Sometimes directors succeed in conveying a rare and rich symbiosis between actor and character—an association that was perhaps neither suspected in advance nor calculated in the moment. D. W. Griffith forever captured on film (in *Broken Blossoms*, for example) the delicate strength of Lillian Gish—the waif as victim, but also as provider. Josef von Sternberg was somehow able to portray both the erotic insouciance and the spirited feminine wisdom of Marlene Dietrich (in, among other films, *Shanghai Express*). Alfred Hitchcock celebrated both the insistent passion and the risky, romantic idealism of Ingrid Bergman (in *Notorious*). Federico Fellini revealed the artless simplicity and the profound humanity of his wife, Giulietta Masina (in *Nights of Cabiria*).

In that tradition, a seasoned director with the painstaking exactitude of William Wyler was needed to evoke from Audrey what is essentially an encoded portrait of herself in *Roman Holiday*, and this revelation was certainly far beyond the intention of either director or actress. In each of her subsequent films, these complementary parts of her character became ever more clarified—the polite and the playful aspects, the dedicated and the willful, the idealistic youth and the grown-up who endures a kind of moral education. In *Roman Holiday* as elsewhere, Audrey is never woodenly consistent. She is not a material girl but a mercurial one, a constant nymph who can be royal or sassy, regal or spirited, depending on the moment.

YET AUDREY COULD not yet be considered a seasoned professional in 1952. Indeed, some aspects of a scene could present special problems. Like many actors, she could not weep naturally on command. For such situations, there have always been vials of certain eyedrops on film sets, manufactured to bring forth the necessary tears.

"When we got to the last scene," Audrey recalled, "we were in the car, and I was saying goodbye to Greg and going back to being a princess. I was supposed to sob my heart out. But I couldn't cry. I was pretending to cry, but it was no good at all. There were no proper tears. They tried glycerin. Take after take, it wasn't any good. Willy [Wyler] came over and gave me absolute hell. 'How long do you think we're going to wait here? Can't you cry, for goodness' sake? By now you should know what acting's about!' I was so upset—he was so angry with me. I just started to cry. He shot it, gave me a big hug and walked off. That's how you learn. He knew with me there was no point in trying to teach me. He would just make me cry."

WHILE THE FILMING proceeded, Gilbert Miller sent frequent reminders to Paramount's offices in Los Angeles and Rome, for he intended to hold them to Audrey's contracted return for the long national tour of *Gigi,* which had been firmly booked across the country for autumn 1952 and into 1953, and she was expected in New York on October 1. These memoranda were not unforeseen, and so Paramount calculated that the last day they could use Audrey in Rome would be September 30. Someone reasoned that if she had to be in New York by October 1, she could depart from Rome by airplane that day, and by regaining the time en route, she would arrive that evening—unable to work, of course, but legally in fulfillment of the obligation that she be physically in New York on October 1. The studio had no obligation to consider her marriage plans, which in any case no one had discussed when the shooting schedule was finalized in late May.

But complications of another sort were threatening.

Beginning in early July, James Hanson had begun to interfere in the matter of Audrey's schedule—to persuade Paramount to hurry along the filming. She tried to deter him from this intervention, but he only became more insistent: he would be her protector and defender against the Hollywood brass, and they would have all the time necessary to prepare for the wedding.

On July 8, Hanson wrote to Henry Henigson, the Paramount executive producer assigned to the picture: "It appears to be possible for Miss Hepburn to return to New York on the *Queen Elizabeth* on September 24. Miss Hepburn hopes to be able to take the boat from Southampton, as she has some affairs to attend to in this country [England] before leaving." He then referred to an earlier letter, in which he had asked if it were possible for the film to conclude in early September, which would allow them ample time for the wedding, which, curiously, he did not mention.

In early August, due to the inevitable delays and the necessary postdubbing at Cinecittà, the completion date of the picture had been pushed back to September 25. This allowed Audrey and James only one week for their wedding and a foreshortened honeymoon before she returned to work in America.

As much as she longed to be married, she intended to honor her contractual obligations: she was sorry, she told James, but she had no control over the shooting schedule, and she was sure he understood the necessity of her resuming the tour. Why could they not be married in New York? she asked. To this he was not agreeable: his family had certain social expectations, after all.

During those torrid weeks, there occurred another kind of interference. The London tabloids featured photos of the handsome James Hanson, with this or that attractive young actress or socialite on his arm, attending a play or a party in London or Paris, or emerging from this or that nightclub.

On August 12, Hanson wrote again to Harry Henigson, this time demanding that Audrey be released in mid-September so they could marry in England before going on to New York and the resumption of the *Gigi* tour: "Our present plan is to leave Rome on September 21 for London"—which, as he had to realize by then, was impossible. Five days later and quite on his own, he issued a press release through his London office: "Audrey Hepburn, the British actress, and James Hanson, whose family operates several haulage and bus companies in England and Canada, will be married on September 30. Miss Hepburn, who is starring with Gregory Peck in *Roman Holiday*, now being made in Rome, said the wedding would take place in Huddersfield parish church, Yorkshire, England."

With that, Paramount's American executives—unaware of any such plans—contacted Audrey. She had asked to be given, at the end of production, the splendid wardrobe that had been designed for her, along with the dozens of accessories, including handbags, shoes, hats and costume jewelry. The studio informed her that they hoped she would accept all this as a wedding gift.

Very soon, the ironies were compounded, for Audrey Hepburn announced the termination of her engagement to James Hanson. "We decided it was the wrong time to get married," she said. "My schedule commits me to a movie here, then back to the stage, then back to Hollywood. [James] would be spending most of his time taking care of his business in England and Canada. It would be very difficult for us to lead a normal married life." In those days, the press made nothing more of the matter.

James's executive manner, his peremptory actions and his other romantic entanglements had cost him his fiancée. But there were other considerations on Audrey's mind. Ella had chosen her two husbands unwisely, and both marriages had ended in divorce— a situation her daughter did not want to repeat. She felt she had to succeed where Ella had failed, and she did not want to subject her children to the confusion and unhappiness she herself had known as a child.

She arrived unescorted in New York on the appointed day. Gilbert Miller and the cast (some of them replacements) noted her exuberance and energy; she was, Audrey said, happy to be back. Yes, the work in Rome had been wonderful, unforgettable; of her private life she said nothing.

For the months ahead, Audrey was not tied down to one spot at all, for the busy national tour of *Gigi* took her across the country, to places she had never visited. Among other cities, she played to audiences in Baltimore, Pittsburgh, Cincinnati, Detroit, Chicago and San Francisco. She was making her way to Hollywood.

Chapter Six

1953

IN 1952, THE UNEXPECTED Broadway success of *Gigi* had delayed the filming of *Roman Holiday* and caused more than the usual financial and logistical headaches for executives at Paramount Pictures. But the tension was eased when *Gigi*'s prolonged national tour, from October 1952 to June 1953, coincided with the final editing and music scoring for *Roman Holiday*; now, the timing could not have been more perfect for the studio. As Audrey made her way across America, she was providing Paramount with extremely beneficial advance publicity. When she began two weeks of performances at the Biltmore Theatre in Los Angeles in March, everyone who had picked up an American newspaper or magazine knew about the imminent release of *Roman Holiday*.

"We were there to shield her from the press when that was necessary and to allow the press access to her when that was helpful," recalled Arthur Wilde, at the time Paramount's publicist assigned to Audrey in Los Angeles. "She was of course very classy and demure with the public, but she knew exactly what she was doing, and she did things in her own way. Audrey was easy to work with, always cooperative and without any high-handed attitude—and she was really her own best publicist. But it was clear that she had no plans to be merely the tool of the studio."

According to Wilde, there was some concern at Paramount over Audrey's flat-chested, almost boyish figure, which was certainly an exception among American stars during the primacy of Marilyn Monroe and Elizabeth Taylor. "I had the unfortunate task of informing Audrey that the studio might ask her to pad her bust off-screen as well as on. But she was adamant that she would change nothing in her appearance—she would be herself or no one at all. Of course she was right. She started an entirely different look in America, and in 1953 she was the one incomparable newcomer. The press had never seen anyone like her."

That year, rumors swirled in and out of the columns about Audrey's next projects. Director Joseph L. Mankiewicz, who had seen a preview of *Roman Holiday*, wanted her and John Gielgud to appear in a film of *Twelfth Night*; Gielgud countered that they might appear to better advantage in a screen version of *The School for Scandal*. At the same time, it was inaccurately announced that Audrey would appear with Laurence Olivier, under Peter Brook's direction, in *The Beggar's Opera*; that she would star in a French comedy, *La Cuisine*; that she would travel to Venice and appear as Yul Brynner's co-star in *A New Kind of Love*; and that she would be Marlon Brando's leading lady in *Desirée*.

To her surprise and amusement, Audrey was also offered the role of a Japanese bride (again opposite Brando) in *Sayonara*, and on this matter she spoke frankly: "I couldn't possibly play an Oriental—no one would believe me! They'd laugh. It's a lovely script . . . [but] I know what I can or can't do. And if you did persuade me, you would regret it, because I would be terrible." None of these enterprises reached the stage of serious discussion, for Paramount already had a second picture planned for their rising star.

THE 1940S AND 1950S were remarkable decades in the theater, and very often New York scouts for the studios conspired with theatrical agents to purchase movie rights to plays even before they opened. In addition to the many successful musicals that reached the screen, there were films based on works by Tennessee Williams (*A Streetcar Named Desire*), William Inge (*Come Back, Little Sheba*), Robert Anderson (*Tea and Sympathy*), Arthur Miller (*Death of a Salesman*), Eugene O'Neill (*Mourning Becomes Electra*) and Carson McCullers (*The Member of the Wedding*), among many others.

Sabrina Fair, a comedy by Samuel Taylor, was scheduled for a Broadway premiere in November 1953, and long before rehearsals began in New York, Paramount snapped up the screen rights. Billy Wilder, a successful director at that studio, agreed to add *Sabrina* (its shortened movie title) to his impressive list of credits that included *Double Indemnity*, *The Lost Weekend* and *Sunset Boulevard*.*

Months before rehearsals began for the New York premiere of *Sabrina Fair*, Samuel Taylor went from New York to Hollywood to work with Wilder on the screenplay. His four-act comedy was

---

* Taylor's title was drawn from no less a source than John Milton, whose seventeenth-century poem *Comus* addressed the goddess of England's Severn River (hence its Latin name, Sabrina):

> *Sabrina fair,*
> *Listen where thou art sitting*
> *Under the glassy, cool, translucent wave,*
> *In twisted braids of lilies knitting*
> *The loose train of thy amber-dropping hair;*
> *Listen for dear honour's sake,*
> *Goddess of the silver lake,*
> *Listen and save!*

the story of the exceedingly wealthy Larrabees of Long Island, a family with two unmarried sons. Fairchild, the family chauffeur, has a dazzlingly witty daughter named Sabrina, who has just returned from five years in Paris and is now "a woman of the world" (the subtitle of Taylor's play). There are two Larrabee brothers who catch sight of the transformed Sabrina—which of them will win her hand, and does she want either of them to do so? The romantic resolution of the play was not nearly so important as the playwright's wise comedic sense that led to that resolution, and the fine interplay among the characters he created. (The play eventually ran for more than nine months and 318 performances.)

Samuel Taylor's literary wit, his elegant language, his essential love of people and the social subtleties of *Sabrina Fair* were doomed in Hollywood. Wilder insisted on a complete overhaul of the play, which of course he was contractually free to do. After two months of work with the director, Taylor saw that his play, his characters and his themes were all becoming unrecognizable. He fully understood the changes, additions, deletions and transpositions that were required for a successful movie, but he could not agree that the wholesale despoliation of his play and its purpose were among the exigencies. (That Taylor was a gifted screenwriter is clear from Alfred Hitchcock's *Vertigo*, which he single-handedly rewrote after a disastrous first draft by another playwright.)

Taylor felt, with considerable justification, that Wilder was vulgarizing his delicate comedy, and—irate but polite as always—he bade Wilder farewell and returned to New York, where he could far more happily attend rehearsals for his play.

Ernest Lehman, who had just completed the script for *Executive Suite* and knew how businessmen and socialites spoke, was then engaged to redraft the script with Wilder. But Lehman, who later wrote superb screenplays for *The King and I, Sweet Smell of Success* (based on his own story), *North by Northwest, West Side*

Story and *The Sound of Music,* could be as stubborn as the director, and their collaboration was thorny when it was not openly hostile. Still, they chugged along on the script, which was still being hammered out even after production finally began in early October.

WHILE WILDER AND Lehman worked on the screenplay of *Sabrina* and Paramount approved an autumn start-date for filming, Audrey concluded her stage tour of *Gigi* with sold-out performances in San Francisco. Edith Head arrived there with costume designs for the new picture, and according to her, "Hepburn now realized that she was a star, and she wanted more say about what she wore" than she had when the two women had met about the costumes for *Roman Holiday*.

Audrey's politely outspoken independence—to which the schoolmarmish Edith Head was not at all accustomed—does not contradict Arthur Wilde's observation that she had developed no high-handed attitude: Audrey simply knew what clothes suited her and her character, and she had a calm confidence in her sartorial choices that she did not always have in her own talent. Her final selection of wardrobe would await her forthcoming journey to Paris, where she would have a look at the new fashions.

As Edith learned, Billy Wilder and Paramount executive Don Hartman had conceded to Audrey's request that she be permitted to buy her wardrobe for *Sabrina* in Paris as if she were purchasing clothes for herself—hence Paramount would neither be forced to give onscreen credit to a foreign couturier nor to pay taxes or duties on imports. (She was also instructed to wear those purchases in Europe so that they could be packed and shipped back with her, as obviously personal items; she would, of course, be reimbursed by the studio on her return.) Meanwhile, Audrey won over Edith by taking her on shopping tours in San Francisco, where they interrupted their excursions by slipping into one of the city's patisseries for French pastries.

On June 20, just as the coronation festivities honoring twenty-seven-year-old Queen Elizabeth II were in full swing, Audrey traveled to London for the British premiere of *Roman Holiday*. There, she stayed with her mother, who was working in South Audley Street. The baroness scheduled several receptions for Audrey, William Wyler, Gregory Peck and the Paramount contingent.

Cecil Beaton, the photographer, designer and memoirist, was among those who attended one such gathering on the evening of July 23; Peck had brought along a friend, the American actor-director-writer Mel Ferrer, who told Beaton that Audrey was "the biggest thing to come down the turnpike." Beaton described her in more original terms:

"At last the daughter appeared—a new type of beauty: huge mouth, flat Mongolian features, heavily painted eyes, a coconut coiffure, long nails without varnish, a wonderfully lithe figure, a long neck, but perhaps too scraggy. [Her] enormous potential cinema success seems to have made little impression on this delightful human being. She appears to take wholesale adulation with a pinch of salt: gratitude rather than puffed-up pride. Everything very simple about and around her: no maid to help her dress or to answer the door to the guests who had now started a slow trickle into the room . . . In a flash, I discovered [her] spritelike charm, and she has a sort of waifish, poignant sympathy."

Beaton became an admirer at once, and eventually became a collaborator. The chemistry between Audrey and Mel Ferrer was not so simple. He told her how fine she had been in *Roman Holiday;* she said that she relished his performance in the film *Lili*. These civilities only lightly concealed a fierce sexual attraction between the twenty-four-year-old ingenue and the courtly veteran almost twelve years her senior, who happened to be married.

SIX FOOT THREE, slender and gallant, Melchor Gaston Ferrer was born into a wealthy and cultivated New Jersey family in August 1917. His father was a respected Cuban American surgeon with a successful New York practice, his mother a prominent socialite. One of Mel's sisters and a nephew eventually worked as editors for *Newsweek* magazine, while another sister became a brilliant heart specialist who went on to develop the life-saving procedure of cardiac catheterization; a brother, José, was also a physician. Mel attended Princeton University for two years, worked as an actor in summer semiprofessional productions, edited a small-town New England newspaper and, in 1940, published *Tito's Hats,* a children's book celebrating the bond between a father and son.

By 1953, Mel had already been married three times. At twenty, in 1937, he wed a sculptress and aspiring actress named Frances Pilchard, by whom he had two children. After divorcing Pilchard, he married Barbara Tripp, who also bore him two children. He then divorced Tripp and, in 1942, remarried Pilchard—to whom he was still wed when he met Audrey that July.

Between September 1938 and December 1940, Mel had played inconsequential roles in three Broadway plays. With his father's supervision and an admirable willpower, he overcame a bout of polio. He worked as a disk jockey in Texas and Arkansas and returned to New York full of theatrical ambitions for which, alas, there seemed little rationale in detectable talents. But Mel was urbane, articulate and stylish, and those qualities impressed the loutish Harry Cohn at Columbia Pictures, who engaged him to direct a disastrous low-budget film in 1945. Returning to New York, Mel then directed the actor José Ferrer (not a relative) on Broadway in *Strange Fruit* and in *Cyrano de Bergerac;* the latter was enormously successful.

Unaware that *Cyrano* had to be completely restaged by another director before its premiere, producer David O. Selznick brought Mel back to Hollywood, where he acted in and directed a few films to no memorable effect. At that time, he met and befriended a number of actors who had been contracted to Selznick—Gregory Peck, Joseph Cotten, Dorothy McGuire and Jennifer Jones (who was then the second Mrs. Selznick). They established an acting company based at the La Jolla Playhouse near San Diego, where they presented a series of astonishingly dull plays. When this enterprise was prudently abandoned, Mel utilized his professional associations to best advantage and turned up at MGM, where he appeared in the popular movie *Lili*.* That summer of 1953, his star, never ascendant, was swiftly diminishing: his most recent film was something called *Saadia*, about a strange Arab girl with romantic powers fatal enough to destroy both her suitors and the movie.

The week they met, Mel, with a lover's temerity, told Audrey that she ought to return to the stage in another French play—but in something more poetic than *Gigi*, something by a more mystic writer than Colette. If such a play could be found, would she be interested in co-starring with him? She was. And so, from her assent and their precipitate romance, Mel inferred a luminous future for the two of them: they would be like Lunt and Fontanne, Olivier and Leigh. He hurried home to Frances Pilchard, to whom he spoke with disarming frankness, thus winning an uncontested second divorce from her.

"It was fascinating to watch Mel move in on Audrey," remembered Radie Harris, a respected Hollywood journalist who had known him since 1936. "After that first meeting [with Audrey], Mel never let go, and they were inseparable."

---

* The La Jolla Playhouse was revived in 1983 on the campus of the University of California at San Diego, where it is a thriving and award-winning regional theater company.

NOT, HOWEVER, as inseparable as Mel desired. He was obliged to return to London to complete the dubbing for his role as King Arthur in *Knights of the Round Table,* while Audrey and her mother departed for a brief seaside holiday at St. Jean de Luz in southwest France, near the Spanish border. From there, they went to Paris, where Audrey sought her wardrobe for *Sabrina*. Her choice of designer forever established the look of Audrey Hepburn in movies—and in private life.

Late in July, she presented herself at the atelier of Hubert de Givenchy, on the rue Alfred de Vigny, opposite the Parc Monceau. A tall aristocrat with movie-star attraction, he had been inspired by the houses of Balenciaga and Schiaparelli and was busily preparing his own first collection that summer. Energetic, refined and highly organized, Givenchy was positively patrician, but without an atom of pomposity or affectation.

His assistant announced that Miss Hepburn had arrived for her appointment. Expecting her namesake Katharine, Givenchy went to meet (as he recalled years later) someone "like a very fragile animal. She had such beautiful eyes, she was so slender—and she wore no makeup!" Audrey was dressed in plain trousers, ballerina shoes, a short T-shirt—and a straw hat beribboned with lettering ("VENEZIA") suggesting a gondolier's boater. Impressed though he was with her quirky charm, the designer had no time to spend with her creating a movie wardrobe. He did, however, invite her to look at his ready-made collection, where perhaps she would find something he had designed earlier. On the racks, Audrey found a gray wool suit—precisely what she wanted for the scene in which Sabrina returns to Long Island, transformed by her sojourn in Paris.

Then she saw the fitted white strapless gown, embroidered with a black silk floral design and a detachable train: this she considered ideal for her character's grand entrance at the party, when at last David Larrabee notices that Cinderella has been transformed into a princess. Finally, Audrey selected a black cocktail dress with a high boat-neck, secured at the shoulders with small bows.

That summer day, Audrey left Givenchy's workrooms with these items for her next picture and, in the bargain, a friendship that never wavered for the rest of her life.* Over the course of forty years, their mutual respect and devotion grew into something beyond that of designer and mannequin or clothier and client. They both cultivated their natural styles—their shared love of gardens, for example, and of good (not necessarily expensive) food and wine—into rare forms of a refined attitude toward life; with them, style became substantial. "There are few people I love more," Audrey said of Hubert. "He is the single person I know with the greatest integrity."

For his part, he felt that "she always knew what she wanted and what she was aiming for. She was a very precise person and a consummate professional. She was never late and she never threw tantrums. Unlike many of her illustrious colleagues, she did not behave like a spoilt star. She knew exactly how to shape her strong, independent image. This naturally extended to the way she dressed, and so she always took the clothes created for her one step further by adding something of her own—some small personal detail that enhanced the whole."

The moviemaking and apparel-design industries are notoriously laced with petty jealousies, and participants often mistake artifice and illusion for reality and substance. To the creation and presentation of clothes that were right for this particular woman,

---

* After *Sabrina*, Givenchy designed Audrey's wardrobe for *Funny Face, Love in the Afternoon, Breakfast at Tiffany's, Charade, Paris—When It Sizzles* and *How to Steal a Million*. In 1954, he made a fittings mannequin that was unchanged for the rest of her life.

Givenchy and Hepburn brought a respect for the individual and a sense of simple elegance that invited others to look for their own (not necessarily expensive) styles, not mutely to imitate theirs.

AUDREY WAS IN New York on August 27 for the national premiere of *Roman Holiday,* whose reviews—more enthusiastic by far than those accorded by the British press—placed her firmly in the hot glow of celebrity. "A remarkable young actress . . . Paramount's new star sparkles and glows with the fire of a finely cut diamond . . . Through some private magic, Audrey Hepburn raises the enterprise to the level of high comedy . . . Miss Hepburn is an actress of considerable eminence."

To her credit, Audrey's eminence was not at all clear to herself; indeed, she had already developed a healthy suspicion about journalistic euphoria. "I have to try to keep a balance about it all," she said at the time, considering the arc of her career so far.

I want to retain the feeling that it is all happening to someone else, and at the same time have an idea of my own value and worth to the company. You see, I have always reached for something just above my head. If I have been able to hold on, it is because I seized every opportunity and worked extra hard. Nothing came easily. In [stage] musicals, I was the tense, rigid girl trained for ballet who had to watch everyone else to find out what to do. In the theatre, in *Gigi,* I acted without acting experience. The play was a success in America and they said nice things about me. But all through the sixteen-month run, I was still learning. By the last night, I was really only just ready for the first night. Then *Roman Holiday*—I was reaching again. Out of that curious studio life of camera, lights, noises and nerves, I had to try to bring a true performance.

As for the critical raves:

This is the most trying time of my life. Just now, I am no more than a publicity star. I have been made by writers. But what they have made me into is a shadow. I cannot become a substance until the public gives its approval.

As usual, the press wanted to know her plans for marriage. "I can't do it just now. Marriage is a full-time job. It takes more talent than acting. I can't do both and do both well . . . I have learned to do without." To a question about Mel Ferrer, who was her constant companion in New York during activities for the premiere—and who was not yet free from his third marriage—Audrey replied coolly that she would never be Mrs. Mel Ferrer, and so she may have believed. When she did marry, she added, no one would ever have to ask if she had been married before: "When I get married, I want to be very married." Meanwhile, however, she was not immune to Mel's charms, and they spent what time they could together before he departed to work on an Italian picture. Well, Ella reminded Audrey, James Hanson, at least, did not have the complication of a *wife*!

SABRINA SEEMED READY to roll into production in September, but there were delays. The screenplay continued to exercise Wilder and Lehman, primarily because the play was being expanded to provide a number of locations in Manhattan and on Long Island. In addition, there was the matter of Taylor's witty, allusive dialogue—apposite for the upper-class characters and fine for New York theatergoers at that time, said Wilder, but lacking the grit and sexy humor that would amuse mass audiences.

The difficulties accumulated. Cary Grant had agreed to play

the role of Linus Larrabee, the fierce industrialist who has no time for romance until he falls for Sabrina; and William Holden, who had already appeared in Wilder's *Sunset Boulevard* and *Stalag 17*, was cast as the playboy brother, David. But Grant, who was about to turn fifty, withdrew as the start date approached, protesting a prior commitment but really apprehensive about playing opposite twenty-four-year-old Audrey. Wilder could not convince him otherwise. (The following year, Alfred Hitchcock had no such trouble, and Grant appeared to great effect in *To Catch a Thief* with Grace Kelly, who was exactly Audrey's age.)

With that, the director made an unfortunate decision: he offered the role to Humphrey Bogart, who was fifty-four but looked sixty-five and had never undertaken light romantic comedy. Never mind, said Bogart's agents when Paramount hesitated: Bogart was a professional—and after all, he was married to Lauren Bacall, twenty-five years his junior (an argument that was a classic irrelevancy). Decades of hard drinking had rendered Bogart weathered, dyspeptic and ill with the first symptoms of the cancer that would claim his life four years later. As it began, the entire production was darkened by his haunted demeanor. Whereas Cary Grant would have rendered a romance with Audrey believable, Bogart made it seem perverse—especially because the movie audience was asked to believe that Audrey would quickly shift her affections from the handsome Holden, then thirty-five, to the battered Bogart. The difficulties were only beginning.

First, Audrey was required to do some singing in the picture, and so she spent the weeks of preproduction studying dialogue with one coach and voice with another. "I had to," she told a journalist at the time. "When I first came here, I had no voice at all. It was terribly monotonous, shrill and inflexible—all of which it still is, only a little less so." The men in dark suits at Paramount politely asked Audrey's new agent, Kurt Frings, if she might not be a bit less forthright about such matters. She had a disarming habit of letting daylight in on magic, as Walter Bagehot memorably said of the British royal family.

That was the least of the matters requiring executive attention.

Martha Hyer, an attractive and versatile young actress, had been signed to play Elizabeth, David Larrabee's fiancée. "I quickly became aware that the set was a battlefield," she recalled years later. "There was much friction, side-taking and intrigue during the filming. I don't know why, but Bogie was almost paranoid in thinking that Holden, Wilder and Audrey were against him—maybe because he was insecure and didn't feel comfortable in the part." Bogart also knew that Hepburn and Holden were rising stars, and that his own career had peaked. Hell hath few furies like apprehensive actors.

In fact, things got off to a bad start after the first day's work, when Bogart poured drinks in his dressing room for a few of the cast and crew, but did not invite Holden, Wilder or Audrey, who met in Holden's dressing room for martinis and after-work chatter. After several days of these separate gatherings, Wilder invited Bogart to join them and was curtly turned away; Wilder had failed to invite him at the outset, and now the lines had been drawn, and henceforth no quarter was to be given. "Bogart thought that a director must humble himself before Bogart," as Bogart's agent Irving Lazar said years later. "But on a Billy Wilder picture, there is no star but Billy Wilder." From that day, Bogart never ceased to complain about the director, his co-stars, the script and the crew. His scorn for the project continued right up to the film's premiere in September 1954.

Bogart was not the only major tippler on *Sabrina*. Holden was a notoriously heavy drinker, too, and, as Hyer remembered, "after a liquid lunch, he had to rest until he sobered up." Bogart, who functioned better, noted an advantage one morning, when Holden was "very shaky, blowing his lines and not really in shape to work."

Bogart at once remarked in a stage whisper, "Methinks the lad hath partaken too much of the grape"—and at once the simmering resentments became open warfare. The men had to be pulled apart, and the makeup crew was hastily summoned for damage control. That department had a much easier task with Audrey each day— and a good thing, too, for they had to devote far more time treating the bleary eyes of Bogart and Holden and reducing their alcoholic flush. Tactful, courteous and uncritical, she accepted the men's damp shenanigans as typical manly behavior, par for the Hollywood course.

There was another reason for her tacit acceptance of Holden's conduct: early into filming, they became lovers, and as Hyer and others remembered, "they were together most evenings after shooting." At the same time, Audrey relocated from her first residence, an apartment hotel at 3435 Wilshire Boulevard (near Paramount Studios), to a two-room furnished rental at 10368 Wilshire (closer to Holden's residence), where their rendezvous were conducted. In those days of the "morals clause" in Hollywood contracts—a paragraph that could destroy a career if public decency was offended by an actor's private life—Audrey and Bill had to be extraordinarily discreet. In this case, the matter was compounded by the fact that he was married and a father. Of Mel, Audrey was uncertain; in any case, no promises had been exchanged, and he was away at work. Playful, romantic and attentive, Bill was, for the time being, irresistible.

BORN IN 1918 into a prosperous Illinois family, William Beedle was the son of an industrial scientist and a teacher who relocated to California when the boy was three. While a college student in Pasadena, he was noticed by a Paramount scout. Rechristened William Holden by the studio, he appeared uncredited in two minor pictures until the leading role in *Golden Boy* (1939) raised him to instant stardom. In 1941, he married the actress Brenda Marshall, who divorced her first husband to marry him, and who subsequently bore him two sons. Nothing about that marriage, which lasted thirty years, seemed authentic—for the most part, in fact, it veered between pathetic soap opera and low comedy.

From the start, Mr. and Mrs. Holden blithely engaged in a dizzying array of extramarital romances, usually with each other's full awareness. These intrigues ended with mutual, tearful acts of contrition—before the next paramour came into view. To prevent the complication of illegitimate paternity, Holden decided, with Brenda's encouragement, to undergo a vasectomy in 1947. This decreased neither his libido nor the number of his conquests, who, for obvious reasons, were delighted with the medical news.

Holden's wife was ordinarily complaisant—until Audrey. In late October, he brought her home for dinner (a curiously repeated pattern in the marriage), and Brenda at once picked up the scent of a real threat. Later, she demanded that he end the liaison, but the lovers simply continued the affair at her apartment and sometimes, more injudiciously, in their studio dressing rooms. "Audrey embodied everything that he admired in a woman," according to Holden's biographer, Bob Thomas. "She was young— eleven years younger than himself. Audrey considered him the handsomest man she had ever known, and she was entranced by his manly charm and gentle humor."

The charisma of good looks, charm and humor can be little more than the main features of seduction, and in this case they were wildly successful. Like James Hanson and Mel Ferrer, Holden was just that much older, and this Audrey inevitably found alluring. And she was completely won over when he promised to divorce Brenda and marry her. In a delirium of happiness that made their onscreen love scenes eminently credible, Audrey at once raised the issue of children: she wanted two, three, four and more—she would abandon her career to have a family. For a few weeks, until their last scenes together, Holden temporized, and then he broke the news of his sterility.

On the spot, Audrey ended the affair. "I really fell in love with Audrey Hepburn," Holden said later, "but she wouldn't marry me. So I set out around the world with the idea of screwing a woman in every country I visited." Years later, Audrey's reaction to his tale of international intrigue consisted of two words only: "Oh, Bill!" Always fond and never censorious of him, she may well have thought it providential that she never became Mrs. William Holden. "They had great careers," Billy Wilder reflected, "but they weren't happy in their personal lives."

THE CONTINUING BATTLEFIELD, as Martha Hyer called it, was rarely without a skirmish. Bogart resented not only Holden but also Wilder and Hepburn. One day, the director brought Bogart some rewritten dialogue. "How old is your daughter?" Bogart asked, scanning the lines.

"My daughter is about seven."

Bogart threw the pages back. "Did *she* write that?"

Things reached critical mass when Bogart mimicked Wilder's accent and referred to him as "a Nazi son of a bitch"—a singularly cruel thing to say because, as everyone knew, the Jewish Wilder had lost his mother, stepfather and other family members at Auschwitz.

Bogart's ill temper even extended to Audrey, who was never unprepared for a scene and almost always word-perfect on the first take. But one morning, after she had just been handed new dialogue, she fumbled a line. "Maybe you should stay home and study your lines instead of going out every night," Bogart muttered with a wicked grin. ("I hated that bastard," said Holden. "He was always stirring up things.") Audrey smiled, defusing the moment, and they continued the scene. Acting with Bogart was never easy for her, not least because Bogart had a lifetime tendency to spit when he delivered his lines. Wilder told Audrey's wardrobe assistant to be ready with a towel after each take—"but to do it discreetly."

With equal discretion about Bogart's saliva, cameraman Charles Lang had to be cautious with back lighting, which tended to reveal the smallest spray of spittle. He was also anxious about Audrey's appearance, especially when she wore the dazzling, strapless Givenchy gown. Production memoranda document the problem of photographing her shoulders and neck so that they appeared sexy instead of bony.

All during filming, Wilder suffered from back trouble and script problems. Ernest Lehman, who preferred order to chaos and the luxury of time to on-the-spot demands for new dialogue, described the production as desperate from start to finish. "It was still being written and shaped as we went," according to Wilder, "and we were falling behind in the writing." To cover himself, he depended on the kindness of Audrey. A long scene with Bogart had to be scrapped on the set. "I had to fill the entire day," Wilder continued, "and I had to stall. So I went to Audrey and I told her the problem."

Risking her own reputation, she at once went to the assistant director. "Oh, I have a terrible headache," she said. "Please let me lie down a bit." Fifteen minutes passed, an hour, then half a day; Audrey was willing to play the prima donna before the entire company, "but she did not care," according to Wilder, "she just did it." And with her help, Lehman and Wilder had time to solve that day's script problem.

"You cannot duplicate her or take her out of her era," Wilder said, adding (perhaps in a reference to the Holden affair and certainly to her unpretentious collegiality), "She was something entirely different on the screen than what she was in life. Not that she was vulgar—she wasn't . . . But there was so much inside her, and she could put the sexiness on a little bit, and the effect was really something."

And then, in late November and right on cue, up popped Mel Ferrer, bearing his divorce decree in one hand and a play in the other. As if to erase all memories of Holden and Hollywood, Audrey accepted Mel's offer to appear with him on Broadway early the following year, in an adaptation of Jean Giraudoux's romantic fantasy, *Ondine*. Ferrer may have been inspired to select this highbrow, obscure work by the fact that—like *Sabrina*—the title character's name is that of a water sprite.

WITH *SABRINA* COMPLETED, Audrey invited Hubert de Givenchy to visit her at Paramount and to attend an early screening of the picture. When the credits appeared, Audrey was mortified and Hubert astonished to read "Costume Supervision—Edith Head." "They showed the film—and my name was mentioned nowhere," he said years later, recalling the studio's blithe discourtesy. "Imagine if I had received credit for *Sabrina* then, at the beginning of my career—it would have helped! But it doesn't matter: a few years passed, and then everyone knew. Anyway, what could I do? And I didn't really care. I was so pleased to dress Miss Hepburn."

Later, salt was added to the wound when, of *Sabrina*'s six Oscar nominations, only Edith Head won—and she had designed only one outfit for the picture. Nevertheless, the indomitable Edith accepted the statuette without so much as a mention of Hubert de Givenchy, that evening or ever after. "Edith always thought she designed everything in town," as Billy Wilder's agent said. "She was notorious for never giving an assistant credit, even if she herself hadn't done a thing."

For her second film under the Paramount deal, Audrey was paid $1,000 weekly—a total of $11,914 when the picture was complete; after her agent, lawyer and manager received their shares and taxes were withheld, she took home a little over $3,000. Her co-stars fared better: John Williams, in the role of her father, received $12,000; William Holden, $80,000—and Humphrey Bogart, $200,000.

Christmas brought Audrey a gratifying present when the influential trade publication *Film Daily* announced the results of its annual poll of movie critics: she and José Ferrer were voted the leading movie stars of 1953. The advance word on *Sabrina* was highly favorable, and when the film was released in September 1954, Audrey and the picture were, it seemed, almost beyond criticism. *Roman Holiday* told the fairy tale in reverse, but *Sabrina* followed the arc of Cinderella's transformation from likable commoner to lovable "princess."

Burdened with the era's requisite exaggerated eyebrow liner, absurdly thick eyelashes and over-the-line lipstick, she found a way through the often tedious thicket of the screenplay. Beside the historic miscasting of Bogart, Audrey had to play a girl—and she is never more than that—who has none of the distinctive eccentricity Samuel Taylor had given the character, and which was precisely the quality enabling forty-two-year-old Margaret Sullavan to captivate theater audiences in New York for forty weeks.

In the clipped cadence of her voice and with her sheer natural winsomeness, Audrey managed to counter Bogart's charmlessness. More than a half century later, moviegoers seem content with the fairy tale, and they ignore the essential hollowness at the core of Sabrina Fairchild's character on screen. Indeed, little more is asked of the girl than that she resemble Audrey Hepburn.

Chapter Seven

~

1954

IN EARLY JANUARY 1954, hours before a fierce winter storm thrashed the city, Audrey and Mel arrived in New York to begin rehearsals for *Ondine*. To present the proper facade necessary at that time, they checked into separate suites at the Gorham Hotel, the first of their Manhattan residences over the next six months. The gossip columns noted their joint appearances all over town, their inseparable social life and, almost as an afterthought, their collaboration on the Giraudoux play. The general public may have chosen to believe that they were friends—a ruse italicized by Audrey's protests that they were just dating—but anyone even remotely connected with the theater knew this was already an ardent love affair. In 1954, dating meant sharing activities like dinner at a restaurant or an evening at the theater—going out together. "Dating" had not yet acquired the connotation of those intimacies shared by staying in together.

Ella arrived from London for an extended winter holiday three days after them; she was installed at the same hotel, for which Audrey paid her bill. Within weeks, she and Mel found their budgets strained almost to the point of debt: their incomes for 1953 were not nearly enough to support this lavish new lifestyle, and their salaries in the theater were substantially lower than that in the movies. Economies were called for, and the first luxury to be sacrificed was fancy dining; henceforth, unless they were invited guests, supper meant a simple meal at an inexpensive watering hole like Dinty Moore's.

ONDINE WAS PRODUCED by The Playwrights Company, which included Maxwell Anderson, S. N. Behrman, Elmer Rice, Robert E. Sherwood, Sidney Howard and (the most recent to join) Robert Anderson, then represented on Broadway by his successful play *Tea and Sympathy.* The director of *Ondine* was the estimable Alfred Lunt, who had acted onstage since 1903 and directed since 1940; he and his wife, Lynn Fontanne, had appeared together in no less than twenty-one classic and modern plays, including works by Shakespeare, Chekhov, O'Neill and Coward. At her husband's request, Fontanne was discreetly present each day of rehearsals for *Ondine,* which began at the 46th Street Theatre in mid-January.

Lynn Fontanne very quickly became a strong support for Audrey, a gentle coach and an ally—much as Cathleen Nesbitt had been during *Gigi*—especially because Audrey was, in her own words, "almost in a panic, thinking I had to be near-perfect to live up to the build-up, which was colossal." Afraid that she was not equal to the public's expectations, Audrey also looked for emotional encouragement to Mel, who was protective (indeed, proprietary); and to her mother, who was neither.

BASED ON AN early nineteenth-century fable by La Motte-Fouqué, Giraudoux's play had been adapted and translated by Maurice Valency. The plot, such as it was, concerned the eponymous water nymph or sprite—like Milton's Sabrina—who comes to earth and falls in love with the knight Hans (played by Mel). Warned that

Hans will die if she proves unfaithful, Ondine mocks the social conventions and hypocrisies of the medieval court and then disappears when she learns that Hans is destined to marry Berthe (Marian Seldes). To humanize herself, Ondine then returns, pretending that she has been unfaithful, and Hans dies. With three sounds from the depths of the waters, Ondine forgets her mortal interlude and returns to the sea nymphs.

A colorful but vague fantasy, *Ondine* has provided a wide field for critical discussion: academics and audiences have never been certain what to make of it, although Ondine seems to represent both the indifference of nature and its elemental oneness with mankind, and the play has elements of a wry satire on marriage and the clash between idealism and reality. However one assesses its merits, *Ondine* depends very much on the appeal of the leading lady.

In 1939, Jean Giraudoux came to America after the Paris premiere and asked the Lunts to play the leading roles of Ondine and Hans; they liked the play but prudently declined, rightly judging the characters too young for them: at the time, Lunt was forty-seven and Fontanne fifty-two. But in 1954, a decade after the playwright's death, they were at last involved, and Lunt relished the chance to direct it.

Robert E. Sherwood supervised the production for The Playwrights Company. "I think Hepburn is absolutely ideal for the part of Ondine," he wrote to Alfred Lunt on November 4, 1953. "She has had ballet training, and I think that is extremely important, as the whole play seems to have a ballet quality."

There was, however, no such enthusiasm for Mel Ferrer, who had brought the play to Audrey and had planned it as the first of their stage and screen collaborations; in exchange for her signature, the Playwrights had to agree to have Mel as Hans. "We had the chance to bring Audrey back to the stage," said Robert Anderson years later, "but the price was Ferrer. It turned out to be far too expensive."

The cost immediately became evident during rehearsals. First, and for reasons no one could fathom, Mel openly objected to Lynn Fontanne's presence at rehearsals. Shamed by his conduct, Audrey wrote her a note: "I am able to step out there with so much more happiness and confidence than ever before, thanks to your patient guidance and encouragement." What she said to Mel is unknown.

Next, Ferrer complained that Lunt was too old to stage the play. He made no secret of his contempt, openly smirking at the director's suggestions to the actors and turning his back on Lunt in the middle of a conversation. "He did not respond to direction as Audrey did," according to Marian Seldes, "and was ungracious to [Lunt] in front of the company at times." Everyone found the situation deeply embarrassing. To make matters still more difficult, Mel then approached Sherwood, demanding that the play be revised to enlarge his role—a request they rejected on the spot. But his arrogance remained untempered. "It was unfortunate," Seldes continued.

> Mel had done some theater as actor and director, and had worked in films, too. In a funny way, he had gotten there first. But now it was quite clear that Audrey was overshadowing him—not through her choice, but through the accidents of fame. He had brought the play to her, and so he took the position that he had masterminded it all.

The rehearsals became more and more confused, for Mel was undermining Lunt's direction during the day by giving his own instructions to Audrey in the evenings. "There was never a flare-up," according to Seldes, "because Alfred was too much of a gentleman."

While the cast found Mel's attitude unendurable, they admired Audrey and developed enormous affection for her. "I sat in the wings and watched her as we rehearsed across the huge expanse of the 46th Street Theatre stage," Marian Seldes recalled, "and I thought she was just gorgeous. But like many great beauties, she did not think her features were particularly beautiful, and she hadn't a drop of vanity."

By the time of the pre-Broadway opening in Boston, on January 29, Mel was so outspoken in his hostility toward Lunt and so obsessed for his part (and apparently so unconcerned for Audrey's status) that he threatened to quit the play and take Audrey with him. "That wasn't jealousy—that was imbecility," said Fontanne. All the while, Audrey wanted everything to go smoothly—but she would do nothing to risk Mel's anger.

At that point, Audrey took an early flight one morning from Boston to New York, where she arrived unannounced at Sherwood's apartment. On the verge of tears, she said she felt that she was really the source of the conflict, and she offered to withdraw from the play. Sherwood finessed the situation with admirable diplomacy, restored Audrey's confidence while scarcely mentioning Mel and sent her back to Boston with renewed confidence. With that, Sherwood sent a telegram to Lunt:

> I HAVE HAD A VERY USEFUL AND SENSIBLE TALK WITH AUDREY HEPBURN AND AM GOING TO BOSTON TOMORROW SATURDAY AFTERNOON TO DISCUSS WITH YOU VALENCY AUDREY AND FERRER ANY POINTS THAT REMAIN IN DOUBT . . . AUDREY SAID TO ME THAT SHE COULD ASK NOTHING BETTER FOR HER FUTURE CAREER THAN ALWAYS TO BE DIRECTED BY YOU AND I TAKE THAT STATEMENT LITERALLY AS EVIDENCE OF HER INTELLIGENCE.

The Boston reviews were rhapsodic, especially for Audrey. And to the surprise of everyone in the production, there was no outcry from the press or the audiences over her third-act appearance in a fishnet body stocking with strategically placed faux seaweed: her costume gave an unmistakable impression of nudity.

On February 18, *Ondine* opened in New York for a limited run, and the critical superlatives for Audrey were almost unanimous. "Audrey Hepburn gives a tremulously lovely performance," wrote Brooks Atkinson in *The New York Times*.

Everyone knows that Miss Hepburn is an exquisite young lady, and no one has ever doubted her talent for acting. But the part of Ondine is a complicated one. It is compounded of intangibles—of moods and impressions, mischief and tragedy. Somehow Miss Hepburn is able to translate them into the language of the theater without artfulness or precociousness. She gives a pulsing performance that is all grace and enchantment, disciplined by an instinct for the realities of the stage.

The unnamed reviewer for *The New Yorker* agreed: "Miss Hepburn's gift is such that everything she says and does has an almost irresistible charm. The frailest joke takes on an extra dimension of personality and becomes hilarious; the most perfunctory and obvious bit of business seems at the moment a brilliant acting inspiration."

Mel did not fare nearly so well. "His playing is curiously uninteresting," wrote Richard Watts, Jr., speaking for almost all his colleagues (except Atkinson). "It lacks vividness, style and imagination almost completely, which is all the more distracting because these are the qualities that the production otherwise possesses so winningly. If Mr. Lunt were just a few years younger, how splendid he would have been in the part!"

Despite the vague poetics of the play and the harsh New York winter, there was rarely a vacant seat at the 46th Street Theatre. Ten days after the opening, Atkinson wrote a second long, critical essay in praise of the production and the players and, apparently smitten, continued his canonization of the leading lady:

> Miss Hepburn gives a magical performance as Ondine. She is a rapturously beautiful young woman, but there is no self-consciousness or vanity in her acting. Sprite-like in the spontaneity of her movement, quick, agile and bubbling, she describes Ondine's ordeal in the human world with candor and grace. Under the enchantment, a keen mind is at work. Ondine is not merely an entrancing creature but a vivid idea, and the acting could hardly be more lucid or admirable.

However much he liked Audrey, Alfred Lunt agreed with critics like Walter Kerr, who thought the production was a failure. But whereas Kerr objected to the play's "philosophical debris" and the oppressive weight of its "succession of speeches," Lunt believed the fiasco was finally due to Mel Ferrer's vulgarization of his scenes with Audrey. "Of course people are disappointed in the love story," he wrote to Robert E. Sherwood that spring. "She jumps on the hero's lap and he holds her like a potted palm—he sits beside her at the table and treats her like a tired waitress. Listen, if he played his scenes on top of her, you'd have the feeling that he was laying a cornerstone. Personally, I'd call the whole show a fucking failure." And to a woman who asked if Lunt had learned anything from directing movie stars, he was quite blunt: "Yes, Madam. I learned that you cannot make a knight-errant out of a horse's ass."

When Lunt had departed New York and the critics turned to other tasks, the play had to continue on its own merit, and at that point, Mel lost all restraint. At the most serious moments, he often took a prop and mimicked Jerry Lewis, then a popular movie and television comic. If he could not take this poetic fairy tale seriously, Marian Seldes wondered, why do it at all? Shamelessly

stealing scenes and upstaging other players—Audrey included—
he disallowed the solo curtain call that Lunt had prescribed for her.
Mel came before the audience holding her hand, as if he knew the
applause for his own unaccompanied bow would have been far less
fervent. It is doubtful that this happened at Audrey's insistence,
for she would not have countered her director's last instructions.
Indeed, word of his astonishing imperiousness may have been relayed by the stage manager to Lunt at his Wisconsin home, for six
weeks later, Audrey was taking solo curtain calls.

There were good reasons for Mel to capitulate. On March 25,
Audrey won the Academy Award as best actress of the year 1953,
for her performance in *Roman Holiday*; to this was added the
equivalent award from the British Academy of Film and Television Arts (and numerous tributes from less august organizations).
Three evenings later, she won the Antoinette Perry ("Tony")
Award for the best performance by an actress in a Broadway play
that season. (For the same production, Lunt was honored as best
director, Richard Whorf best costume designer and Peter Larkin
best scenic designer.) "I can't allow [the awards] or all this public
acclaim to turn my head," she told a journalist, "or induce me to
ease up in working toward my life's ambition—to become a truly
great actress."

Mel gave every sign of pride and delight in her prizes; the
Baroness van Heemstra did not. "She came to the play," Marian
Seldes recalled, "and although she seemed to want to be the agent
and manager of Audrey's life and career, she was not warm or
maternal at all. She was very correct, beautifully dressed and
coiffed—but daunting, rather aloof and undemonstrative." Such
was the usual assessment of Ella over many decades.

Audrey's success did not mean security. "It's like when somebody gives you something to wear that's too big, and you have to
grow into it," she said. "I wouldn't say I've learned to act yet.

Often I think I'll never learn anything. Some of the things I do onstage depress me beyond measure." Indeed, as the season continued, she became more nervous, even depressed, despite her awards, her celebrity and the gratifying offers pouring into the office of Kurt Frings (formerly a lightweight boxing champion in Europe).* By April, Audrey was pale and shaky, and her smoking had increased from two to three packs daily. The company doctor told The Playwrights Company he feared she might be headed for a complete physical and emotional breakdown.

The Oscar and the Tony were not an unmixed blessing: henceforth, every Audrey Hepburn undertaking was expected to be hugely successful, commercially and artistically. Not yet twenty-five, she had attained a level of accomplishment toward which seasoned professionals often work for years or even decades. How could she possibly sustain this height of achievement? In fact, she told members of The Playwrights Company that spring, she was so spent by the experience of *Ondine* that she would never appear in a play again. She kept her word.

"There was enormous pressure on her, from the press and from Mel," Marian Seldes remembered, "and despite the praise and affection showered on her, there was a subtext of unhappiness in her life." Seldes wrote Audrey a note, offering any kind of help, or just a friendly chat. Audrey replied gratefully, signing her name with a drawing of the water sprite of the play—but she never confided in her colleagues.

The ongoing pressure from Mel now had to do with marriage, for he had proposed and was pushing for a favorable reply; Audrey hesitated. At the same time, reporters plied her about rumors of an impending wedding, but as usual she parried with generalities:

---

* Audrey had briefly been represented by Lew Wasserman at MCA, but she preferred a smaller agency with a European sensibility.

Marriage is like signing a long-term contract. Unless you know your innermost thoughts, you can't give yourself to anyone. I'm still learning about myself . . . I don't know lots of things yet, but I will. That's why I don't want to be tied down to one spot, or even to one man.

"She had given up Hanson," said Seldes, "but she wasn't ready for Mel." Audrey's mother, and her friends Anita Loos and Cathleen Nesbitt, strongly advised against marrying him.

As scheduled, the last performance of *Ondine* was given on July 3. At a farewell party, the entire company noticed, with alarm, Audrey's frail, distracted condition. She smoked one cigarette after another, had a hacking cough, her hands shook almost uncontrollably and she left the gathering after a polite interval. Ten days later, with her mother and Mel, she left New York for a quiet refuge in Switzerland, far from the strains of New York and the stresses of Hollywood. When *Sabrina* was released in September, Audrey was not involved in promotional activities.

Her absence from public view was soon explained. In Bürgenstock, Switzerland, on the shores of Lake Lucerne, Audrey Hepburn married Mel Ferrer: a civil service was held in the town hall on Friday, September 24, and there was a brief Protestant religious ceremony next day, in a private thirteenth-century chapel. For the church service, she wore a white organdy dress with a high, round neckline (designed by Givenchy) and a simple wreath of white flowers. Only a few of their friends were invited. Mel had selected the picturesque town for its privacy, its cool, healthful air, its limited access for the press and general public—and because he was working through August and September in Italy, in a film called *Proibito,* which solved their immediate financial dilemma.

But her withdrawal from public life was not occasioned merely by planning her wedding.

From late June in New York and throughout that summer in

Europe, Audrey had endured what was then called a complete nervous breakdown—a popular but not a proper description of clinical depression. In her case, the quiet weeks in Switzerland did not immediately restore her energy nor alleviate what Marian Seldes and others described as a kind of chronic unhappiness. Audrey slept long hours—sometimes an entire night and day—but that brought little refreshment, and then she could not sleep for an equivalent period. She ate well and then for days had no appetite at all. Like an anxious child, she had bitten her fingernails to the quick; she smoked incessantly and often wept uncontrollably, sometimes for no apparent reason. The baroness simply prescribed self-discipline and walks in the cool morning air. They had been through the war, she reminded her daughter: what had she to be depressed about now?

A reply could not easily be given, but a young woman of Audrey's exquisite sensitivity and physical fragility would eventually have found almost unendurable the demands of eight performances weekly for five months, the crush of interviews surrounding her awards and honors, the frenetic pace of social life imposed by the accident of fame and the general lack of privacy. In addition, there was the conflict over Mel, a zealous, self-appointed overseer of her career. When he visited from Italy for a day or two that summer, he invariably came with a cache of plays and scripts for them to consider, and he agreed with Ella that perhaps the best remedy for her illness was to return to work. For the remainder of the year, that would be out of the question.

By the time of her wedding, Audrey had improved, and she admitted to a journalist friend that indeed she had suffered a "complete breakdown in New York," from which she now felt she was emerging.

Because of Mel's work schedule, their honeymoon was limited to three days at a chalet. Then, on Tuesday, September 28, they traveled to Rome, where Mel returned to work. Besieged by paparazzi for details of the wedding, Mel was ready to answer until Audrey interrupted. "This is our marriage, not the public's," she said, ending the discussion.

The couple retreated to a rented villa near the seaside resort of Anzio, about thirty miles south of Rome; there, Audrey read scripts, tended a garden, looked after a menagerie of pets, supervised three servants, learned how to cook Italian specialties, wrote letters and hoped for an early pregnancy.

She accepted one invitation for a public appearance, and that was in Amsterdam, on November 2. To raise funds for Dutch war invalids, Audrey agreed to sign photographs of herself at a department store. She and Mel had to flee the scene when the younger members of the crowd went wild, smashing showcases as they pushed and shoved to be near the movie star. For several years to come, Audrey kept her promise that day, not to make any public appearance unless there was adequate planning, security and crowd control. Meeting strangers was always awkward and difficult for her; from that day and for the rest of her life, it was also something that threw her into stark terror.

DURING THE RUN of *Ondine,* Audrey and Mel were visited backstage by Michael Powell, whose partnership with Emeric Pressburger had brought to the screen *The Red Shoes* and *Black Narcissus,* among other impressive postwar British films. "She was whole-hearted in her love for him," Powell said of Audrey and Mel—"the kind of woman who gives all or nothing. I don't know how he lit this torch, but by heaven it flamed."

Powell had the idea to make a film of *Ondine*—but one based on the La Motte-Fouqué fairy tale, which was in the public domain (not on the Giraudoux play, whose movie rights would have to be purchased). "They snatched at the idea," according to Powell, who also invited Mel to appear early the following year in a film version of *Die Fledermaus,* called *Oh—Rosalinda!!* (The film was made, to no great or enduring life.) Powell's idea for *Ondine* had everything to do with Audrey: Mel, he thought, had none of the charisma of Louis Jouvet, the original Hans in the 1939 Paris production. "When Jouvet paused, we all paused. When Mel paused, the play stopped. It was Audrey, in spite of her small voice in that big theater, who carried the play."

In Rome that November, Powell and Pressburger visited Audrey and Mel at their villa to plan *Ondine,* for which the actors had been promised a very handsome salary. They had a merry dinner, and the guests were shown to quarters. Next morning, they all set to the task. "We talked, wrote and worked," Powell continued, "continually interrupted by telephone calls and hysterical servants. Audrey and Mel were, amiably, the worst listeners in the world. They were always wandering off in the middle of a sentence, and none of us allowed any of the others to finish one."

As they developed the scenario, Powell recalled,

Mel was beginning to declare himself, and his tactics were only too obvious: the play, the play and nothing but the play [he insisted]. Somehow every idea, every scene, became inextricably bound up with the play, and Mel was the knight in shining armor defending *Ondine,* defending it from rape and disaster at [our] devilish hands. Audrey looked at him adoringly. There had obviously been extended pillow-talk throughout the night . . . Fortunately the knight and his water-sprite wandered away and gave Emeric time to collect his thoughts: "They don't seem to know the difference between a play and a film."

"Of course they don't [Powell replied]. They're actors. They've learned the part and spoken the words to an audience, and it worked. They think that's all there is to it. We have to educate them."

The hosts returned, and Pressburger began a brilliant exposition of his idea for the film, emphasizing that the screenplay was based on La Motte-Fouqué and not on Giraudoux. "Mel could see his most cherished lines tumbling into the basket . . . Audrey's hand crept into Mel's and stayed there." When Pressburger was finished, they all went for a walk in the hills, and the subject of conversation changed. Mel and Audrey had invited two other couples to join the group for the evening—producer Dino de Laurentiis and his wife, actress Silvana Mangano; and producer Carlo Ponti with Sophia Loren, whom he was to marry.

During dinner, the telephone rang. Paramount Pictures had agreed to finance more than half of the film of *Ondine,* provided that Mel and Audrey, Powell and Pressburger put half their salaries in escrow until the picture turned a profit. And then Mel said something odd: he advised the producers to negotiate with Giraudoux's widow for film rights to the play.

"He still wants to make a photographed version of the play," Pressburger said to Powell as they traveled to Paris next day. "That is why you have to see [Madame Giraudoux]. If he could afford to buy the rights himself, he would. With a film of the play, he would be sure of himself and Audrey, [and] that is why he wants us to buy the rights for him, so that he can cut our bloody throats."

Their train sped through the Alps, and Pressburger came up with an idea: to transform the myth of Ondine into a modern-dress movie, set in Monte Carlo. They would replace the medieval dukes, knights and kings with millionaires, racketeers and scuba divers, gamblers and fading film stars. There would be dramatic underwater photography and all sorts of cinematic tricks. But in Paris, Madame Giraudoux made hilariously inflated demands for the screen rights to her late husband's play, and the producers politely departed without a deal, which was fine so far as they were concerned. They had tried to do Mel's bidding, but Madame had been the flounder, not the sprite, in the sea.

Audrey and Mel arrived in London on December 31, 1954—to further the discussions on *Ondine* and for Mel to begin acting in *Oh—Rosalinda!!* Powell and Pressburger joined them for a New Year's Eve party at Ella's flat in South Audley Street. "The baroness was a bit stiff," Powell recalled, and he left the party before midnight.

On the last day Mel worked on *Oh—Rosalinda!!,* he, Audrey, Powell and Pressburger met at the studios of Hein Heckroth, the producers' production designer. Mel said, speaking for two, that he and Audrey were not pleased with the costumes: he also wanted a completely new approach to the story and the design of the picture—he wished, in other words, to film the play. "We realized that Mel had been leading up to this for months and was now coming in for the kill," according to Powell. "He was acting the part of producer." And that was the end of the project.

On February 4, Audrey went to Paris for the French premiere of *Sabrina,* planned to coincide with "collection week," when the forthcoming spring/summer fashions were presented by the couturier houses.

Paramount's French offices, where Gallic ingenuity joined American marketing genius, drummed up all sorts of advertising plans. For one thing, the studio offered prizes to any mother who gave birth to a girl on the day the film began its Paris run and named the baby Sabrina. Then a contest was held, for a cash reward, in which young women believed they could affirmatively reply to the question "Do You Look Like Sabrina?" Next, record albums with the songs from the picture were displayed in shop windows. The high point of all this revelry was the appearance of Audrey herself, safely cordoned off and kept at some distance from journalists, who answered some polite questions during a press conference at the Ritz Hotel; it was a scene lifted from the final moments of *Roman Holiday.* That same month, Audrey was nominated for an Academy Award as best actress for *Sabrina;* Grace Kelly won, for *The Country Girl.*

In March—just weeks after learning the wonderful news that she was pregnant—Audrey suffered a miscarriage. "That was the closest I came to feeling like I was going to lose my mind," she said years later.

Chapter Eight

1955–1956

IN EARLY 1955, Audrey and Mel signed a long lease on a three-story country house in Switzerland called Villa Bethania, near Bürgenstock, high on a hilltop overlooking Lake Lucerne. As it happened, they spent almost no time there that year.

During a brief holiday at St. Moritz that April, the Ferrers met with the American film director King Vidor, who had made sixty-one movies, among them *The Big Parade*, *The Crowd* and *Duel in the Sun*. Just when Audrey and Mel invited Carlo Ponti and Dino de Laurentiis to join Powell and Pressburger for dinner, Vidor was concluding negotiations with Paramount, and those two Italian producers, for an epic production of Tolstoy's novel *War and Peace*. By late March, the project was being hastily prepared, while two similar plans (by David O. Selznick and by Mike Todd) were forthwith abandoned.

Ponti and de Laurentiis had seen Mel's film *Proibito* and told Vidor that he would perhaps be right for the role of Prince Andrei. This was a shrewd move: with Mel's influence on Audrey, she would certainly accept the role of Natasha, around whom develops the moral and psychological focus of the story. She was happy for Mel's employment, but she never shared his ambition—indeed, she would have been content to live quietly at home as wife and, she hoped, mother.

"Audrey's career always came second," said Henry Rogers, who that year became her publicist and a good friend.

> She never had the burning desire to become and remain a movie star, as do most actresses, but instead cared only for personal happiness, peace, love, her children, a husband whom she loved and who loved her . . . Although she loved acting, she wanted to work less and spend more time in private . . . She was filled with love, [but] Mel was filled with ambition, for his wife and for himself.

It had been Mel's idea to engage Rogers, but when the publicist arranged interviews and magazine features, "she was uncomfortable [and] always bridled whenever I mentioned the need for an interview to be done, or a photo session. I tried not to push her into a lot of publicity activity, realizing that she considered it to be an unpleasant chore." Selecting only crucial publicity activities for her, Rogers always felt in an awkward position between the spouses—caught "between Mel's insatiable desire for Audrey's new publicity and her reluctance to give interviews or pose for photographs."

Like Marian Seldes and others who knew and worked with Audrey, Rogers added, "Rarely did I ever see her happy." Perhaps unaware of her childhood misfortunes, her extreme sensitivity and her recent miscarriage that year, he recognized only one basis for her despondency—a misconceived marriage:

> It was no secret that her marriage to Mel was not a happy one. It seemed to me that she loved him more than he loved her, and it was frustrating for her not to have her love returned in kind. She had confided these feelings to me and a number of

other intimate friends many times. She never complained, but I always saw the sadness in her eyes . . . During the years she was married to Mel, she was Trilby to his Svengali.

That allusion may have overstated the case, but it was an impression held by many who knew them; there can be, after all, a fine line between mentorship and domination. In this regard, Audrey's marriage confirmed her in a relationship with a man like James Hanson, who (unlike Mel) had no connection to or understanding of the movie world at all, yet who capriciously inserted himself into the scheduling of *Roman Holiday* and usurped the role of managing agent and producer. Hanson's manipulative manner effectively earned his dismissal from her life—an action that was now unimaginable in the case of her husband.

Mel Ferrer never exerted the sinister, hypnotic influence over Audrey that the Hungarian musician Svengali wielded over the young singer (in George du Maurier's novel *Trilby*). And Mel's intentions were certainly benevolent. But remarkably often, her cause coincided with his own best advantage. It seemed never to have occurred to him that their deepest aspirations were, in the final analysis, incompatible.

"I had the feeling that Audrey needed somebody to make her decisions for her," said Vidor. "He did all the talking for her. He knows what is right for her. He knows how much money she should be getting. I believe he collected her salary personally."

AND SO, ESSENTIALLY for her husband's sake, but also because they needed the money, Audrey capitulated and agreed to play the role of Natasha. With no resistance from the producers, Kurt Frings quickly obtained for her a salary of $350,000 plus an expense allowance of $500 weekly—the highest fee paid to any actress in the world and thirty times her payment for *Sabrina*. (Mel was to receive $100,000.) "I'm not worth it—it's impossible!" she said to Frings. "Please don't tell anyone!" But the deal was as much to her agent's advantage as to hers, and he announced it all over Hollywood. At once, the press was trumpeting her historic fee and she was receiving messages of congratulations—first, from Henry Fonda, who had been signed to play Pierre, Natasha's true love. Fonda was fifty years old.

Audrey's reaction to the news did not spring from false modesty. She always considered herself an apprentice and had no high estimation of the gifts that were being refined by experience, by earnest preparation and by gravity of purpose. She knew she was fortunate to be offered good roles in premium movies and was aware that she was not easy to cast: she had neither the opulent figure nor the demeanor—and certainly not the desire—to play the sexy protagonists of that time. Nor had she the age or eccentricity for character roles.

A fresh type with a unique look and an elegance of which audiences might grow weary, Audrey felt that she must prove herself anew with each undertaking. And with two performances nominated by the Academy and one awarded, she knew she would be more critically assessed by critics and producers than many of her colleagues. That spring, she turned twenty-six, and she often wondered if her career had any further to go. This was not a depressing thought, for the business was never her priority. She would choose carefully, or she would not choose at all.

At that point, the Ferrers applied for and received permanent residency in Switzerland, which offered major tax advantages: had he continued to file a return in America and she to pay British revenues, they would have forfeited ninety percent of their income.

THE PROBLEMS ON *Sabrina* were due to clashing personalities and ornery temperaments; those on *War and Peace* were logistical.

With lavish designs on paper, but no script in hand, Ponti and de Laurentiis nevertheless insisted that filming begin on July 1, with exteriors to be shot in Italy and Yugoslavia and interiors in Rome. Vidor immediately had to supervise the completion of casting more than fifty speaking roles, while fifteen thousand extras were outfitted in period costumes made by ninety tailors working around the clock; in addition, animal trainers from all over Europe were summoned to provide more than eight thousand horses; and 2,876 cannons were hauled out of theatrical storage and military museums. The producers urged Vidor and his cameraman, Jack Cardiff, to remain calm, for they had (they said) an ingenious method of having a screenplay finished in record time.

Their ingenuity was as reckless and unrealistic as the start date. To Vidor's astonishment, Ponti and de Laurentiis took a translation of Tolstoy's fourteen-hundred-page novel about Napoleon's assault on Russia, cut it into equal segments like so many wedges of Italian sausage and assigned each slice to a different team of Roman writers. Demanding that each complete his section within three weeks, the producers then hauled the result—*ecco fatto!*— into Vidor's office. The result was a script wildly uneven in tone, inconsistent in character development and lacking anything like a coherent viewpoint.

The length of a typical screenplay is from about 100 to 130 pages: the first draft of *War and Peace* was 506 pages. Paramount, nervous about the schedule and eager to recoup its $6 million outlay, rubber-stamped its approval of the vast text, but Vidor was horrified when he glanced at the unshootable tangle of pages. He put the script in a drawer, summoned the writers Bridget Boland, Robert Westerby and Irwin Shaw and began the task anew, pledging to transform the novel into a film in weeks. That they did not collapse under the strain is nothing short of astounding.

The producers wanted an epic to end all epics; that was understandable in 1955, when moviemakers were in a collective panic over the massive defection of audiences to television. Hollywood responded with a proliferation of Technicolor, stereophonic sound and Cinerama; wide-screen processes like CinemaScope and VistaVision; gimmicks like 3-D; and a mercifully short-lived contraption variously called Smell-O-Vision and AromaRama. Long movies with casts of thousands and eye-catching sequences, like *The Robe, Demetrius and the Gladiators, The Ten Commandments, The Greatest Show on Earth, Around the World in 80 Days* and *Ben-Hur* were calculated to offer moviegoers the sweep, scale and hint of eroticism that television, in that stricter era, could not.

In this commercial rush for spectacle, the result was often merely expensive, mammoth, colorized, loud, big-screen tedium. Over time, this development led to a profusion of computerized fantasies and action movies, violent assaults on eye, ear and intelligence. This was not always progress, as human stories with adult dilemmas and sensibilities were gradually sacrificed to court a younger audience; meanwhile, grown-ups (as Samuel Goldwyn said in another context) began to stay away from the movies in droves. In 1955, this was an evolution in its first stages, and that spring, Vidor did what he was being paid to do: he tried to come up with a saga of majestic grandeur. The odds were against him from the beginning.

A grand and enduring portrait of the Russian soul, Tolstoy's novel is a monumental work in which historical and philosophical themes are explored through an enormous variety of more than five hundred characters from every social level. Part of the author's genius was his management of all this in a story of striking vibrancy and emotional authenticity; the movie, on the other hand, became an assemblage of expeditions, extended battle sequences and strategic military conferences, occasionally and ineffectively interrupted by characters with very little recognizable sentiment. Even the chronology seemed confusing.

Great hopes to the contrary, and the continuing attempts of

Vidor notwithstanding, *War and Peace* reached the screen as three and a half hours of empty spectacle. "Oddly mechanical and emotionally sterile," was the critical consensus, "[and] the characters seem second-rate people, hackneyed and without much depth . . . The human stories are sketchy and inconsequential." Audrey, in an underwritten and unmotivated role, could not escape criticism, too: "She goes from smiling innocence to tearful innocence," wrote a senior London critic, lamenting that both character and actress seemed not to mature, which was much the point of the novel. Still, no less a group than the New York Film Critics Circle nominated her as the best actress of the year. (Ingrid Bergman won, for *Anastasia*.)

Filming lasted from July to November, and the conditions were persistently uncomfortable. Amid the stifling heat of the Italian summer, tons of artificial snow were brought in for the scenes of the wintry marches, while Audrey and her colleagues smothered under heavy gowns and furs; even the studio interiors were unpleasant places, for the air conditioning at Cinecittà was erratic at best and often inoperative. Despite the exhaustion of ten-hour workdays, Audrey was a serene presence to whom the entire company looked for encouragement. Few noticed that her serenity masked constant anxiety for her performance.

The ball sequence, for example, with its many setups over several days, required her to appear romantically energetic during a long and complex shot. Audrey rose to the occasion with an unfailing patience that impressed her director. "It was of course inconceivable to have anyone other than Audrey Hepburn as Natasha," said Vidor at the time. "She has a rhythmic grace that is a director's delight." There was never a cross word between them, which could not be said of his collaboration with her male costars. Both men seemed gloomily inappropriate in their roles: Fonda played Pierre as depressed instead of introspective, while Ferrer—whose eyes were notably expressionless—recited his lines flatly and, wearing period costumes, somehow managed to look absurd instead of impressive.

For all her docility and politesse, Audrey could be stubborn. During the ballroom sequence, for example, she wore a low-cut gown that revealed her clavicle, upper ribs and hyoid bone. "She really had no breasts—she was a model and very thin," recalled Cardiff. "I suggested she wear a necklace or something with this low-cut dress, but she said, 'Jack, I'm just me. I am what I am, and I haven't done too badly like this.' " Cardiff was anxious about the scene "because you could really see her ribs." So could de Laurentiis, who was infuriated with the result, but by that time, the sequence had been filmed and the set dismantled. "She was very silly," Cardiff concluded, "because there was no need to accentuate her ribs."

THE FERRERS COMPLETED their roles in *War and Peace* in late November and then proceeded to Paris, where they took a suite at the Hôtel Raphaël. Mel immediately went to his next job—a role in *Eléna et les hommes,* starring Ingrid Bergman and directed by Jean Renoir. On February 27, 1956, a month before he finished working, Audrey traveled alone to Los Angeles. Tired though she was, she had been offered an opportunity she could not reject—to sing and dance with no less a partner than Fred Astaire, in a romantic musical called *Funny Face*. It was certainly a fine script, and it would be her finest performance since *Roman Holiday*. Despite the fact that it was another Cinderella story with a fragile narrative and one-dimensional characters, *Funny Face* retains a naïve charm and, half a century later, remains one of the most inventive, colorful and lively movies of the 1950s. But it almost did not happen, and it was not produced easily.

In 1951, screenwriter Leonard Gershe had completed the libretto for a Broadway musical called *Wedding Day,* with book and lyrics by Ogden Nash and music by Vernon Duke. The work remained unproduced, and Gershe sold his story rights to Metro-Goldwyn-Mayer. There, producer and composer Roger Edens—who had won the Academy Award in 1948, 1949 and 1950 (for scoring *Easter Parade, On the Town* and *Annie Get Your Gun*)—had a superb reputation for producing extravagant and appealing musicals.

Edens and Gershe decided to abandon the Nash-Duke contributions and to substitute popular songs by George and Ira Gershwin. Turning first to the 1927 Broadway show *Funny Face* (which had starred none other than Fred Astaire and his sister Adele), they took its title, the title song and four other numbers but ignored the original story in favor of *Wedding Day*. (In 1927, *Funny Face* had been Astaire's suggestion for both the song title and the name of the show; it was his nickname for his dancing partner, Adele.)

To direct the hybrid project, Edens and Gershe easily interested Stanley Donen, who was responsible for the success of (among other musicals) *Singin' in the Rain* and *Seven Brides for Seven Brothers;* this team set about transforming *Wedding Day* into an MGM project.

The completed screenplay was several things: both a satire and an endorsement of high fashion (perhaps only a Hollywood movie can have it both ways); a spoof of the coffeehouse "beatnik" intellectualism popular in the 1950s; and a tribute to the genius of photographer Richard Avedon. The story told of Dick Avery (Astaire), hired to use his cameras in service to the editor of *Quality* magazine (Kay Thompson). Jo Stockton (Audrey), a plainly clad, somewhat naïve Greenwich Village bookstore clerk with a fondness for a social philosophy known as "empathicalism," is selected to be transformed into a high-fashion model for the coming season—"she's new, she's fresh," says Dick. Whisked off to Paris, she is (thanks to Givenchy) changed into a stunning runway mannequin, and—are we surprised?—she falls in love with Dick, who belatedly responds.

This thin premise was punctuated with stylishly inventive scenes that invariably succeed, thanks to Givenchy's designs; Avedon's clever, multicolored fashion photography, seamlessly woven into the story; and amiable song-and-dance sequences. These latter were variously droll ("Think Pink," which imagines the women of the world outfitted in clothes that seem dyed in Pepto-Bismol); touchingly wistful ("How Long Has This Been Going On?" and "He Loves and She Loves"); and romantically old-fashioned (the title song and "'S Wonderful"). Because the romantic heart of the story is set in Paris, the movie had ample opportunity for a colorful tour of sites such as the Opéra, Montmartre, Notre Dame, the Place de la Concorde, the Tuileries gardens and the Eiffel Tower (the final location for the snappy musical number in which the leading trio dart about the city singing "Bonjour, Paris").

THE PROJECT'S CREATIVE TEAM, presuming from the start that Fred Astaire would rush to sign a contract if he was told that Audrey Hepburn was ready to join, prepared the script specifically for him. Fresh from his latest hits (*The Band Wagon* and *Daddy Long Legs*), Astaire would be making his twenty-eighth film since *Flying Down to Rio* almost twenty-five years earlier. To secure his participation, the producers resorted to a traditional, if somewhat disreputable, Hollywood maneuver.

Gershe's new screenplay had been submitted to Kurt Frings, who was legally obliged to send it on to Audrey in Paris. But after he sat down with his copy of the text, Frings said that it was trash and that he would advise his client not to do it. Audrey, however, read it during her Christmas holiday, loved it, said so to Frings and eagerly signaled her willingness—especially (and here was the ruse) when the producers told her they had signed Fred Astaire, which they had not. As a matter of fact, they had gone to Fred Astaire at precisely the same time, informing him that they already had Audrey—which they had not. This was risky business, and on the shady side of ethical, but in this case the stratagem worked.

Astaire and Hepburn were now aboard, but other complications arose. For one thing, Audrey was under contract to Paramount, which refused to loan her out to Metro; for another, the rights to the Gershwin score were owned by Warner Bros. Tricky negotiations continued daily from November through February, and finally Warner sold the song rights for a hefty sum to Metro, which in turn set up the package of Roger Edens, Leonard Gershe, Stanley Donen, Fred Astaire and Audrey Hepburn and sold the project to Paramount. Besides a truckload of cash, MGM also got the right to use Audrey for a picture of their own within three years.

After two months of vocal and dance rehearsals, and recording sessions of the songs (which the actors would silently mime during playback on the set), filming began at the Paramount studios in Los Angeles in April 1956. In Mel's absence, Audrey demonstrated a strength and determination not always evident when he was there. She had, for example, definite ideas for each scene—almost all of them welcomed by her director.

Only one sequence occasioned a dispute. For her long and complex dance number set in a Paris café, Audrey was to wear a black sweater and black leotards; to this outfit, she wanted to add black ballet slippers without socks. No, countered Donen, the effect of your dancing will be much diminished—he preferred that she wear white socks, the better to highlight her intricate steps against the dark, smoky background. This was her only dance number without Astaire, and he wanted viewers to see her every move.

Audrey was astonished. "Absolutely not!" she cried. "It will spoil the whole black silhouette and cut the line at my feet!"

"If you don't wear the white socks," Donen replied calmly, "you will fade into the background, there will be no definition to your movement and the dance sequence will be bland and dull."

She burst into tears and ran to her dressing room but later regained her composure, wore the white socks, returned to the set and continued. After seeing the rough cut of the sequence, she wrote Donen a note: "You were right about the socks—Love, Audrey."

"Audrey was very serious," according to Kay Thompson. "The poor thing was doing something monumental in a hurry. Fortunately, the songs were perfect for her." She sang "How Long Has This Been Going On?" in her thin, slightly tremulous mezzo—a timbre that could never fill a theater, but her rendition was surprisingly affecting. For once, the audience understands that the question refers not to a romance in progress, but to the sudden rush of romantic feelings that a simple kiss stirs up.

As THE CAST continued their long workdays that spring, Audrey marked her twenty-seventh birthday—and Fred Astaire his fifty-seventh. A curious pattern was emerging, and one with few counterparts in Hollywood history: for the third time, this young actress was paired with a leading man old enough to be her father. The situation was very like the tradition of medieval and Renaissance religious art, in which the youthful Virgin Mary is represented alongside her husband, Joseph—represented as a venerable old man, bearded and avuncular. The relationship, therefore, seemed chaste, free of the taint of carnal congress.

This is precisely why the image of Audrey Hepburn in films is strangely unerotic—not because *she* is undesirable or aloof, but because she was so often shown with much older men who seemed incapable of matching her exuberant energies (thus far, Bogart,

Fonda and Astaire—later, and more to the point, Gary Cooper).*
Only when Audrey was past her twenties and audiences demanded
just a bit more sensuality (if not sexuality) was she cast with Albert Finney, Peter O'Toole and Sean Connery. If she had any
thoughts about the older men and the egregious lack of onscreen
heat, she never expressed them—to do so, she may have thought,
would have been offensive to the actors.

In Audrey's case, she was presented as something of a stained-
glass window figure, radically different in face, voice and form
from (for example) Marilyn Monroe and the opulent stars of the
day. With Gregory Peck, the thwarted romance was credible because he, too, was never a sex symbol in the movies. It was almost
impossible to imagine her in a passionate embrace with Bogart,
Fonda or Astaire—even their kisses seemed perfunctory.

Billy Wilder may have sensed this conundrum, for he had ignored a fundamental rule of romantic moviemaking in the last
shot of *Sabrina*, aboard the ship bound for Paris. The embrace of
Hepburn and Bogart was photographed not in close-up, nor even
in a medium shot, but with the camera several meters away. For
once in this movie, the director seems to agree with us: Hepburn
and Bogart are literally incredible together—they do not inhabit
an intimate space, they are figures in a seascape, remote from us
and one another. Indeed, the image of them as a couple is frankly
disagreeable, and Wilder (always the cynic) may have wondered if
the romance was doomed. We see them from a distance; there is
nothing with which we are invited to identify.

In Fred Astaire's career, his persona was perhaps best summed
up by the famous trick sequence in Donen's *Royal Wedding*, in
which Astaire calmly, joyfully seemed to cover the floor, walls and
ceiling of a furnished room with gravity-defying steps. That scene

---

* The ageless Cary Grant, in *Charade*, was the egregious exception: the twenty-five-year
age difference seemed not to matter.

perfectly illustrates our perception of his place in the universe: he seemed to exist above natural man. His was the form of a medieval saint, too: there was nothing erotic or even sensual about him. In each of his films, his dancing partners, to shift the metaphor, were his fairy goddaughters. And his deportment always suggested that he was, in some odd way, beyond mere physicality: Fred Astaire was a gentleman up there on the screen—so much a gentleman, in fact, that there was never an atom of erotic appeal about him. That is precisely why the final shots of *Funny Face* succeed so well, as Fred and Audrey literally float downstream in the forest of Chantilly, photographed in a haze of diffused light and attended by snow-white doves and swans. This is the stuff of sheer Hollywood fairy tale, and it has its own charm. But it is so calculated that there is something oddly antiseptic about it—there is, in other words, nothing to take seriously.

Astaire was always a kind of Peter Pan, ignoring the physical laws of the universe: he strode, he leaped and he tapped his way through movies, and in *Funny Face*, Audrey was his Tinker Bell. Watching him, it looked easy to overcome the burden of the body, and he did what (it seemed) could not be done. One of the enduring images of his career is the final shot of *The Story of Vernon and Irene Castle*, in which he and Ginger Rogers cakewalk into eternity. Visually, it is (as Ben Hecht would have said) a lot of hooey; it is also irresistible.

THE FAIRY TALE existed only on the screen.

From the first day of filming, Audrey was in awe of Astaire and worked double-time to please him. For his part, he resented the love she at once evoked from the director, the crew and the other actors. He knew that the production team would hasten to please her, because, as he said, "Audrey is a lady who gets her way."

Once filming began, Astaire became anxious about their age difference and hence the credibility of the romance: the idea of appearing with Audrey had been irresistible, but now reality intervened. She looked younger than her age, and he felt older than his. When the cast members greeted one another warmly each morning and gathered collegially around Donen for coffee and chatter, Astaire arrived and was noticeably irritable. "What do you want me to do?" he asked Donen brusquely, or "What is he [or she] doing over there?"

In fact, Astaire (not Donen) interrupted his dances with Audrey several times during filming. "What are you doing?" he asked her in a loud, irritable voice. "Fred was impatient," according to Kay Thompson, "and he wanted to be great in front of Audrey. Those scenes at Chantilly, of Fred and Audrey crossing the water on a little raft—Fred stopped her four or five times right in the middle of the scene and said, 'What are you doing?' After Fred had yelled at Audrey a couple of times . . . finally the scene was over." Later that evening, Audrey confided to Kay that she found her work with Fred "a bit of a strain"—something to which she never publicly alluded.

The entire company happily anticipated filming the exterior locations for *Funny Face* that summer. But in Paris, things could not have been more frustrating. Rain drenched the city and environs day after day, and even a slight pause in the downpours had to be fiercely seized despite dark clouds, for time and money were at stake. A scene in the Tuileries, for example, was obviously photographed during a rainy interval, but Donen had to make a virtue of necessity. The weather did not improve Astaire's disposition.

As for Audrey, the work in Europe was her caviar, for she was always more comfortable there than in Hollywood. Delicate and droll in the New York sequences of *Funny Face,* she did not, however, seem entirely natural in the burlap-and-corduroy informality of Greenwich Village. She was more suitable for Paris, and Hollywood knew it: part or all of six Hepburn films were made there or at least located there.*

Ella came from London to Paris to watch some of the filming. "She had great humor and so did Audrey," recalled Leonard Gershe, who took the baroness for a drink and befriended her that summer.

> But unfortunately, they didn't have it together—they didn't share laughs. I adored her mother, but Audrey didn't like her very much . . . Ella played the role of stern mother. She was a different person when she talked about Audrey—judgmental—and she took her role of baroness quite seriously. On the other hand, Ella could be very silly when she wanted to be, and so could Audrey. But Audrey never knew that woman. They didn't know they were really very alike.

Although Ella believed that her daughter was a wonderful actress, Gershe continued,

> She couldn't tell her that. Audrey once told me that she never felt loved by her mother, but Ella did love her, believe me. Often people can't tell the object of their love that they love them; they'll tell other people instead. I probably would have hated Ella as a mother—but I loved her as a friend.

Audrey completed *Funny Face* in late July. She had a few weeks' holiday with Mel in Bürgenstock before he took on two consecutive roles that required him to work in Spain and France. At the same time, Audrey accepted an offer to work again with director

---

* *Sabrina, Funny Face, Love in the Afternoon, Paris—When It Sizzles, How to Steal a Million* and *Bloodline.*

Billy Wilder, on condition that the film be made entirely in Paris, where she and Mel could be reunited on weekends. Wilder sold her on the picture before she read the finished screenplay by informing her that Gary Cooper, for many years America's movie ideal of the dutiful, ordinary man, was to be her co-star; again, Cary Grant had rejected Wilder's bid.

Love in the Afternoon, based on a novel by Claude Anet, was about a wealthy, aging American businessman and Don Juan named Flannagan (Cooper) who, without feeling or conscience, pursues affairs with women around the world; he has, thus far, successfully avoided marriage. In Paris, his indiscretions provide work for a private detective (Maurice Chevalier), who has a virginal daughter named Ariane (Hepburn), a music student. At first, she is fascinated by his exploits; then, she falls in love with him and, to convince him that she is a worldly woman, invents a history of her own lovers. Finally, Flannagan can no longer ignore his attraction to Ariane. Leaving Paris, he is about to abandon her on the train platform but then sweeps her up into his arms.

Tall, rangy, laconic, shy and full of a sex appeal of which he was (only apparently) unaware, Cooper was the most enduringly popular American male star for almost thirty years. In 1956, he was fifty-five but looked more than a decade older. After Grant had rejected the role, Wilder—with typical perversity—chose Cooper for the unappealing role of an incurable womanizer. Still married to his only wife, Cooper was nevertheless a busy bee who buzzed from one Hollywood flower to another over many years: his lovers included (among others) Lupe Velez, Barbara Stanwyck, Merle Oberon, Carole Lombard, Paulette Goddard, Marlene Dietrich, Ingrid Bergman and Clara Bow.

Before she began work on the new picture that September, however, Audrey traveled from Paris to New York, to see her friend Cathleen Nesbitt in the musical *My Fair Lady,* starring Julie Andrews and Rex Harrison. "What Audrey is hoping for," reported Edwin Schallert of the *Los Angeles Times* after speaking with her, "is that her husband, Mel Ferrer, will play the professor and she the cockney heroine—a striking contrast to their work together in *War and Peace*."

Returning to Paris, she greeted Wilder, and prepared for *Love in the Afternoon*. Gratitude to him for the success he had provided in *Sabrina* may have been Audrey's primary motivation in agreeing to this picture: given her care in selecting scripts and her stated desire for a variety of roles, it is otherwise difficult to understand what might have been persuasive reasons not to do it. Indeed, with this movie, critics and audiences were finally becoming impatient with the casting of much older men opposite her; for the first time, and despite her wardrobe by Givenchy, Audrey's appearance seemed statuesque, nearly frozen into a kind of blank perfection. Indeed, Ariane's clothes should have been selected off the rack— or designed as if they were; instead, they are almost hilariously unsuitable, far too opulent for an unemployed student whose father struggles along as a private detective.

From the start of production that autumn, in the studios just west of central Paris, Wilder had a serious technical problem that could never be resolved. Although he had supervised makeup and wardrobe tests with the male lead, Cooper's status had made those tests little more than a formality. But when he arrived for the job, the actor unwittingly brought Wilder and his cameraman a depressing reality. No matter how heavy the cosmetics, no matter how carefully the lights were arranged and rearranged, Gary Cooper appeared a haggard old man, angry at the emptiness of his life and ravaged by indulgence. This had been the problem with Bogart in *Sabrina*, but now there were extended love scenes, and love scenes cannot always be rendered from a distance.

What to do? Filters were placed on the camera, but that was insufficient. And so, for almost every shot in which his face appears in close-up, Gary Cooper had to be photographed in deep shadow, or from behind, or through gauze, or partly obscured by a prop or a wall, a curtain or a door. Fifty years later, some aesthetes strain for meaning in all this subterfuge, seeing the desperate measures as the perfect metaphor for Flannagan's character. Wilder always had contempt for such excuses, and in any case they would have been entirely inappropriate for what was intended to be a comedy. As for Cooper, this was the ninety-ninth picture he made since his silent-movie debut in 1925—hence his experience told him precisely what was happening when his scenes required numerous setups and there was continued muttering behind the camera. More and more uncomfortable in the role, he always looked (as one of his biographers wrote) as if his shirt collar was too tight. Cooper had turned his standard of unexpressive, almost monotonic line-readings to his best advantage over the years; this distinctive quality was no help to him in this case.

"He and Billy Wilder were connoisseurs," Audrey said later of her co-star. "They talked about food and wine and clothes and art. I was never included in their rapport. I have the greatest respect for Mr. Wilder, but I don't know him personally really well. I couldn't speak with him in the way I could with King [Vidor]." And so, in addition to the awkwardness between the leading players, Audrey now felt that she had lost her earlier, easier association with this director; predictably, that, too, affected her own performance.

Wilder's stated intention with *Love in the Afternoon* was to honor his mentor, the filmmaker Ernst Lubitsch, who had been such a splendid satirist; instead, this comedy is about as amusing as Wilder's *Sunset Boulevard,* which is to say not at all. Bleak and melancholic, it has an unappealing premise that seems only more disturbing with the passage of time. With a running time of two hours and ten minutes, it seems more like four hours; utterly lacking narrative crispness, storytelling economy or romantic credibility, it is difficult to believe that it came from Billy Wilder and was both created and advertised as a charming romantic comedy.

In addition to the miscast Cooper, the problems with the movie accumulate from the first scenes, in which every bit of exposition is repeated three times—a device that continues throughout the film. Rendering everything more tedious still is the presence, in scene after scene, of an unsmiling quartet of musicians playing "Fascination." They were intended as comic relief, but their presence simply stops the film.

Like few other movies, *Love in the Afternoon* makes romantic rendezvous seem joyless and dispiriting. And it is difficult to appreciate the creation of the character of Ariane (by Wilder and his co-writer, I.A.L. Diamond) as a virginal student, devoted only to her cello and ignorant of romance. A girl with the looks of Audrey Hepburn? in Paris? in 1956? and not in a convent?

The deepest problem, however, is Ariane's attraction to the scoundrel Flannagan, a man who exploits and discards women. Why is this clever, sensitive girl drawn to an aging lothario who cares so little for women that he boasts of forgetting their names? The film comes close to presenting Ariane/Audrey as little more than a masochist straight from the pages of *Les liaisons dangéreuses*.

When the film was released in 1957, audiences loved Audrey Hepburn and Gary Cooper too much to notice that they both played profoundly disturbed characters. In other creative hands and with a different cast, this might have made an interesting psychological case study; after all, 1957 was the year of *The Three Faces of Eve*. This was to have been a Wilder comedy—*Sabrina* on the rocks with a twist—but the film's static compositions erased humor from this damp, unengaging tale. As usual, however, Audrey was silent about its failings and effusive in her praise of colleagues.

THE FINAL SCENE is the ultimate Hollywood cliché. Ariane sprints alongside the train that will forever take Flannagan away from

Paris and from her. Protesting through her tears that she will be just fine, thank you, and repeating her already exposed lies about the many men in her life, her appearance melts his stony heart, and he sweeps her up into the train and into a final, smothering kiss.

Thoroughly exhausted after two demanding pictures in one year, Audrey was, she told Mel at Christmas, ready for a long hiatus. But they had agreed to appear in a lavish play on American television, and early in 1957, they flew to New York for rehearsals.

Part Three

ACHIEVEMENT
[1957–1970]

The embassy ball sequence of My Fair Lady.

Chapter Nine

~

1957

A<small>T A QUIET</small> dinner before the Ferrers left Paris for New York in January, Hubert de Givenchy presented Audrey with a small gift box. In her honor, he had supervised the invention of a new perfume bearing her name. *"Mais, c'est interdit!"* she cried: "Oh, but you can't!"—a polite exclamation on opening a lavish present of which the recipient feels undeserving. So that the fragrance would be hers alone for a year, Givenchy said that he would refrain from marketing it until December. When he did, he presented it to the public as L'Interdit, its name memorializing not only her astonished gratitude but also the fact that it was forbidden to others for a year. The name also whimsically connoted a bouquet so intoxicating that it ought to be banned.

A<small>LWAYS EAGER TO</small> take on projects concerning his native Russia, Anatole Litvak had, by 1957, directed the films *Tovarich*, *The Battle of Russia* and *Anastasia*, which had just been released and for which Ingrid Bergman won her second Academy Award. Twenty years earlier he had also made a popular film entitled *Mayerling*, the name of a notorious Austrian village linked to a romantic tragedy. At a royal hunting lodge there, in 1889, Crown Prince Rudolf—desperate over his father's command to put away his teenage mistress, the Baroness Marie Vetsera—shot her to death and then killed himself. The misfortune may indeed have been a murder-suicide, but perhaps it was a political assassination, or even the result of a lunatic family vendetta: scholarship is still catching up with the facts.

In any case, *Mayerling* had already been the basis for no less than five motion pictures when Litvak suggested it to the National Broadcasting Company in New York. He also proposed that a real-life married acting couple undertake the leading roles, and so someone at NBC contacted Kurt Frings, who negotiated a lucrative deal for the Ferrers. For two weeks of rehearsal and a week of taping in January, Audrey received $150,000 and Mel $100,000.

On Monday evening, February 4, the ninety-minute drama was broadcast in color, which was then a premium reserved only for exceptional programming; it was later released theatrically in Europe. But the production was not favorably reviewed in America and soon disappeared. "A more pallid or elementary version of [the story] would be difficult to imagine," wrote one senior critic. "It was as if two pleasant young people were walking through an operetta that did not have a score." The production values and cast of more than one hundred were impressive, the dozens of sets and multiple wardrobe changes for Audrey spectacular. But the overstuffed luxury of this *Mayerling*, with its grand ballroom sequences and lavish court settings, was incongruous for an intimate tragedy—it was, in other words, all style and no substance.

As for Audrey and Mel, the critics considered their Maria and Rudolf a curiously dispassionate couple: "they never really came close to the tragic content of the romance that could not be." Some reviewers and even members of the crew thought there was a surprising coolness, even a distance, between the Ferrers themselves. Mel was never a convincing onscreen hero, for a certain awkwardness rendered him unconvincing; and although Audrey had developed a certain technique for playing a distressed young lover, it failed her in this case. The rehearsals were polite and perfunctory, the finished production the same.

And with that, Audrey Hepburn and Mel Ferrer never again appeared together in a project. She began a year's interval away from movie and television cameras, she managed to elude the press, and she instructed Henry Rogers to turn aside all requests for interviews. Meanwhile Mel completed two films in 1957, one of which required his presence in Mexico. There, the couple resided at the Villa San José in Michoacán, which had famously lush gardens (the single feature that always attracted Audrey to inns or resorts), but, to her happy surprise, no telephones.

During their holiday, she learned of the enormous success attending the premiere of *Funny Face.* "Those are marvelous notices," she wrote in response to a packet of reviews sent by Roger Edens.

I also saw the front page item in Variety *about the breaking of box-office records!!!! I am deeply grateful. Hurray! Hurray! Please congratulate Kay [Thompson] for her fab[ulous] reviews (and so they should be). May it mean many more successes for her . . . Thank you, and I am so very happy for you . . .*

Although there was no telephone at the Villa, communication was possible by telegram, and that is how Kurt Frings reached Audrey that spring. He knew that she was concerned about her future, and she was aware that roles for her were becoming alarmingly repetitious: she was either the alluring nymph to a much older man (*Sabrina, Funny Face, Love in the Afternoon*) or an aristocrat in a period piece involving a political-romantic predicament (*War and Peace, Mayerling*). Since her Oscar for *Roman Holiday,* a certain stasis had affected both her range and her appeal. Always conscious of her image and unwilling to play in movies that were coarse or offensive to her, Audrey had neither the age nor the quirkiness for character roles, and she was not at ease in movies that tested the limits of sexual frankness in the 1950s.

Hence when Kurt Frings sent her a wire about an altogether different sort of role, in a forthcoming movie based on one of the most popular and respected novels of 1956 (still high on best-seller lists in dozens of languages), Audrey agreed, by return wire, to read the book. Three days later, it arrived. Profoundly affected by the story, its literary merit, honesty, courage and poignancy, Audrey finished *The Nun's Story,* by Kathryn Hulme, in two sittings; to his credit, Mel was equally impressed and told her that this was the role of a lifetime—if only Paramount would free her to work for Warner Bros., which had acquired movie rights to the book.

The Nun's Story, a novel based on one woman's true history, concerned a devout young Belgian named Gabrielle van der Mal, daughter of a famous surgeon, who entered a religious order in 1927. After her cloistered period of training, she pronounced her vows as a nun. Henceforth known as Sister Luke (named for the saint who is invoked as the patron of her father's profession), she was first trained as a psychiatric nurse and worked in one of the order's mental asylums. Respected, dedicated and effective, she was then sent to study tropical medicine before being assigned to work with the poor in the Belgian Congo. This she did with admirable distinction for almost nine years before returning to the congregation's Mother House in Belgium. During World War II, Sister Luke felt drawn to aid the Underground and the Belgian resistance, but the nuns were expected to care for both friends and enemies with equal skill and compassion: wounded Nazi soldiers had to be treated with the same care as Allies. Sister Luke found this injunction increasingly difficult, and so, with permission from her superiors and Vatican authorities, she was released from her vows and found a new vocation as a lay war nurse.

Audrey found much to admire and even to identify with in *The Nun's Story*. Like the heroine, she was born in Belgium; both women lost their fathers, and both had brothers taken prisoners of war. Most of all, Audrey was captivated by Sister Luke's fierce dedication to her conscience, and to her interior life. The novel did not present her struggle as due to a loss of faith; rather, the poignancy of that struggle sprang from the reality of faith. Sister Luke and Audrey Hepburn were deeply introspective souls, increasingly uncomfortable with mere appearance. And just as Sister Luke never believed that the traditional religious habit defined her vocation, so Audrey Hepburn never believed that Hollywood finery—even her beloved Givenchy's designs—defined Audrey Hepburn. The garments were simply part of the image.

In the novel as in life, Sister Luke never lost her Catholic faith, never believed that her departure from the institutional religious life meant her "divorce" from God or His abandonment of her. "Christ will not abandon me if I go out [from the convent]," Sister Luke tells her chaplain in the novel. "I have given too many cups of water in His name and He knows I would go on doing it, whether working for Him as a nun or as a war nurse."

Audrey was never a traditional observer of any religion, but she was certainly a woman with an elemental kind of faith in the universe: she loathed war, she took enormous delight in the simplest realities of nature and, as her life progressed, she experienced profound changes that resulted from deep struggle and introspection. "I am like Sister Luke in many ways," she said. It was a wise professional decision to undertake something so completely different from her previous roles, and the subsequent experience of filming, as she herself wrote, forever changed her life. Any reference to *The Nun's Story*, in conversations with family or strangers, always evoked Audrey's unambiguous, enthusiastic comments.

⌒

FRINGS ALSO INFORMED Audrey that dramatist and screenwriter Robert Anderson, a member of The Playwrights Company whom she had met during the run of *Ondine,* had been commissioned to write the screenplay for *The Nun's Story.* It would be helpful, Frings added in a subsequent telegram, if Audrey would come to Hollywood for a meeting with producer Henry Blanke and with Anderson, who was there, completing an earlier assignment and getting important background information from Kathryn Hulme, then residing in Los Angeles.

Hulme had met the real-life Sister Luke, a woman named Marie Louise Habets, a year after she had left the convent. (In actuality, Marie Louise had been known as Sister Marie Xavérine and had been a nun from 1927 to 1944 in a Belgian community known as the Sisters of Charity of Jesus and Mary.) In July 1945, both were working for the newly formed United Nations Relief and Rehabilitation Administration (UNRRA). Later, both women worked at Wildflecken, a former Nazi facility that had been transformed into a refugee camp for more than twenty thousand displaced, seriously ill patients from all over Europe.

Until that time a writer of a few respectable books with not much lasting shelf life, Hulme was on her own path to spiritual development. She had been in Paris during the 1930s, studying with the mystical philosopher Gurdjieff and joining one of his subgroups, a small band of lesbian writers Gurdjieff called The Rope. Kathryn (who preferred to be addressed as Kate or Katie) was now earnestly considering how to integrate her unconventional private life within both her spiritual and her professional ambitions.

Marie Louise, whom friends always called Lou, gradually confided in Kate the story of her seventeen years of formal religious life. During their six years of work in Europe, both Kate and Lou continued their own inner journeys of "conversion" to find their own true selves and thus, as they put it, to turn wholly toward God. They also found that they were indeed soul mates. In 1952, they came together to America. Kate resumed her career as a writer, while Lou worked as a nurse.

Quite on her own and with no pressure from her companion, Kate subsequently converted to Catholicism, which sealed her association with Lou on every important level. It was not long thereafter that Lou suggested her own story to Kate as subject for a book—"because it might do some good," as Lou said. "These were the words of a nun," Kate wrote later in another book dedicated to Lou, "words of faith and hope, illumined with the sweet charity of wishing to share her hard-earned treasure of impregnable belief with all those who—in the words of Gurdjieff— were 'hungry for something else.' "

The result of the former nun's suggestion was indeed "something else." When *The Nun's Story* appeared in 1956, it quickly sold over three million copies in English and many more millions in foreign languages. Kate Hulme and Lou Habets remained important players in the life of Audrey Hepburn, who was deeply impressed by both women and maintained a long and affectionate connection to both.* In early June 1957, Audrey agreed to go to Los Angeles to meet with them and with Robert Anderson to discuss *The Nun's Story*.

ROBERT WOODRUFF ANDERSON, who had just turned forty that April and was therefore exactly Mel's age, was—also like Mel— tall, gallant and courteous. Born in New York, he took his B.A.

---

* Lou and Kate lived together for more than thirty-five years, sharing a strong and unsentimental Catholic faith and an unwavering commitment to human welfare. "My neighbors say that I am still a nun," wrote Lou to the author of this book in 1984, three years after Kate died at eighty-one, in 1981; Lou died a decade later at eighty-six; her double name, Marie Louise, did not have the hyphen habitually and incorrectly added by others.

and M.A. degrees at Harvard and completed all requirements for his doctorate in literature before he joined the navy during World War II (in which he was awarded the Bronze Star). Before that, in 1940, at the age of twenty-three, he married the theatrical producer and dramaturge Phyllis Stohl, who was ten years his senior.

After the war, Anderson's writing career flourished under the loving tutelage of his wife: his plays, mostly lyrical narratives about adults in romantic dilemmas, were produced off-Broadway and in regional theaters—until 1953, when *Tea and Sympathy* began a two-year New York run before its long and equally successful tour and many foreign productions. Dedicated to his work and known for his uncompromising professionalism, he was, in 1957, much in demand as playwright and screenwriter. But his marriage had a heartbreaking finale. Just when *Tea and Sympathy* opened, Phyllis was diagnosed with cancer, and for three years Anderson nursed her during her agonizing decline before her death.

Her loss left Anderson a shattered man, haunted by her memory and even obsessed with their marriage for the rest of his life: he spoke of Phyllis daily, to friends and acquaintances, to students during his many lectureships and to the press in interviews. This habit, often sometimes indiscreet, continued even after his second marriage, in 1959, to the actress Teresa Wright; her prize-winning career on stage, screen and television spanned from 1938, when she was twenty, to her death at eighty-six, in 2005.

Phyllis had died on November 28, 1956, and within days, Bob was very close to complete nervous collapse. At that time, Ingrid Bergman was preparing to appear in the Paris production of *Tea and Sympathy*. Bob's agent was that legendary wise woman Kay Brown, who had been responsible (among other memorable achievements) for convincing David O. Selznick to import to Hollywood Alfred Hitchcock from England and Ingrid Bergman from Sweden. Among the most prestigious names in American stage and screen history, Kay Brown now represented both Anderson and Bergman.

Weeks after Phyllis's death, Kay contacted Ingrid in Paris, where preparations for the French premiere of *Tea and Sympathy* had been briefly postponed when the actress required an emergency appendectomy. After Kay told her about Bob's depression, Ingrid at once picked up the telephone and rang him. "I think you belong over here," she said. "It's Christmas, and you shouldn't be alone. The play will give you a purpose and a family." She booked a room for him at the Hôtel Raphaël, where she was lodging (as had Audrey and Mel), and when Bob arrived in Paris on December 10, Ingrid was at the airport to meet him.

She had recently been through a different kind of distressing experience: her troubled marriage to director Roberto Rossellini had finally reached critical mass when he flaunted his affair with an Indian actress he intended to marry, even bigamously if necessary. Ingrid had left him and relocated to Paris, where she was now free to accept offers to appear on stage and screen—invitations Rossellini had hitherto discouraged or flatly forbidden. However debated their artistic merits, Rossellini's films had left him bankrupt, and they had three children to support. This responsibility Ingrid assumed at once: she accepted Jean Renoir's offer to star in *Eléna et les hommes* (with Mel), and Twentieth Century–Fox invited her to assume the title role in Anatole Litvak's *Anastasia;* her French dramatic debut in *Tea and Sympathy* was to follow. At forty-two, Ingrid Bergman was beginning a triumphant second act to her distinguished career.

As Ingrid and Bob discussed the play and shared their recent heartaches, it is perhaps not surprising that these two sympathetic people became ardent lovers. "One Paris critic reviewed Ingrid favorably," Anderson recalled, "but he didn't much like *Tea and Sympathy,* and so he wrote, 'Ingrid Bergman saves the play.' Later, I wrote her a note: 'Ingrid Bergman saved the play—and the playwright, too.' "

Bob was, as he said, madly in love with her—but Ingrid was more pragmatic and knew that the relationship had a term. "I realized very quickly that he was a man who couldn't cope any longer with anything," she recalled, "and I did all I could to help him survive. He was very close to me in those days. Maybe I was in need, too. I knew [our relationship] was important perhaps to both of us." She also knew that his base was in the American theater and that he was now accepting important Hollywood offers—professional developments that would help his emotional recovery.

More to the point, she saw that their affair had sprung mostly from his desperate neediness. "I want you to get hold of yourself alone," she wrote to Bob on January 26, 1957. "I can't help you. Right now, you must fight it out alone. To be in Paris again [with me] would just be to hide away with one person. But you know it would only be worse afterwards. There would always come the time when you have to face the loneliness."

Ingrid was, after all, still Mrs. Rossellini, and some time would intervene before she was free to marry again; in addition, her professional life, like Bob's, would require long and distant separations between them—she in Europe, he in Hollywood. But to the credit of both, when their romance ended, they transformed it into a warm lifelong friendship.

While in Paris, Bob at last sat down with *The Nun's Story*, which Phyllis had read not long before her death, telling him that he ought to write the screenplay. At the same time, Kay Brown was eager to find as much work as she could for Ingrid, too—and so she suggested that Ingrid play the leading role in the film. At Christmastime in Paris, Ingrid and Bob read the book together. He liked it enormously and saw marvelous dramatic and moving possibilities, but Ingrid recognized at once that she was too old to play Sister Luke.

Instead, Ingrid proposed Audrey Hepburn. Bob relayed the

idea to Kay, and Kay contacted Kurt Frings, who then sent a telegram to Audrey. By January, Kay had made the deal for Bob, and Frings was negotiating with Warner, who was delighted that Paramount, which had just suffered considerable losses with *War and Peace*, had turned down *The Nun's Story*. The picture, Paramount reasoned, would require the considerable expense of filming in Europe and Africa, and so they agreed to loan out Audrey to Warner in exchange for adding a picture to her contract.

For the moment, things were happening quickly.

In the spring of 1957, Bob Anderson had just completed the script for the Robert Wise film *Until They Sail* and was commuting between his home in New York and visits to Hollywood for research and meetings on *The Nun's Story*. At the same time, Warner signed Fred Zinnemann to direct. Zinnemann had begun his career in Europe, and after coming to America, he had directed a number of important films—among them, *The Men* (Marlon Brando's first film), *High Noon* and *From Here to Eternity;* he had already won two Academy Awards and would earn two more in his long, distinguished career. Zinnemann was a meticulous craftsman who did protracted, detailed research; he was also known for his quiet courtesy with actors; he had a highly refined European sensibility; and he insisted on the finest production values.

By late April, Jack Warner, Henry Blanke, Fred Zinnemann and Robert Anderson were awaiting word on Audrey's participation. Finally, the potential problem with Paramount was settled, but another occurred: Audrey had promised Mel that she would star in a film of the exotic romance *Green Mansions,* which he wanted to direct in fulfillment of Audrey's obligation to MGM. First Mel had to complete his acting assignments and then travel to Mexico and South America for research for *Green Mansions* even before fixing a start date. As it happened, Audrey was able to complete *The Nun's Story* before beginning *Green Mansions*.

⌒

IN EARLY JUNE, Audrey arrived in Los Angeles to meet the creative team so far assembled. Robert Anderson, who had just returned from a research trip to convents in Belgium, met her at the airport, as Ingrid had once greeted him—and with the same result. Bob's affair with Ingrid had ended as gently as such things can. Now, that summer in Los Angeles, Audrey Hepburn and Robert Anderson began a long, intense romance.

Over the course of several years, Bob confided the details of the affair to this author, asking that it not be set down until after Audrey's death. "My novel *After* [published in 1973] really tells the whole story of my affair with Audrey," he said. Indeed, the book is a lightly coded document of the entire range of their intimacy, often in astonishingly frank sexual detail.

After tells the story of a writer named Chris Larsen, in his early forties (Bob was forty in 1957); in the opening chapters of the book, he nurses his cancer-stricken wife until her death—just as Bob had done for Phyllis. Chris then meets a twenty-two-year-old actress named Marianne: Audrey was twenty-eight and had just played the role of Ariane. The novelist's description of Marianne is a perfect description of Audrey: "The first thing you noticed was 'style.' She was tall and slender and held herself beautifully, almost like a dancer. Her dark hair was worn in her own particular style, not the style of the day . . . I saw her large dark eyes . . . The entire effect of her was striking. She had style, dedication, real excitement."

In *After*, Marianne dresses as did Audrey that summer in California and as she preferred to dress, in private, all her life: "She had changed into blue jeans and a faded scarlet turtleneck sweater." Bob's reaction to Audrey that summer was also memorialized in Chris's words: "I didn't think about anything except that there was this extraordinary girl out there who had dropped into my life. She was life, not death, and for some reason I could not understand, I functioned [sexually] beautifully with her."

Bob and Audrey met privately at the home of one of her friends who was away for the summer. "She was a very tidy girl," he wrote of Marianne/Audrey in the novel, "insisting on cleaning up after breakfast and wanting to go beyond that and clean the whole kitchen." Most of all, however, he recalled that "she was sad—beautiful and sad and romantic." The description could have been offered by Audrey's son, who later wrote of "the inner sadness she had always carried inside her."

In the novel, the subject turns to Marianne's past: in passage after passage of the novel, Bob wrote of Audrey speaking of herself:

> There's not a great deal that I want to talk about. My ideas on marriage were formed very early . . . I never saw my father. Oh, I've seen pictures of him, all I could get my hands on. Very handsome. Good family, whatever that is . . . My mother tells me that there was a marriage and a quick divorce, and some money changed hands. She never married again. She has a very low opinion of men . . . [Father] turned into a bit of a hermit, I understand. Strangely, I don't feel much bitterness towards him. My mother used to go on and on about how horrible he was, but since I couldn't understand her, I instinctively got very defensive about him. His image has been very important to me. I fantasize that he's somewhere in Europe, living alone, writing day and night on a great body of important work, and one day—one day he'll show up at a stage door where I'm playing.

As Audrey and Bob devoted time each day to discussing Sister Luke, so he memorialized her professional devotion in his novel. "What I want in this world," says Marianne, is to devote my life to some one or some thing. Complete, whole. Dedication. When I was a girl, I thought of becoming a nun. Their concentration and dedication excited me. I get the same feeling about some dancers, musicians, artists. To give up everything to do one thing well, and not make anyone else pay for that dedication.

And the reaction of Chris/Bob was immediate: "I adored her. I was in awe of her talent and her dedication to her talent."

Since her childhood, Audrey had always loved bicycles, and that was her preferred mode of getting about at movie studios, on location and along the streets of Beverly Hills that summer. The bicycle became a recurring prop in *After*, the means by which Marianne arrives and departs at Chris's summer house. Like Audrey's that summer, Marianne's was "a red bike with a basket." In tribute to that summer, Bob created several scenes for Sister Luke and her bicycle in *The Nun's Story*. Years later, he recalled these pleasant memories and their poignant conclusion.

Robert Anderson spoke privately and wrote in fiction with disarming frankness about his affair with Audrey Hepburn—an affair encoded in his novel.

"We mustn't be apart again," says Chris after one long, intimate afternoon.

"She drew back and looked at me with a questioning frown, then nestled her head against my shoulder. She was loving and passionate but, I thought, a little reserved."

As Anderson said years later, "That was Audrey."

That summer of 1957, Audrey recognized (as had Ingrid) that Bob's great passion for her, and his extravagant expression of commitment—despite her marriage—was based on a terrible loneliness. According to him, she spoke in precisely the terms Marianne uses when Chris professes his adoration of her in a love letter:

You don't know me . . . You may think you feel [this adoration] because of the situation, but I don't think it has anything to do with me. I mean, to adore, to want to put one's life in someone's hands . . . Your situation is so unusual. You're so susceptible. Your feelings are lovely, but I don't think the letter was addressed to me but to some terrible need in you to fill the void, the emptiness. To belong to someone again.

In many ways, *After* is as much a courageous admission of the author's psychological state after his wife's death, and his obsession with her, as it is an acknowledgment that his affair with Audrey was (like that with Ingrid) doomed. But during that summer, the end of the real-life romance was yet to come.

IN EARLY JULY, Audrey returned to meet Mel for a brief holiday in Europe; finally, she signed her contract with the jubilant Jack Warner in late summer—she was to receive $250,000 plus ten percent of the film's gross receipts, which eventually earned her almost $4 million over four years. Bob traveled with her as far as New York, where they stayed for a few days at his apartment on East 79th Street. She then went to join Mel, while Anderson completed the first draft of *The Nun's Story* and prepared to go to Africa for research with Zinnemann and art director Alexandre Trauner.

Aware that there would of course be changes and revisions, Bob also continued his constant correspondence with Kate and Lou, plying them for details about how a young woman in Belgium, circa 1927, took leave of her family on the day she entered a convent; how nuns donned their veils; how the ceremony of haircutting was accomplished; how they managed the layers of antique garb in their habits; how rules and regulations determined the course of everyday life; and asking for some reflections on the rhythms of prayer, work, recreation and silence in the lives of nuns dedicated to nursing.

"Trying to shape your excellent book for the screen is a tremendous challenge," Bob wrote to Kate. "Actually, your story line is so excellent and so dramatic in itself, that the major work I'll have to do is putting words in mouths where you have simply narrated scenes. You have written it with such a sense of drama, that you have given us the majority of the scenes—it will only be for us to make them work in terms of action and dialogue." Anderson shaped the screenplay with complete fidelity to the book, and almost all the dialogue in the film may be found on the pages of the novel. His great achievement, however, was the judicious excision of scenes from the book for cinematic economy.

With *The Nun's Story,* Audrey wished to be involved in every aspect of the film's creation, and so in late September, she met Zinnemann and Anderson in Rome for research. They had just returned from Stanleyville, in the Belgian Congo, where they scouted for the proper locations and found local doctors who provided them with operating room equipment dating from 1930. Zinnemann was a perfectionist in every detail, and under the proper tutelage, Audrey learned precisely how surgical instruments were used and handled, just as she was learning every detail of convent life. There was also a unique challenge for cosmetician Alberto De Rossi, who had to devise makeup for Audrey and the dozens of actresses who were playing nuns: the intense interior lighting for Technicolor film required them to wear makeup—but they had, of course, to look as if they were wearing none at all.* Audrey also attended meetings with Trauner, then supervising the design and construction of dozens of interior sets at Cinecittà Studios.

---

* Audrey requested and was given as her dresser a woman she had befriended named Adelia Buonis, who had performed the same function during *War and Peace.* She also asked that her former assistant, Carlo Pierfederici, be her driver during the filming of *The Nun's Story.* "He needs the work and he is a gem," she wrote to Henry Blanke.

Returning to California, she rented the home of Deborah Kerr (who was then working on a film in England), at 685 Elkins Road, in the Brentwood section of Los Angeles, high in the hills above Sunset Boulevard. From there, she made frequent visits to Kate and Lou, asking them questions and learning about wardrobe, rituals and gestures—how to walk, kneel and bow, and what were the proper aspects of convent deportment. But the camaraderie between her and the two older women did not come easily.

"She didn't really want to meet me at first," according to Lou. "She felt the story was too much of my private life. She just sat there and looked at me and didn't ask any questions." She and Kate put Audrey at ease, asking questions about her own life and career and talking about Belgium. Soon, Audrey relaxed, and the three women shared a warmth and familiarity their friends referred to as the 3-H Club.

Also in Los Angeles, Audrey read the second draft of the screenplay, which contained Zinnemann's emendations. Her response to him indicates the depth of her understanding of the role and her extraordinary sensibility about making this character credible, sympathetic and yet faithful to the true story.

"I think we have a slight difference in the conception of Sister Luke," Audrey wrote to Zinnemann on November 19.

I am bothered by the fact that Sister Luke calls herself a "failure" at the end of our story. She is too intelligent to display what sounds to me like false humility. I still wish she could somehow express herself as having failed as a nun but that her hopes and faith have been reborn at the thought of being able to function as a free human being and consequently with more devotion than before. I still would like to feel the start of something new and strong at the end of the story, instead of a sense of dejection and defeat on her part and a kind of artificial whitewashing of the Order. Like you, I want the final situation to be fifty-fifty, so that neither the nun nor the Order becomes a villain.

Audrey was on the mark, and appropriate changes were made. In the finished film as in the book, it is quite clear than the departure of Sister Luke—who had always expected too much of herself—was not at all a matter of failure, much less of sin. When the film was released, however, virtually every reviewer and most audiences discussed the wonderful Hepburn film about a nun who failed in her vocation.

But it is not at all about failure: it is about transformation.

"You've got to learn to bend a little, or you'll break," says Mother Christophe (played by Beatrice Straight), her sympathetic superior in nursing duties at the mental asylum. Sister Luke's first vocation, she was told, was to the institutional religious life. After seventeen years of selfless work there, she was a woman of whom the superior general, Mother Emmanuel, said, "Your sisters love you, the doctors trust you, and your students respect you enormously." And when she felt drawn to help the resistance during the war, her second vocation took her out of the convent but not away from lifelong commitment to selfless work: "I have given too many cups of water in His name and He knows I would go on doing it, whether working for Him as a nun or as a war nurse."

As the year ended, Audrey prepared for the filming of the most challenging role of her career—the most difficult, the most physically painful and the most exhausting. What Kate and Lou called Audrey's own "dear soul" was about to flourish and deepen, certainly beyond even her own expectations.

Chapter Ten

January – June 1958

"WE GOT TOGETHER and talked about the character of Sister Luke," Fred Zinnemann recalled, speaking of January 1958. He, Audrey and Bob Anderson were in Rome for the first two weeks of that month, visiting convents and psychiatric hospitals and conferring with clergymen engaged both as expert advisers and as insurance against the possibility that some Catholics—those who knew very little about the formal religious life of monks and nuns—might be offended by the account of a nun released from vows. "We talked about how Sister Luke develops, and how she reacts to other characters. It took many hours of going into lots of details. We also spoke about what Sister Luke was thinking . . . so she gradually started to live with that, and she found the role in concrete form in the convents, when she saw the nuns."

Regarding the assistance and approval of Catholic clergy and nuns, Warner, Blanke and Zinnemann not only wanted to represent accurately the details of Catholic rituals and of convent life: they also wanted to avoid any censure or disapproval of the film for the way it treated its controversial subject matter—especially since no one in any major capacity on *The Nun's Story* was Catholic.

Zinnemann and Anderson were especially gratified that month when a number of highly respected priests—like Rev. Harold C. Gardiner, the Jesuit scholar and literary editor of the weekly magazine *America*—read the screenplay. Not only did he and his colleagues have no objections, they praised it as a deeply spiritual scenario that would make for an important film. In addition, the Cinema Office in Rome, which handles requests put to the Vatican for assistance or tacit approval, assigned a group of Dominican priests to work with the production company. Anticipating sensationalism and not known for leniency, especially in matters of clerical image, the Dominicans were surprised to find that only one or two matters of detail warranted their comment. "Eventually," Zinnemann added, "caution gave way to trust and finally to most generous help [from the Dominicans], without which the film could not have been made."

Meanwhile, the director engaged a magnificent cast of internationally esteemed actors: Dame Peggy Ashcroft, Dame Edith Evans, Peter Finch, Mildred Dunnock, Beatrice Straight, Patricia Collinge, Ruth White, Margaret Phillips, Niall MacGinnis, Lionel Jeffries, Barbara O'Neil, Colleen Dewhurst and Stephen Murray. The production archives disclose that all these players quickly agreed to participate, for two reasons: the opportunity to assume roles that were vividly written, and the prospect of working with Audrey. Peggy Ashcroft's recollection was to the point. "I rarely accepted film roles at that time," she said years later, "but this was not to be turned down. I admired Audrey Hepburn enormously, and I found the screenplay irresistible."

Zinnemann was also fortunate in assembling appropriate non-speaking bit players for the scenes of the entire community of nuns: he personally interviewed more than seven hundred women and then selected 109 ladies who walked with unselfconscious dignity and who comported themselves with natural but formal decorum. "Twenty dancers were also borrowed from the ballet corps of the Rome Opera and were drilled by two Dominican nuns, one of them a university professor. For the nuns' close-ups, faces of great character and personality were needed. We found them mostly among the Roman aristocracy: a lot of principessas and contessas turned up in their Rolls-Royces or Mercedes at five in the morning. Dressed as nuns, they looked marvelous." The local sisters who trained these laywomen were so pleased with the results that, on returning to their convents, they became impatient with the young nuns. "You should do better than that," they told the juniors. "Mr. Zinnemann's nuns are perfect!"

Patricia Bosworth was a young New York stage actress who had been recommended by Anderson for the role of Sister Marie Christine, a novice who departs on the eve of Vow Day. She joined Audrey and others in the cast for a unique kind of preparation: "Fred Zinnemann arranged for us to visit convents in Rome, and to observe procedures at the Salvator Mundi Hospital, where we learned how nursing nuns were trained." Bosworth also recalled the ubiquitous presence of a priest adviser on the set all during principal photography, instructing the "nuns" how to walk, move and bow.

After two weeks in Rome, the women proceeded to Paris, where extraordinary and unprecedented arrangements had been made for Audrey and others to have long discussions with nuns and even to live for several days in convents. "One of the French religious orders," Zinnemann recalled,

> gave us permission to have each of our key actresses stay in a different convent for several days, going through the entire ritual of the day, starting with the first prayers at 5.30 a.m. until the Grand Silence at the end of the day. I stashed my "nuns" away at different convents, each one separately . . .

Making the daily rounds to see how they were doing, I'd arrive in the warmth of a taxi (it was mid-January in Paris, the winter was intensely cold and the convents were hardly heated), and all of them would come out of the cloisters absolutely purple with cold but fascinated by what they were involved in and very excited by the way they were getting prepared for their characters.

This entire time of preparation was, Zinnemann added, "an interior voyage of discovery and an enormous personal experience" for everyone working on *The Nun's Story*.

After the cast and crew had been immunized against tropical diseases, they proceeded to the Belgian Congo, where filming began on January 28, 1958, and continued until February 23. During those weeks, scenes were shot at the old railway station in Stanleyville, at a native market, in a hospital, at a mission school, in several villages and at an island leper colony. All the nonspeaking Africans in the film were locals, many of them often confused with all the paraphernalia of moviemaking but nonetheless eager to cooperate with their strange visitors. The heat and humidity were oppressive, and giant bugs and dangerous snakes were ever present during filming.

"It was very hard, unglamorous work," Audrey said later, recalling the "sometimes almost dangerous exhaustion. But it was my best memory of any film set, because of our close community spirit in the Congo." Another kind of danger occurred during the filming in Rome, on March 23, when Audrey collapsed at Cinecittà in excruciating pain. Her condition was diagnosed as a critical attack of kidney stones, and she was given morphine to relieve the pain. For an entire day, there was considerable alarm that she might have to submit to serious and risky surgery, but the kidney stones eventually passed. The production was shut down for several days, but Audrey made a quick return to work.

In a long letter to Kate and Lou, Fred's Zinnemann's wife, Renée (present during the entire production), detailed the circumstances of working in the Congo that February. Several scenes involved surgery in a native hospital: "The girls [Audrey and others] and Fred have watched some pretty gruesome operations—a cancerous tumor and a Caesarian section (the baby died). It was quite a traumatic experience for all, as none had been around operating rooms before except Fred."

Forever after, Fred Zinnemann cherished the memory of his leading lady.

After more than twenty-five years, I am struck by the fine, firm line of development in Audrey's performance. The subconscious quality of independence is present in all her actions. When she comes running in late [for a scene in which the postulants are going to chapel], her haste betrays the inner calm she should be developing. Or when the girls prostrate themselves on the floor in front of the Mother General, Audrey peeks out of one eye, curiosity getting the better of her.

Audrey's performance was in fact composed of countless such moments that seemed to erase the distance between actress and character.

FROM HOLLYWOOD TO New York, then on to Rome, Paris, Brussels and the Congo, Bob Anderson had pursued the affair with Audrey, and she had responded passionately. Bob was, after all, a man she admired: cultivated and handsome, he was a serious and respected playwright, screenwriter and essayist; he had given her the finest script of her career; and he was attentive and courtly, but not annoyingly deferential, in his obvious adoration of her.

But then there was an ironic and poignant repetition of the past.

One evening in May, Audrey spoke to Bob of her intense longing to be a mother. Mel did not enter the conversation, but it was clear to Bob that her marriage was deeply and perhaps irreparably troubled. He took this as an implication that—were she to leave Mel for him—she wanted and expected to have children. With great sadness, Bob told Audrey that he could never be a father: he was congenitally sterile. It is unlikely that she did not, at that moment, think of William Holden.

That was the heartbreaking conclusion to the affair that might have become a marriage. There was no long, difficult conversation—no explanations or recriminations. "We kissed good-bye and I exiled myself in London and wrote a play," Anderson said years later. Unlike Ingrid, Audrey made a clean break with Bob, and they met only once more; she seems to have been so deeply hurt by this revelation that she could not sustain even his friendship. She simply wanted to end this chapter of her life and perhaps even to forget it. "If you hear from Audrey," Bob wrote in a sad letter to Kate and Lou, "give her my best. I'm anxious to hear from her. She was magnificent—a great actress and a great sport. She went through hell."

APART FROM ITS sustained reflection on the primacy of conscience, *The Nun's Story* is a tender elegy for a kind of religious life that once was the norm among certain groups of nuns, but is now rarely found in the Roman Catholic Church. The practice of humiliations, the suppression of personality, the attempt to put aside normal human feelings and the unnatural efforts even to ignore one's own past: these were, from about the seventeenth century in Europe and later in America, taken for granted as guaranteed paths to holiness in some religious orders of monks and nuns. To good effect, almost every community later abandoned those practices, under encouragement from the Vatican itself. *The*

Nun's Story and Audrey's recognizably human Sister Luke offered neither a gratuitous endorsement nor a smug disapproval of this rarefied life of long ago.

When the picture was released, one of the director's advisers—a nun named Mother Marie-Edmond—wrote to Zinnemann from her Paris convent after seeing the film with her community. Her critical comments represent the common judgment of European and American religious women in 1959:

> The discipline of postulants seems exaggerated—at times, it looks like living in barracks! And everything seems directed toward personal perfection [rather than] the love of God. Audrey Hepburn realizes her difficult part admirably and with perfect tact. There is nothing ridiculous about her or any other actress, whereas most pictures portraying nuns do not avoid that danger . . . But Sister Luke and the other nuns give the impression of living under constraint: they quench everything which is simply human and they seem just to live through formalities and routines (except in the Congo). They have hardly any friendly relations. This is sometimes a little true of the religious life, which necessarily imposes certain constraints *on the novices,* but this is *totally false* as to the whole of the life.

Audrey's achievement was indeed "realized admirably"—in fact, it was nothing short of inspired. She had neither a sophisticated wardrobe by Givenchy nor even an Edith Head suit to command viewers' attention—indeed, only her remarkable face and her expressive, delicate hands were visible. Instead of high key lighting to glamorize her, there were only the lineaments of her own inner life: she created a compelling portrait of spiritual anguish and maturing integrity, and this she accomplished only with her eyes and the subtlest gradations of expression; almost everything was internal.

This was a performance vastly superior to any other before or after in her career; in fact, it is defensible that Audrey Hepburn's Sister Luke is one of the greatest performances in the history of film. Not only is the character far more profound that anyone she ever portrayed: she also located correspondences within herself that revealed, possibly far beyond her realization, some of the depths of Audrey Hepburn, and what she took with utmost gravity in her life.

Almost always, while watching movies, viewers make adjustments of perception, trying to close the gap between actor and role; but for the most part, we watch actors pretending to be someone, and however unconsciously, we cannot entirely suspend our understanding that the performer is not the character. We see someone "playing" (the word is significant), affecting someone else's identity, and we admire, or we do not, the technique, the tricks of the trade, the fake tears, the lighting, the judicious editing, the supporting music—all the components movies employ to help us accept as authentic what we see. Our assessments of performances, therefore, are usually simple: we say that an actor was effective *as* so-and-so—in other words, we admire the pretense, the "playing." Apart from documentaries, we very rarely accept that the person on screen and the character portrayed are one: that occurs only when we observe very gifted artists.

In the case of Audrey Hepburn in this role, however, something very rare occurred. We are not, in the final analysis, watching her pretend. To the contrary, we proceed with her reality every step of the arduous, honorable journey, as Gabrielle van der Mal becomes Sister Luke and embarks on a transforming spiritual adventure with a deeper knowledge of herself and therefore, as the film affirms, of what might be called God's active and ongoing guidance of her life and destiny. The division between actress and role has indeed been entirely erased.

"The idea of the cloister is a repellent one to those who believe that earthly life is the purpose and value of earthly existence," wrote the critic Stanley Kauffmann when the picture was released. "But the film's strength, sustained by Miss Hepburn's performance, is such that even the unconvinced will feel a tug of envy for those who have found the assurances which he can never accept. And that, after all, is the point of Sister Luke's story."

The exterior similarities between Audrey and Sister Luke, which she learned from the book, from the screenplay and from her friendship with Lou, doubtless gave her powerful starting points for discovering that a very important part of herself was indeed like this nun. Both Audrey and Sister Luke were born in Belgium; both left home at a young age to pursue a career. Both were transplanted to alien countries, where they flourished while working constantly. Both were caught in the violence of the war in Holland; both had brothers captured by the Germans—and both lost their fathers. Hence there was, right from the start, a symbiosis of accidents that, in very deep ways, joined character and actress. "My mother had always impressed on us that one has to be useful," Audrey said years later, "and that giving love was more important than receiving it. As Sister Luke, it was enormously helpful for me to remember that. And I found that something happened when I put on the habit of a nun. Once you do that, you feel something."

"Audrey has reached a new maturity," wrote Zinnemann to Kurt Frings toward the end of production. "I have never seen anyone more disciplined, more gracious or more dedicated to her work than Audrey. There was no ego, no asking for extra favors; there was the greatest consideration for her co-workers . . . She has proven herself a great actress in a very difficult and exacting part." He and several others in the cast (Peggy Ashcroft among them) exchanged letters over the ensuing years in which they praised Audrey's almost uncanny comprehension of each scene.

Those involved in the production noticed that Audrey became

quieter, keeping more and more to herself as the weeks passed after Bob Anderson's departure. She trusted her makeup crew and never used a mirror; nor would she listen to the radio or phonograph records, "because Sister Luke would never do these things," she said. Audrey was not playing at being a nun: part of her true self was paradoxically a nonreligious nun. Several lines from the film punctuated her own conversations for the rest of her life, among them this part of the exchange between Sister Luke and Mother Christophe, superior of the mental asylum:

SISTER LUKE: I thought that one would reach some sort of resting place where obedience would be natural and struggle would end.

MOTHER CHRISTOPHE: There is no final resting place, ever. But you must have patience with yourself.

She would, making these words her own, speak not of obedience but rather of courage; of her lifelong attempt to rid herself of paralyzing fear and radical insecurity.

Audrey needed both qualities that January, for she had to cope with debilitating exhaustion during the Congo filming. "Audrey is in almost every shot," Zinnemann wrote to Warner executive Steve Trilling. "I tried to force the pace and to extend the working hours once or twice, but I found that even Audrey, with her fantastic stamina and her discipline, cannot go beyond seven p.m. without looking and feeling very badly the next day. In all my years in this business, I have never seen such dedication."

Although she was nominally, generically Protestant, Audrey proclaimed no denominational allegiance; in any case, she was more than receptive to those transcendent realities toward which authentic Christian belief reaches—and which were at the heart of Hulme's novel. That Audrey possessed a sense of awe before the simple things in nature was acknowledged by all who knew her. That she sympathized with suffering; that she saw herself as no better than any ordinary woman; that she was never haughty with her colleagues and the public but always considerate and serene despite her own anxieties; that she took pleasure in material things and in her own sexuality, and yet did not depend on them for ultimate happiness—these were qualities recognized by her intimates and colleagues. And she was most certainly, that year, "hungry for something more," which is the clearest sign of that much abused and devalued word *spirituality*. "The part [of Sister Luke] was suited to my nature," she told the press.

Audrey Hepburn and Fred Zinnemann were deeply moved by the faith of the nuns they met in Paris and in Africa—"the marvelous serenity," as he said, with which they went about their duties and devotion. Some of those who provided medical care for the poorest, he recalled, "themselves lived under the most primitive conditions in the steaming forest." He also remembered a clinic for lepers, run by an elderly Dutch nun who had been working with the outcasts for thirty-five years: "She exemplified all the joy of life, even though she spent her days among people who were dying. I asked if she had ever been back to Europe. She looked at me in amazement: 'Why should I go back? I have never been sick!' That was the only possible reason that occurred to her. Such serenity, fastness of purpose and devotion were awesome qualities for an outsider to witness, especially for a movie director."

Audrey was equally moved. "After looking inside an insane asylum, visiting a leper colony, talking to missionary workers and watching operations, I developed a new kind of inner peacefulness."

Indeed, she was being changed by this role, and she knew it. On April 7, Audrey wrote to Kate and Lou from Rome, where the interiors of the movie were being filmed.

. . . All I can tell you is that any resemblance between the present Hepburn and the former one dating back to January 1st of 1958 [before

filming began] is purely accidental. I have seen, heard, learnt so much and have been so enriched by a milliard experiences that I am and feel a different person. . . .

Delving into the heart and mind of Sister Luke, I have also had to dig deep down in myself. Thereby having done a bit of ploughing of the soul—so to speak—the seeds of all I have experienced have fallen on neatly prepared ground, and I hope will result in harvesting a better Audrey . . . Hope this doesn't sound too flowery, but my vocabulary is, I'm afraid, too poor to accurately describe the constant joys and gratitude of your happy postulant . . .

Lots of LOVE,
Audrey

And in an Easter telegram to the same friends, Audrey wrote: "Joyous happy Easter from your ever loving Sister Audrey."

HER PERFORMANCE, one critic hoped, would "forever silence those who have thought her less an actress than a symbol of the sophisticated child-woman. In *The Nun's Story,* Miss Hepburn reveals the kind of acting talent that can project inner feelings of both depth and complexity so skillfully you must scrutinize her intently on a second and third viewing to perceive how she does it." And the critic for *Variety*—a trade publication not known for seeing much beyond commercial possibilities—acclaimed "a soaring and luminous film [in which] Audrey Hepburn has her most demanding film role and gives her finest performance."*

---

* Audrey, her director and many who contributed to the film were awarded prizes worldwide, but Oscars eluded them; she did, however, receive top honors in 1959 from the British Film Academy and the New York Film Critics Circle. That was the year of *Ben-Hur,* which, perhaps to no one's surprise, won eleven Academy Awards: a traditional Hollywood "religious" movie, it was burdened with mere spectacle and self-conscious pieties, and it lacked the depths of Zinnemann's film—none of which seemed to matter in the voting. Simone Signoret was voted Best Actress for her performance in *Room at the Top.*

From first to last scenes, *The Nun's Story* deals with its profound subject matter as few films have ever done. Mediocre talents—those of the writer, director and cast—might well have sentimentalized Sister Luke, or been contemptuous of her, or melodramatized her. But the picture remains a model of fidelity to Kathryn Hulme's meditative literary novel and to the true story of the remarkable woman on whom that novel is based.

The movie also sustains its own careful structure. It opens, for example, as Gabrielle van der Mal prepares to leave home to enter the convent: in close-up, she is seen removing a friendship ring, or perhaps an engagement band, from her finger; she then places the ring beside a small framed photo of a young man named Jean (the French form of Ian, Audrey's half-brother, whose picture it is). She snaps shut her valise and puts on a cloche hat. At the last moment of the film, we see her remove her nun's ring, place a plain hat in her valise and close it.

The picture has many such small but significant moments that reward careful attention. When Gabrielle descends the staircase at home to depart for the convent, she sees her father in the parlor. He stands distractedly at a piano, playing with one finger the first notes of *"Voi che sapete"*—Cherubino's aria from Mozart's opera *Le nozze di Figaro*. Then she steps toward him and, standing at his side, she continues the melody. In various orchestrations, this music recurs at key moments in Franz Waxman's powerful, evocative score for the film. The text of the aria perfectly italicizes the core of the opera and this movie, for just as Cherubino sings to the Countess and Susanna, so Gabrielle may ask of the nuns: "You ladies who know what love is, see if that is what I have in my heart."

And at the last moment of the film, there occurs something that is very nearly breathtaking in its aptness and poignancy. As Gabrielle walks slowly from the convent into the world, Audrey gave the film its final, most memorable and poignant moment. We remain with the camera in the room as she walks away from us. But she cannot overcome seventeen years of custom: about to descend the step from the convent to the street, she reaches back to gather the long nun's skirts she once had—and she hesitates briefly, the subtlest sign of her realization that now she is wearing a laywoman's much shorter dress and coat. At last she continues on her way. Shown from a distance, from behind the actress and in silence, this moment is all the more effective because of that distance. Then we hear the deep tolling of a bell, and the film ends as it began.

Robert Wolders, who was very close to Audrey in the last years of her life, found the picture difficult to watch after her death. "I think the film that reflects Audrey the most is *The Nun's Story*. For all her sense of fun, she was extremely introspective, as is Sister Luke. What I see in the film and in the character is so close to Audrey in those moments when she was in turmoil, when there was something she could not resolve." And Audrey's son Sean recalled his mother's opinion of the picture and her role in it. "I think my mother was proudest of *The Nun's Story*. It was a wonderful, serious script, not at all fluffy, and she thought it was an important film."

Audrey turned twenty-nine during filming and was, as Kathryn Hulme said, "hungry for something more." In the role of Sister Luke, the actress felt that hunger—she sensed, too, that she was heading somewhere, although the goal and the direction were unclear and her bearings still unsure.

But one thing was certain: Audrey had to know about her father, whose death had been rumored among Ella's friends. She wrote to Mel, asking if there was some way to learn more—and to do so without alerting the press. He said he would contact a friend at the International Red Cross, a man who had located several missing relatives of Hollywood colleagues.

It may or may not be merely coincidental that Audrey's inquiry to Mel, and her longing to know about her father, coincided exactly with two of the last scenes she filmed for *The Nun's Story*. There had been touching sequences between her characters and their fathers in *Sabrina*, *War and Peace* and *Love in the Afternoon*, but none were so deeply felt as those in the Zinnemann picture.

"Goodbye, Father," says Gabrielle as she enters the convent. "I'll do my best—I want you to be proud of me."

"I don't want to be proud of you—I want you to be happy," he replies.

"I am happy," she says.

The poignancy of this scene, with the haze of tears in the eyes of both actors and the gentleness in their voices, is tragically carried forward toward the end of the film. Sister Luke receives written notice that her father has been gunned down by Nazi soldiers on a road, while he was tending the wounded. Alone in her convent cell, she cries aloud, "Father! Father! Father!"—each time more loudly and desperately. The scene then changes to Sister Luke's conversation with the convent chaplain: she intends to leave the religious order. As Gabrielle van der Mal, she will take up the struggle begun by her father. Her loss of him is not the sole reason for her departure, but his death at least partly provokes her decision.

Recollecting these scenes is not meant to imply that they were the reasons why Audrey wanted to contact her father. But no actor, certainly not one of her exquisite sensitivity, can leave her personal life and her net of memories outside the studio when she plays a role. Ruston's disappearance from her life remained an unresolved source of anguish, a sharp and vivid wound that had to be healed.

Chapter Eleven

July 1958–December 1960

AUDREY COMPLETED HER scenes for *The Nun's Story* in late June. For six months, she had worked constantly, but for a few days of illness in Rome and for travel between filming in Europe and Africa. But as July approached, there was to be no summer holiday, no rest from her exhausting round of obligations. She had promised Mel that she would play the leading role in *Green Mansions,* which, after research and background filming in South America, he was ready to direct in Los Angeles, beginning on July 15. Audrey had not worked in Hollywood in five years, since *Sabrina;* nor was she eager to return. En route to Los Angeles, she took a detour to their house in Bürgenstock, where she stocked a dozen large valises full of personal effects, tableware and bibelots, the better to make their temporary California residence more homelike.

Mel was probably aware of Audrey's affair with Robert Anderson. Film production companies have few secrets, and some cast and crew members knew about her comings and goings. Certainly Fred Zinnemann knew about it, for he and Bob were good friends and held each other's confidence, but others grasped the situation, too. It is, after all, unusual for a screenwriter to be present during virtually the entire time of filming—unless the script is fraught with problems and in need of daily improvisation, which was far from the case with *The Nun's Story*. Anderson and Zinnemann had completed their research journeys well before filming began, and the screenplay was in almost perfect shape: the writer's presence for almost all of production had to do with Audrey, not because a few rewrites were necessary here and there; and no other writer worked on it.

More to the point, Audrey gave Anderson the impression that she and Mel had a tacit (or perhaps even an explicit) understanding about extramarital relations when they were separated for long periods. The marriage from the summer of 1959 had a twofold objective—to provide Mel with the cachet of Audrey's professional collaboration, and to afford her the opportunity to bear a child by a man she knew who was not infertile. She was twenty-nine, she had endured at least one miscarriage and she began to express considerable anxiety about the prospects for maternity. Perhaps most of all, she believed that a child would bring to the marriage what she believed she could not.

As for the occupational partnership, Mel's choice of a literary property for her movie was both comprehensible and bizarre. Published in 1904, *Green Mansions* was the best-known work by W. H. Hudson, a naturalist and novelist born in Argentina to American parents. He took British citizenship at the age of sixty and wrote mostly about subjects having to do with the mysteries of nature: *Green Mansions* found wide readership for decades, especially among young women. The story tells of Abel, a political refugee who encounters a mysterious teenage girl named Rima in the South American rain forest. Her tropical habitat has put her in a kind of mystic communion with the natural world, but her experience of human love is dormant until Abel falls in love with her. Much of the novel's appeal doubtless had to do with its tragic ending, for Rima is killed by a band of jungle savages.

Since the 1930s, various Hollywood producers and studios believed that a lush production of *Green Mansions* would translate into abundant green currency, but their attempts to film it had collapsed when suitable scripts were not forthcoming. In 1959, movie rights were once again available, but by then it was such a conventional tale that no director was interested. Mel, however, believed it was just the right project for Audrey: her candid ingenuousness and her image of maidenly innocence would be just right for this fey story set in the exotic jungle. And so this was the project chosen to fulfill Audrey's obligation to MGM (because the rights to *Funny Face* were sold to Paramount). "I have become greatly dependent on Mel's taste and guidance," she said without further explanation.

Casting the hero was easy for Mel: he signed twenty-six-year-old Anthony Perkins, who readily undertook the chance to play opposite Audrey. Lanky, boyishly earnest and slightly odd, Perkins had played sensitive, sometimes confused or even aberrant young men on Broadway and in Hollywood.* At the same time, Dorothy Kingsley—an MGM contract writer available that season—was commissioned to create the screenplay. Once a comedy writer for Bob Hope and Edgar Bergen, Kingsley had written scripts for Metro musicals and for no fewer than seven aquatic spectacles starring Esther Williams. Perhaps no one would have been the right choice to transfer this story to the screen, but Dorothy Kingsley was categorically the wrong one. Her script, approved by the studio and handed over to Mel, was as impenetrable as its jungle setting. But Mel soldiered on, confident that he could supply in visual ingenuity what the dialogue, with its long stretches of silence, so manifestly lacked. Before a foot of

---

* The defining role of Anthony Perkins's career would, of course, be Norman Bates in Alfred Hitchcock's *Psycho*, filmed in 1959.

film rolled through the camera, *Green Mansions* was tangled in creative and commercial troubles.

With his script, his cast in place and his background shots completed in British Guiana and Venezuela, Mel began filming Audrey, Anthony Perkins and the other players not on location in the tropics of South America, nor even in those of Mexico or Florida. The unenchanted forest of the picture was instead filmed on Stage 24 of MGM Studios, in Culver City, California.

"Many friends asked me how such an artistically touchy situation would turn out," Audrey said later. "I answered that I wouldn't know until the picture was finished. Now I can say that it was pleasantly uncomplicated. I found that being directed by Mel was as natural as brushing my teeth." Audrey's observation that the endeavor was "pleasantly uncomplicated" and her analogy to routine dental care are remarkable. Had she meant that the project was rewarding or challenging or in some vague way a step forward in her career, she certainly had the expressive vocabulary to communicate that. Her understatement, on the other hand, is perhaps emblematic of her indifference.

Green Mansions (the first and only time Mel directed his wife) was a failure critically and commercially, notorious for its lack of dramatic tension, its strained dialogue and its supercilious tone: Audrey/Rima: "It is love I feel . . . Now I know that." It is equally difficult to accept her hysterical declamations to the spirit of her dead mother. Barefoot throughout, Audrey was made to wear a diaphanous shift and a long, dark wig; the entire effect was that of an early flower child from Haight-Ashbury. Perhaps most alarming is the obviously fake studio jungle and the lack of chemistry between the principals. Anthony Perkins could not manage to make the shortest love scene credible: kissing Audrey, he seems cool enough to have air-conditioned all of MGM, and there was much bumping of noses. By this time, Mel may have lost hope, or in light of so many circumstances, he may not have wished to direct his wife in a love scene even with so diffident a performer. Most significantly, Mel was out of his depth as director: the pacing is languid, and the entire film lacks anything like credible emotion.

A movie shot almost completely in the studio could easily have been completed in six weeks; in this case, the production shuffled along from July 15 to November 6. The day before the first scenes were put on film, Audrey drove as usual from their rented house to the studio. As she approached the corner of Beverly Drive and Santa Monica Boulevard, a car raced toward her from the left. To avoid a collision, Audrey had to speed across the intersection, where she crashed into a car driven by a woman named Joan Paladini, a young actress known as Joan Lora. Mrs. Paladini brought suit against Audrey, contending that she suffered neck and back injuries. The matter came to trial over two years later when Audrey appeared in court to give her account. The jury returned a verdict in favor of Mrs. Paladini and awarded her $6,250 in damages. From July 14, 1958, Audrey never again sat behind the wheel of a car except on screen.

WHEN *GREEN MANSIONS* was completed and screened for the studio publicists early in December, they had no idea how to promote this dreary, lackluster movie. Near to desperation, they settled on one production detail. In her forest primeval, Rima is everywhere accompanied by a tiny faun. To ensure that the animal would stay at Audrey's side in each scene, she nurtured and raised it before filming began. She then kept it with her at home all during filming and was seen with the little creature all over town. Hence national magazines carried cute photographs of Audrey and Ip, her name for the faun because it uttered high-pitched "ip-ip-ip" sounds.

MGM decided to release *Green Mansions* as swiftly as possible, at Radio City Music Hall, New York, on March 19, 1959. During its run there, more than half of the auditorium's 6,200 seats remained empty. Fortunately, the film's tepid reception was completely eclipsed by the triumph of *The Nun's Story*, which had its premiere at the same theater on June 18. "There was plenty of excitement at the Music Hall yesterday," Bob Anderson wrote to Kathryn Hulme and Marie Louise Habets on the nineteenth. "The lines were almost up to Fifth Avenue most of the day, and thousands of people were turned away. It was one of their biggest opening days . . . Fred [Zinnemann] and I sat together at the evening show. Of course, *The Nun's Story* will never be over for us."

For a month, double lines coiled around the streets of Rockefeller Center and audiences waited as long as five hours for tickets. The film was extended to theaters nationwide in July, and as the accountants at Warner Bros. calculated their earnings, it was clear that this was beyond doubt the most profitable motion picture in the studio's history.

THE FERRERS SPENT Thanksgiving with Mel's children in California and then traveled for the Christmas holiday to Bürgenstock, where they learned that Audrey was pregnant. Although she expressed unqualified delight, her private reaction was more complicated—indeed, the event seems to have been unintended, for in January she was to begin work in Mexico on an arduous movie: a cowboy-and-Indian shoot-'em-up, of all things. Since she had agreed to do her own horseback riding for the film, it is not likely that pregnancy, however ultimately desired, was planned for this precise time.

Contrary to much that has been written, Audrey was actually of two minds about motherhood at this point in her career. On one hand, she was resolutely determined to undertake as wide a variety of challenging roles as possible—hence, after portraying a nun and a jungle primitive, she accepted the offer to appear in a Western directed by John Huston. Indeed, as she arrived for the filming in Mexico, she was beginning her third film since the previous January.

At the same time, she said she was desperate to have children—but the timing had to be carefully planned; indeed, she often said privately that she was hurrying to complete her contractual obligations so that she might retire permanently to raise a family. The pregnancy of late 1958 was almost certainly a surprise in light of the commitments she had already made, which would engage her through all of 1959.

HAVING ALREADY DIRECTED twenty films (including *The Maltese Falcon*, *The Treasure of the Sierra Madre*, *The Asphalt Jungle*, *The African Queen* and *Moby Dick*), Huston was certainly qualified to manage a dramatic outdoor epic set in the Old West. Nevertheless, something went terribly wrong, and as so often in these cases, the problem was a confusing, illogical stew of a script that was long on atmosphere but short on character development and motivation.

Soon after filming began, Burt Lancaster, whose production company backed the film and who had the leading male role, briefly considered canceling the picture, but too much was at stake commercially and personally. Lillian Gish, then sixty-six, had been D. W. Griffith's greatest star during the silent screen era; she had appeared in ninety films since her debut in 1912, and there was little she did not know about moviemaking. But even Gish could not understand *The Unforgiven*—indeed, no one during or after production had the remotest idea what the title meant. They had all accepted their roles based on an extended prose summary of the story and the prospect of working with Huston, who assured them that the screenplay would be finely tuned before the first day of shooting in the desert outside Durango, Mexico, six hundred miles northwest of Mexico City.

A lucid screenplay was never produced. Writer Ben Maddow

(working from a novel by Alan Le May) had collaborated with Huston before, and they continued their efforts day and night in Mexico, but the only result seemed to be hangovers. In addition, Huston had wanted to make a different film from the idea Maddow had sold to MGM. Audrey and Lillian tried to counter their anxieties with whispered black humor about the picture—to the annoyance of Huston.

The project was virtually impossible to salvage. Audrey, who had little more to do than react to events around her, was woefully miscast in the role of a prairie girl who learns that she is really a Kiowa Indian. Occasionally, she managed the hint of a midwestern twang, but for the most part, she sounded like a perfectly polished maiden home from a British boarding school. To make matters worse, her makeup was surprisingly irregular: for some sequences, her skin was painted as dark as a Native American's; for others, she seems as fair as an English rose. Nor was she assisted by the fatuity of a film in which apparently important characters appear and disappear and—marvelous to relate—a herd of cattle somehow leaps from the ground onto the roof of a house and then to an adjacent overhanging precipice. Equally nonsensical are scenes in which Lillian Gish, in defiance of Indian drums, plays Mozart on an antique piano that has conveniently been left outdoors, presumably just for this disputatious purpose.

A terrifying accident interrupted filming on January 28. Huston set up a scene in which Audrey was to ride her horse close to the camera and then dismount. After several attempts to get the shot right, horse and rider approached the proper spot. At that point, a member of the crew jumped in front of the horse, waving his arms to signal the animal to stop. Instead, the horse bucked, and Audrey went flying through the air, landing on the ground with a terrifying thud. In horrific pain, she was frightened that she would lose her baby; everyone else feared that she was paralyzed.

Neither mishap occurred, but there was serious injury. Rushed to a hospital in Durango, she awaited her husband and a doctor, who flew down next day from Los Angeles, where Mel was completing a role in *The World, the Flesh and the Devil*. With the two men was Marie Louise Habets, whom Mel had telephoned and who had immediately offered her nursing skills. She lovingly attended Audrey for the next month, both in Mexico and in California.

After several days of tests in Durango, it was finally determined that Audrey had four fractured vertebrae and a badly sprained foot. On February 2, she was flown in an ambulance airplane to Beverly Hills for treatment and rest. "I'll ride that horse again before the picture is finished," the game girl told waiting reporters. To her immense relief, she had not lost the baby.

Without complaint or requests for special treatment, Audrey returned to Mexico and *The Unforgiven* on March 5 and resumed her role four days later, riding the horse, as she had promised. By this time, her job was only something to be endured.

Twenty years later, Huston was both forthright and on the mark. After describing Audrey's accident and the near-drowning of two actors, he admitted that "in the end, the worst of it was the picture we made. Some of my pictures I don't care for, but *The Unforgiven* is the only one I actually dislike . . . the overall tone is bombastic and over-inflated [like Dimitri Tiomkin's musical score, he might have added] . . . I watched it on television one night recently, and after about half a reel [ten minutes], I had to turn the damned thing off. I couldn't bear it."

Critics and public were likewise unimpressed when the film opened in April 1960. "Ludicrous, feeble and disconcerted" were typical adjectives used in America, while the British press lamented the film's "portentousness." Even Audrey could not escape reproach: "She is just a little less incongruous than the grand piano," wrote a London reviewer. ("But the horses are vigorous," observed *The New York Times* coolly.)

Fulfilling his contractual obligation, Mel left Mexico on March

11 to promote the unfortunate *Green Mansions*. Audrey completed the Huston picture in April and joined Mel in New York; together, they returned to Switzerland to await the birth of their baby.

FOR SEVERAL YEARS, Audrey had hoped to appear in a film directed by Alfred Hitchcock, and during the mid-1950s, she pursued that idea after admiring several of his recent pictures (especially *Rear Window*, *To Catch a Thief*, *The Man Who Knew Too Much* and *North by Northwest*, which she saw in a preview screening in New York and which followed *The Nun's Story* into the Music Hall). Since November 1958, Hitchcock had been working with none other than Samuel Taylor (author of *Sabrina Fair*) on the screen version of Henry Cecil's novel *No Bail for the Judge*. This was the story of a London magistrate, wrongly accused of a murder but ultimately saved from the gallows when his daughter goes underground to smoke out the real villain in the demimonde of London's prostitutes.

After learning of Audrey's interest in working with him, Hitchcock (who coincidentally had a deal with Paramount) proceeded with her in mind to play the loyal and resourceful daughter. After reading Hitchcock's summary of the story in February 1959, she signed a contract to star in his picture. At the same time, Laurence Harvey consented to play her accomplice and love interest; and John Williams, who had portrayed her father in *Sabrina*, agreed to do so again, this time as the beleaguered judge. Production was to begin in London that summer, with Audrey's participation as soon as possible, very likely in late August or early September, after her baby's birth.*

---

* The discrepancies between this account of Audrey's planned participation and that given in my book *The Dark Side of Genius: The Life of Alfred Hitchcock* (1983) are explained by the fact that, in 2004, previously unreleased details concerning *No Bail for the Judge* were at last made available to the public from the Paramount archives.

She was resting at Villa Bethania, Bürgenstock, when, on May 11, Kurt Frings sent a telegram to Paramount's vice president, Y. Frank Freeman, confirming that Audrey would indeed "comply with [her] contractual obligations" to appear in *No Bail for the Judge* late that summer. Frings sent a copy of this message to Audrey.

But then she did something uncharacteristic. Unwilling to proceed immediately from the imminent delivery of her child to another film assignment—and thus to short-circuit what she anticipated as the joyful first days of motherhood—Audrey informed Frings, on May 19, that she would not appear in the Hitchcock picture after all. The stated reason for this, which Frings issued to the press, was that her doctors ordered complete rest until and for some time after the baby's birth. That was true— but it was not the whole story.

Since *Sabrina*, Audrey had the privilege of script approval before beginning work. On or about May 15, Paramount sent her the draft of *No Bail for the Judge*, in which her character was to be nearly strangled with a necktie. This upset her enormously: variety she savored, but violence like this she loathed. "When she read it," said Herbert Coleman, Hitchcock's associate producer, "that was it—the Hitchcock film was virtually canceled from that minute." Instead of asking Frings to negotiate the matter with Hitchcock, she simply withdrew from the production *tout court*— doubtless very much aware that the scene was central to the film and that Hitchcock did not welcome story counsel from actors.* When he learned of Audrey's defection, Laurence Harvey also withdrew, and Hitchcock canceled the production.

For years it was said—primarily by Hitchcock—that the departure of his two leading players was the reason that he could not

---

* The attempted or achieved murder of a woman by strangulation occurs in no less than a dozen Hitchcock films, as well as in projects that were planned but never realized.

proceed with *No Bail for the Judge*. But that is not the case. For one thing, Hitchcock very often lost actors he had counted on to work in this or that film—most recently, for example, he had prepared *Vertigo* (also written with Samuel Taylor) for Vera Miles; when she announced the pregnancy that forced her to withdraw from the film, Hitchcock offered the role to Kim Novak. The decision to shelve *No Bail* was finally made, as Taylor recalled, for quite another reason. Recent laws in Britain exacted harsh penalties against prostitutes for public solicitation. Important scenes in *No Bail* depended on candid importuning and were thus rendered implausible by the new ordinances. More to the point, Hitchcock intended to shoot these scenes on location in London, and in 1959, authorities informed Paramount that they would not approve the filming of such sequences. This chain of events, rather than Audrey's decision alone, sabotaged the picture.

A FEW DAYS LATER, Audrey went into labor, but with a sad outcome—the child was stillborn. The loss pitched her into a depression so acute that Mel feared for her emotional and mental stability. She smoked more than three packs of cigarettes a day, bit her nails to the quick and weighed little more than eighty pounds; suddenly, at thirty, she looked much older. "I still must spend much time in bed," she wrote to Hollywood columnist Hedda Hopper in June, "but I am filled with gratitude that I can have others—and for my husband, [a] gentle and tender nurse."

With the approval of her doctors, she agreed to attend the London premiere of *The Nun's Story* in July. "Audrey looked beautiful but a bit weak," Renée Zinnemann wrote to Kate and Lou. From there, the Ferrers went on to Ireland, where—after a year of effort—Mel's contact in the International Red Cross had finally tracked Audrey's father.

They arranged to meet Ruston in Dublin, where he lived with his wife, Fidelma Walshe. The reunion, in the lobby lounge of the Shelbourne Hotel, was unrelievedly awkward, without warmth or tears or a sense of reconciliation. In the words of his grandson, Audrey's father was "totally disconnected, as he had been for most of his life . . . in reality an emotional invalid." When they finally met, according to the grandson, "she realized that whether he had been there or not, it wouldn't have made a difference. He was an emotionally scarred man, and he never would have been the kind of father she wanted. She made peace with that."

Audrey left feeling that there had been no establishment at all of the relationship that never was. "We can go home now," she said quietly to Mel as they left the hotel. But her efforts, and her sheer generosity toward the man, never ceased: she sent a monthly stipend for the rest of his life; she wrote letters to him and Fidelma over several years; and she visited him once again, not long before his death.

AUDREY HAD ACCEPTED an invitation to appear in an upcoming issue of *Harper's Bazaar,* and her morale improved when she and Mel proceeded from Dublin to Paris. There, Richard Avedon photographed her over several days as she wore eighteen outfits by Dior, Guy Laroche and Pierre Cardin. (Givenchy's absence was occasioned only because he was not among those to be included in the magazine's September issue.) They then returned to Villa Bethania before driving to Montreux, on the shores of Lake Léman, where Mel met with Dorothy Kingsley to discuss a movie project that never materialized. When they returned home, Mel replied on August 14 to a letter from Kate and Lou. "Audrey badly needs to catch her breath," he noted. She did just that when the Zinnemanns, whom she loved dearly, arrived for a five-day visit;

Renée dispatched household chores and Fred created a relaxed atmosphere in their home while Mel fielded telephone calls and tried to confirm several deals for future work. "Audrey looks brown and healthy now," Renée wrote to Kate and Lou on August 23.

By November, the Ferrers were in Los Angeles, where Mel tried to find movies to direct even while he was acting on television. "Audrey looks superb," wrote Kate to the Zinnemanns, "and seems to be enjoying her momentary rest period with no film in the works as yet."

The respite from work was prolonged once again by doctors' orders: in Los Angeles, Audrey again learned she was pregnant. She and Mel returned to Villa Bethania for Christmas, and there she remained, in almost cloistered seclusion.

ON APRIL 4, 1960—the date for bestowing the annual Academy Awards—Audrey wrote a five-page letter, in her own clear handwriting, to Marie Louise Habets:

Dearest most precious Lou,

Tonight is the big night and you will all know the results when we are snoozing away . . . No news will ever be more glorious for me, though, than when I heard I was going to play Lou/Luke—or when you said you'd come and nurse my broken back (and me). . . .

I long for many accolades for Fred—he worked so hard and so tirelessly and with such devotion, pouring his soul and endless sensitive talent into something of which he had a vision no amount of Warner Bros. pressure was ever allowed to blur or distort for him. As for you two angels with gallant souls and witty tongues—no one will ever know how much you have meant and been to it [the film] and us all. . . .

All all all our love—
Audrey.

The next message to Lou and Kate was a telegram from Mel, dated July 17, 1960—from the Lucerne Maternity Clinic:

BOY SEAN BORN TWO FORTY THIS AFTERNOON NINE POUNDS AUDREY BEATIFICALLY HAPPY LOVE MEL.

The two women replied at once:

WE HAVE DISPATCHED SEVEN THOUSAND GOOD FAIRIES TO STAND AROUND SEAN'S CRADLE. WE REJOICE MADLY FOR YOU THREE—LOVE LOU AND KATE.

Wearing a baptismal robe specially designed for him by Givenchy, the infant was christened Sean Hepburn Ferrer, in the same chapel and by the same clergyman who had presided at the wedding in 1954. "On a brilliant Sunday, after a rainstorm, our strong, well-made son was born," Audrey said years later. "Like all new mothers, I couldn't believe, at first, that he was really for me and that I could keep him . . . Even when I was little, what I wanted most was to have a child . . . And I wanted lots of babies. That's been a theme in my life . . . I'm sure it's wonderful when you're 18—but if you wait years, the joy is impossible to describe . . . My miscarriages were more painful to me than anything, ever—including my parents' divorce and the disappearance of my father. From the time I had Sean, I hung onto my marriage because of him, and more and more, I began to resent the time I spent away from him on location. That was always the real me. The movies were fairy tales."

Strongly recommended by Mel, the next fairy tale required Audrey to be on location in New York and then in Paramount's Hollywood studios from October to the end of the year. They traveled together, for he had all sorts of movie projects on the boil, and both baby and nanny went along.

But Audrey was, once again, of divided mind. She did not want to work, but she wanted to work; tempted to play it safe, she simultaneously wanted always to attempt something new. She wanted to be a full-time mother, but she knew that, at thirty-one, good roles would not always be offered, and so she was responsive to Mel's persuasion to reach for a new gold ring. In addition, she needed the money—not to indulge her whims, but for her son's future.

Audrey's work in New York and Los Angeles that autumn was for what became her signature role—Holly Golightly, in *Breakfast at Tiffany's*, the picture that immediately erased the critical and popular disappointment over *Green Mansions* and *The Unforgiven*. Thanks to the wardrobe designed by her friend Givenchy, the picture made her a fashion icon forevermore: in *Breakfast*, her status as the reigning queen of chic surpassed even the position she attained through what, by contrast, seemed the black-and-white constraints of *Sabrina*. Audrey was henceforth considered a key arbiter, standard and model of elegance and vogue. That this should have been a byproduct of *Breakfast at Tiffany's* is, in a way, the height of improbability, for in it she portrayed a prostitute—or tried to. Audrey's Holly may on occasion be a garrulous, silly girl, but she could not make audiences believe that she sold herself for cash. Publicity photos showed her overdraped with ropes of faux jewelry, and soon Tiffany's saw a good opportunity and asked her to accept a handsome contract to advertise for the store. "My image will never be Miss Diamonds," she said, rejecting the offer.

Based on a hundred-page novella by Truman Capote, the film altered the book a great deal. The finished product concerns Holly Golightly, once a teenage Texas bride named Lulamae Barnes, a girl of poor and murky background who comes to New York, and longing to marry (eventually) the richest man in the world, she plies the world's oldest profession. Her only constant companion is a nameless cat she picks up. Sometimes Holly returns to her apartment from a liaison just as people are beginning their workday, and then she munches breakfast right on the street in early daylight, gazing avariciously at the jewelry in Tiffany's showcase windows, as in the first scene.

Holly meets a struggling young writer named Paul (played by George Peppard), whose struggles are alleviated by the subsidies he receives from a wealthy, predatory older, unnamed woman (Patricia Neal). The writer falls for Holly, who is interested only in jewelry and cash but not love and stability—until the last moments of the picture. Capote's story was both acerbically witty and affectingly simple, cool in its assessment of lost souls yet warm in the author's sympathetic character delineation. The movie exchanged the edge and the subtlety for a celebration of New York and a comic infatuation for Audrey Hepburn.

"I read the book and liked it very much," she said. "But I was terribly afraid I was not right for the part. I thought I lacked the right sense of comedy. This part called for an extroverted character. I am an introvert. But everyone pressed me to do it. So I did. I suffered through it all. I lost weight. Very often while I was doing the part, I was convinced I was not doing the best job."

It was precisely this disconnection that made her uneasy. "Despite her obvious insecurities, there was a strong core to Audrey," recalled director Blake Edwards. Those insecurities were evident almost from the first day of work. Edwards had to reassure her— as he did when he and composer Henry Mancini informed her that a song was being especially composed for her to sing while accompanying herself on a guitar. The prospect of this intimidated Audrey, for her voice had darkened and become thinner since *Funny Face;* accordingly, she studied with a vocal coach and a guitar teacher for weeks, delaying the recording of "Moon River" until she felt less uncomfortable.

Mancini encouraged her: the melody was limited to a one-octave range, he said, and that could be transposed down if necessary. "I knew what to write by reading the script," Mancini recalled. "And Audrey's big eyes gave me the push to get a little more sentimental than I usually am. Those eyes of hers could carry it, I knew that. 'Moon River' [with lyrics by Johnny Mercer] was written for her. No one else ever understood it so completely."

When the film was previewed for the Paramount brass the following spring, Mel and Audrey were present. "One thing's for sure," said Martin Rackin, head of Paramount production, at the conclusion of the screening. "That fucking song's gotta go!" According to Mancini, Audrey sprang from her chair, and Mel had to restrain her. "Over my dead body!" she cried, her voice trembling. The song, of course, stayed in the picture.

From the day *Breakfast at Tiffany's* was released, the image of Audrey Hepburn, sitting at her open window, strumming her guitar and singing "Moon River" in her tentative, wistful mezzo, is perhaps the single most enduring emblem of the enchantment she brought to a legion of moviegoers, then and later. Without pretense or pose, she seemed through the music to suggest a fusion of reminiscence, of loss and of longing that even Holly cannot quite fathom. Indeed, we are not listening to Holly singing: this is Audrey, and it is her song, delivered directly from her own introspective personality. According to everything that precedes and follows it, Holly could not be still for the length of any melody. And absent "Moon River," in fact, Audrey rarely seems at home in this expensive, fabricated escapade. Her rendition of the song, which Mancini always considered the best among more than five hundred renditions, was certainly a factor when she was nominated by the Academy as best actress—for a fourth time. (Sophia Loren won, for *Two Women*.)

Although the song was not excised, battles still raged, for Paramount wanted to cut a major portion of Mancini's atmospheric (but often excessive) background music. In this Audrey demon-strated what Edwards called her "strong core," sending pleading and even angry memoranda in support of Mancini, to whom she then wrote:

A movie without music is like an aeroplane without fuel. However beautifully the job is done, we are still on the ground and in a world of reality. Your music has lifted us all up and sent us soaring. Everything we cannot say with words or show with action you have expressed for us. You have done this with so much imagination, fun and beauty. You are the hippest of cats—and the most sensitive of composers! Thank you, dear Hank.
    Lots of love,
    Audrey

For the most part, relations during production were friendly—except for George Peppard and Blake Edwards, who disagreed openly. Audrey and Patricia Neal, however, became friends, and one evening Audrey invited her home for dinner. "I remember our supper was on a work night," according to Neal. "Mel was very strict with her during production, so the evening was one drink, a light meal, and good night. I don't think the sun had set by the time I got home."

IN THE TRANSFER from page to screen, there were major alter-ations to Holly's character, to the tone of the story, and to its melancholy finale. "The book was really rather bitter," said Ca-pote, "and Holly Golightly was *real*—a tough character, not an Audrey Hepburn type at all. Marilyn Monroe was my first choice to play her. I thought she would be perfect for the part. Holly had to have something touching about her—unfinished. Marilyn had that. But Paramount double-crossed me and gave the part to Audrey Hepburn." Capote also regretted that Hollywood turned his seriocomic tale of a lonely, restless Manhattan call girl into "a mawkish valentine to New York City."

In addition, the movie changed the book's dispassionate narrator into the young writer played by Peppard, who is subsidized by a wealthy woman he subsequently leaves when he falls for Holly. At the end of the book, Holly is abandoned by her Brazilian fiancé but nevertheless flies off to South America and continues onward from there (as we learn summarily from the narrator at the end), in a constant cycle of seeking and losing and traveling. In the film, however, she is abandoned by her Brazilian fiancé but then accepts the love of the writer. The final raining scene on the page is part of the story's rueful melancholy; the drizzly conclusion on the screen shows the lovers kissing passionately, lushly attended by Mancini's romantic music.

The riot of colors used for *Breakfast at Tiffany's,* the high style of Audrey's outfits and coiffures, the surprising character she agreed to portray, the impossible romance of the story in light of its bold content: these elements were irresistible to audiences in 1961. Entertainingly packaged, they attracted a new generation of moviegoers at a time when America was developing new fancies for everything from food and drink to music and movies, from social aspirations to economic expectations. And the foundations were only just beginning to shake.

Director Blake Edwards and screenwriter George Axelrod knew precisely how to ensure the movie's success and yet remain within the boundaries of convention. They counterpoised sophomoric vulgarity with down-home sweetness—the former in recurring scenes with a grotesque Japanese neighbor, ludicrously overplayed by Mickey Rooney; and the latter in the romantic final sequence, which gave Audrey her best moment in the film.

PAUL: Holly, I'm in love with you!

HOLLY: So what?

PAUL: So what? So plenty! I love you—you belong to me!

HOLLY: No, people don't belong to people.

PAUL: Of course they do!

HOLLY: I'm not going to let anyone put me in a cage!

PAUL: I don't want to put you in a cage—I want to love you!

HOLLY: It's the same thing.

PAUL: No, it's not! Holly—

HOLLY (crying aloud): I'm not Holly! I'm not Lulamae, either—I don't know *who* I am! I'm like Cat here—we're a couple of no-name slobs. We don't belong to anyone and no one belongs to us—we don't even belong to each other!

There was a moving arc of authentic sentiment when Audrey sang "Moon River," and, in the finale, there is a heartbreaking plangency to her outburst. Never mind that her Holly is not the book's: Audrey rendered this confused girl—who is not yet a woman—as a credible, needy soul. Paul finds her irresistible and so, just in time, does the audience.

DESPITE CHARACTERS fundamentally driven by venality and sexual commercialism, the film neatly exemplifies a venerable Hollywood double standard. Wild parties, drunkenness, exotic dancers, sexual freewheeling and an egregious kind of selfish autonomy are presented as merely the high jinks of New York sophisticates—but at the end, orthodox propriety is (however implausibly) affirmed by the two lovers. They remain fixed in our memories, drenched by rain as if it were a sign of heavenly benediction. A dependable movie cliché, the last scene affected millions of moviegoers in 1961; years later, is still seems, for the most part, astonishingly foolproof.

Audrey, age ten (1939).
Photo by Lady Manon van Suchtelen. Courtesy of Joke Quarles van Ufford.

Dance recital,
Holland (1943).

With her mother
(1945).

Rehearsing in London, with Babs Johnson (1948). *British Film Institute*

In *Sauce Piquante*, London (1950).

Advertising model (1951).
British Film Institute

As Eve Lester, in *Young Wives' Tale*, with Helen Cherry, Nigel Patrick and
Derek Farr (1950). *British Film Institute*

As Nora
Brentano, in
Secret People
(1951). *British
Film Institute*

With James Hanson (1952).
British Film Institute

Relaxing with Gregory
Peck, during *Roman
Holiday* (1952). *Courtesy of
the Academy of Motion Picture
Arts and Sciences*

With William Holden, during *Sabrina. Courtesy of the Academy of Motion Picture Arts and Sciences*

Publicity photo with William Holden. *Courtesy of the Academy of Motion Picture Arts and Sciences*

With Billy Wilder and William Wyler (1953). *Courtesy of the Academy of Motion Picture Arts and Sciences*

With Mel Ferrer, in
War and Peace.
Courtesy of the Academy
of Motion Picture Arts
and Sciences

Rehearsing the ballroom
sequence for *War and
Peace. Courtesy of the
Academy of Motion Picture
Arts and Sciences*

With Fred Astaire,
as Mel Ferrer
reviews Audrey's
publicity photos for
Funny Face (1956).
*Courtesy of the
Academy of Motion
Picture Arts and
Sciences*

As Jo Stockton,
in *Funny Face*.
*Courtesy of the Academy
of Motion Picture Arts
and Sciences*

With Mel Ferrer (1956).
*Courtesy of the Academy of
Motion Picture Arts and Sciences*

With Hubert de Givenchy (1957).
*Courtesy of the Academy of Motion
Picture Arts and Sciences*

Publicity photo (1957).
*Courtesy of the Academy of Motion
Picture Arts and Sciences*

With Henry Blanke (producer), Kathryn Hulme, Robert Anderson and Fred Zinnemann, discussing *The Nun's Story* (1957). *Courtesy of Robert Anderson*

As Gabrielle van der Mal/Sister Luke, in *The Nun's Story* (1958). *Courtesy of the Academy of Motion Picture Arts and Sciences*

While filming interiors in Rome (1958). *Courtesy of the Academy of Motion Picture Arts and Sciences*

With Mel Ferrer, preparing *Green Mansions* (1958). *Courtesy of the Academy of Motion Picture Arts and Sciences*

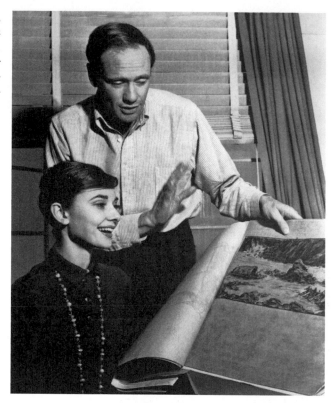

Singing "Moon River," in *Breakfast at Tiffany's* (1960). *Courtesy of the Academy of Motion Picture Arts and Sciences*

With George Cukor (director), Mel Ferrer, producer Jack L. Warner, costar Rex Harrison, Rachel Roberts (Mrs. Harrison) and costume designer Cecil Beaton, at the start of *My Fair Lady* (1963). *Courtesy of the Academy of Motion Picture Arts and Sciences*

Moments before a scene in *My Fair Lady. Courtesy of the Academy of Motion Picture Arts and Sciences*

As Joanna Wallace,
in *Two for the Road*
(1966).

With Albert Finney,
during *Two for the Road*.

With Andrea Dotti
in Rome (1972).

With William Wyler, recipient
of the American Film Institute
Life Achievement Award, and
actress Merle Oberon (1976).
*Courtesy of the Academy of
Motion Picture Arts and Sciences*

With Robert Wolders and U.S. Committee for UNICEF president Lawrence Bruce, Jr., transporting grain to Tigre, Ethiopia (1988). *©UNICEF/HQ88-0090/John Isaac*

With Christa Roth, at a UNICEF fund-raiser (1989). *Courtesy of Christa Roth*

With poor and ailing children in Vietnam (1990). *©UNICEF/ HQ90-0081/Peter Charlesworth*

With children in Bangladesh (1989). ©*UNICEF/HQ89-0476/John Isaac*

With refugee children at a displaced persons camp in Baidoa, Somalia (1992).
©*UNICEF/HQ92-1184/Betty Press*

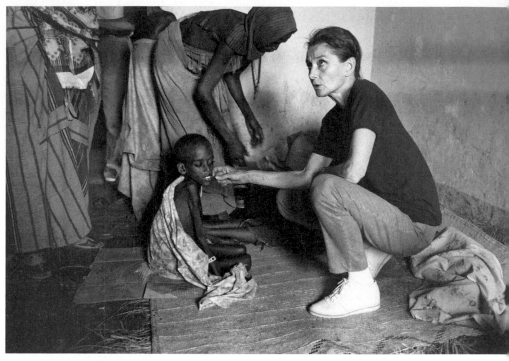

With a malnourished child at a
feeding center in Somalia (1992).
©UNICEF/HQ92-1193/Betty Press

With another starving child,
who died in her arms a few
moments later. ©UNICEF/
HQ92-1199/Betty Press

Chapter Twelve

1961–1962

URING THE CHRISTMAS holidays at Villa Bethania, Audrey
received her gratifying reviews for *Breakfast at Tiffany's,*
which had its premiere the previous October, and her
fourth Oscar nomination was announced later that winter. Mel,
meanwhile, still hoped—in vain, as it turned out—that one of his
writing and directorial projects would come to fruition. "It was
not easy for Mel," said Hubert de Givenchy, discreetly terse.

"Of course it's a problem when the wife outshines the husband
as Audrey does me," Mel admitted, as if he were elaborating on
Givenchy's statement. "I'm pretty sensitive when producers call
me up and say they want to discuss a film with me, when in reality
they're angling for Audrey and using me as bait." As for *Green
Mansions,* he was a master of understatement: "It was not a great
success."

Meanwhile, close friends of the Ferrers, and visitors to Bürgenstock, knew what was happening that year. As Audrey continued
to be in demand, Mel had only the second-rate occupations of
acting in minor European horror films and grade-B costume
dramas—"work acting," he called it in a letter to Kathryn Hulme
and Marie Louise Habets on March 7, 1961. But there were, it

seems, social diversions: he was photographed, merry and mannerly as always, squiring female co-stars with whom he briefly worked on one picture or another. "Pretense that all was well [between Mel and Audrey] became patently absurd," wrote Joseph Barry, a journalist who knew them both.

The tensions were certainly at least partly responsible for Audrey's almost constant anxiety. "Audrey has been the cook here for us all," Mel added in his letter of March 7, "so I am afraid she has not put on any of those kilos that Sean has packed on so rapidly—he is over ten kilos and has six teeth." On March 8, mother, father, baby and nanny went to Rome, where Mel was completing his scenes in a picture and where, as he wrote to friends, he hoped Audrey would indulge in the pasta she so loved and thus regain a few pounds. She ate it, but no weight was added.

Her extreme thinness was evident even beneath the neck-to-knee costumes prepared for her next picture. In that, she was to wear a simple shirtwaist dress, a suit and a wool sheath—none of them amplifying or flattering her reed-thin figure. These outfits, completely deglamorizing her as had Sister Luke's habit, were designed for her first black-and-white movie in five years: a film of Lillian Hellman's first play, *The Children's Hour*.

In agreeing to assume the role of Karen Wright, Audrey was to portray yet another controversial figure, as she had in *The Unforgiven* and *Breakfast at Tiffany's*. Shirley MacLaine, five years Audrey's junior, was to be her co-star, in the part of Martha Dobie.

Screenwriter John Michael Hayes was remarkably faithful to the play. Karen and Martha, friends since college, administer a small boarding school for girls. One of their young charges, a spoiled, willful and spiteful child, concocts a rumor that Karen and Martha are lovers. Horrified, parents and relatives at once withdraw their children from the school, despite the fierce and truthful denial of this gossip by the two women. Even Karen's fiancé is tainted by the general suspicion. Finally, Martha believes that perhaps the rumor has some foundation: in an emotional scene, she admits to Karen that she has indeed had romantic but unexpressed feelings for her friend. Fearing the loss of friendship and deprived of her career, Martha takes her own life.

The strength of both play and film was its interweaving of three narrative planes. First, there is the action of a malicious child who fabricates a destructive rumor. Second, there is the devastating influence of gullible and intolerant adults, quick to believe a mendacious child and to ostracize women they wrongly believe to be lovers. Third, there is the ironic truth that the scandal forces Martha to admit to herself that she has had a sentimental attachment to Karen.

Two years after the successful Broadway premiere in 1934, William Wyler had filmed a screen version of it, but the newly enforced Motion Picture Production Code imposed such constraints that *These Three,* as it was titled, became the rather tame story of a heterosexual love triangle—not a powerful dissection of the spite, prejudice, intolerance and rumor that can ruin lives. Twenty-five years later, Wyler now wanted to revisit the play, and he quickly obtained Audrey's consent to participate: after all, he had guided her to an Oscar for *Roman Holiday,* and she trusted him and his creative judgment.

And so, by late March, the Ferrers were back in Hollywood, again staying at the home of Deborah Kerr on Kemridge Road, in the mountains above Beverly Hills. (Kerr was making several films back to back in England and was pleased to have her friends in residence.) John Michael Hayes, whose many worthy credits included four superb scripts for Alfred Hitchcock, gave Wyler the finished screenplay for *The Children's Hour* on May 15, and a week later, rehearsals began at the Goldwyn Studios in Hollywood.

After a mutually cautious introduction, the two leading ladies established an easy rapport, and neither of them was at all squeamish about her role. "I conceived Martha's character," recalled

Shirley MacLaine, "to lovingly build her adoration and emotional involvement with the character of Karen so that the audience would realize early on what was going on. In fact, Martha was unaware of her feelings . . . until the little girl exaggerated Martha's behavior into a lie. Within that lie was the ounce of truth."

But when Wyler saw the first cut of the picture, he feared the film would not receive a seal of approval from the Motion Picture Production Code, which expressly forbade any story about (or that even mentioned) homosexuality; the lack of the Code's seal would mean that the movie could not be screened in almost every American theater. "Willy got cold feet about the lesbian subject," MacLaine continued. "He cut out all the scenes that portrayed Martha falling in love with Karen." Scenes in which Martha lovingly cared for Karen's clothes, brushed her hair, baked cookies for her—all these were excised. "In eliminating those scenes, Willy gutted the intention of the film"—and if not the intention, surely the helpful signs to the audience of Martha's growing attachment that would have made the final declaration of love more credible, not to say more sympathetic. If audiences had been shown the poignancy of the situation—even in 1961—they might not have been so alienated from the tragedy.

But apart from the commercial expediency that forced Wyler's editorial hand, there may well have been another reason for the excisions he mandated. After all, Wyler understood the ambiguities of Hellman's play and wanted to preserve them in his film. Martha may of course be regarded as a repressed lesbian, forced to confront her true feelings for Karen only when there is the ill-founded rumor of romance. But the dialogue suggests that Martha thinks the accusation *may be true* only when it is made:

MARTHA: There's always been something wrong.
KAREN: Stop the crazy talk.

MARTHA: I'm guilty.

KAREN: You're guilty of nothing!

MARTHA: I've been telling myself that since the night we heard the child say it—I've been praying I could convince myself of it. I can't, I can't any longer. It's there. I don't know how, I don't know why. But I did love you. I do love you. I resented your marriage—maybe because I wanted you.

KAREN: It's a lie. You're telling yourself a lie. We never thought of each other that way.

MARTHA: No, of course you didn't. But who says I didn't? I never felt that way about anybody but you. I've never loved a man. I never knew why before. Maybe it's that.

KAREN: You are tired and sick.

MARTHA: It's funny—it's all mixed up. There's something in you, and you don't know anything about it because you don't know it's there. I couldn't call it by name before, but I know now. It's there. It's been there ever since I first knew you. I don't know. It all seems to come back to me. I've ruined your life and I've ruined my own. Oh, I feel so damn sick and dirty I can't stand it anymore!

KAREN: All this isn't true. You've never said it—we'll forget it by tomorrow.

Martha moves from "maybe" to certainty—but it is "all mixed up." Seen from this perspective, Martha is like an innocent and wrongly convicted prisoner who feels guilty for something she now feels she is somehow responsible for. The guilt then enables her to see everything in her past as supportive of her interpretation of the present. One of the merits of Wyler's *The Children's Hour* (released in Great Britain as *The Loudest Whisper*) is that it mostly maintains these ambiguities. On the one hand, the ironic tragedy of the situation is that a lie exposes a grain of truth; on the other hand, the lie is so monstrous that it unbalances a lonely woman and forces her, quite wrongly, to believe that her "unnatural" self deserves death. However one takes the characters, the play (as critic and historian Bernard Dick has rightly said) "is about the effects of a lie that activates suppressed feelings that suddenly surface when one is faced with an accusation of something that is not true, but could be."

Matching Shirley MacLaine beat for beat, Audrey gave her most centered and delicately shaded performance since *The Nun's Story*. Disallowed designer clothes, she relied only on the subtlest facial expression of inner confusion and on effective variations in vocal tone; the result was a character of moving and remarkable density. Her scenes with recalcitrant pupils, for example, have no touch of the movie schoolmarm; her love scenes with her fiancé (James Garner) have an exquisite physical tenderness hitherto unseen in any of her films; her icy indictment of bigotry is tinged with the right amount of pain; and her deep love for her friend is everywhere evident. This last achievement makes almost unbearable her discovery of Martha's body. Audrey's tears, her shutting of the eyes against the horror of what she has seen, the modulation of her voice from shrieking cries to muted sobs—this is a moment that could be beneficially studied by all students of film acting. Wyler considered her achievement nothing less than brilliant.

Decades later, Audrey's acting and the film are, unjustifiably, held in low esteem. The reason for the critical disfavor may be a triumph of what has been called political correctness. For one thing, audiences for the most part accept neither the apparent passivity of the young women nor Martha's suicide. Homosexuals certainly ought not to be driven to suicide because of ignorant social censure, so (the reasoning runs) they ought not to be *shown* committing suicide. That objection misses the point: Martha has lost her career and is afraid to lose her friend, who is about to marry. The drama shows what occasionally pushes people beyond their endurance. In the final analysis, *The Children's Hour* reveals not what all of life is like, but what some of life is like, and what all life is in constant danger of becoming—in this case, a sacrifice to cruelty, bigotry, deceit and self-hatred. Hellman had drawn her title from Henry Wadsworth Longfellow, whose 1860 poem of the same name describes a devoted father's late afternoons with his three young daughters:

> *Between the dark and the daylight,*
> *When the night is beginning to lower,*
> *Comes a pause in the day's occupations,*
> *That is known as the Children's Hour.*

The dramatic situation, however, had been inspired by something far darker: an incident in Scotland, in 1810, in which a schoolgirl accused her teachers of lesbianism. The child's grandmother spread the libel and ruined the school.*

The film was completed in mid-August, and on Saturday, September 2, the Ferrers left for a month in Villa Bethania. Three days before their departure, Audrey wrote to Marie Louise—"just to tell you and Kate [Hulme] how much we love you both."

AUDREY, SEAN AND the nanny spent the six weeks in Rome because Mel was there completing scenes in *I lancieri neri* (*The Black Lancers*), and they then accompanied him to Paris for his work in *The Longest Day.* From this time, Audrey traveled economy class by air and purchased only a Volvo or Audi, not a large, expensive car—which someone would have had to drive, for she was fearful after the accident in Beverly Hills.

---

* The case was reported in William Roughhead's *Bad Companions* (1830).

There was additional companionship: Audrey's beloved York-shire terrier, named Famous, had been killed after darting into Los Angeles traffic; Mel replaced the loss with a puppy of the same breed, Assam—a name based on the Sanskrit word for "irregular," and so named by its breeder because of slightly irregular eyes and ears. Until the following spring, the family's only time in Bür-genstock was a week at Christmas.

During that holiday, Audrey's publicist, Henry Rogers, visited Villa Bethania. After lunch, Mel began to discuss his wife's future roles—what he advised, what he urged her to consider and, inci-dentally, what did Henry think? Audrey, meanwhile, continued to feed Sean. "She was always reluctant to get into discussions of this sort and was angry with Mel and me," Rogers recalled.

Then Mel changed the subject. He had always resented that Audrey received no compensation for allowing Givenchy to use her name and likeness to promote L'Interdit, the perfume created in her honor: "For Christ's sake, Henry, she doesn't even get a dis-count on the clothes he designs for her. As for the perfume, wouldn't you think he would send her gallons of it—as a gift? She buys it herself—retail!"

Rogers had just come from a meeting in Paris with Givenchy about this very matter: unknown to Audrey, Mel had asked him to work out some kind of honorarium—which Givenchy had read-ily agreed to do.

"Neither of you seems to understand," Audrey interjected. "I don't want anything from Hubert. I don't need his money—he's my friend. If I've helped him build his perfume business, then that's exactly what one friend should do for another. If someone else offered me a million dollars to endorse a perfume, I wouldn't do it—but Hubert is my friend. I don't want anything. Yes, I even want to walk into a drugstore and buy the perfume at the retail price."

At that moment, another guest arrived, on schedule—Robert Favre Le Bret, general administrator of the Cannes Film Festival, who was trying to convince Audrey to attend the opening ceremonies the following spring. Rogers was opposed to the idea: she had no film coming to the festival, and she neither desired nor needed the publicity. Rogers added that Audrey's presence would be criticized as a bid for publicity, and that she would outshine the younger actresses who would be there to promote their films and careers.

Mel persisted, pushing Rogers to withdraw into another room and negotiate a deal for Audrey's visit to the festival. "Le Bret is very important, Henry," said Mel, "and he wants her very badly. Maybe someday we'll need a favor from him." Audrey, indifferent to the entire matter, took Sean up to bed.

"I need a reason for her to attend," Rogers told Favre Le Bret, "otherwise in all good conscience I cannot recommend to Audrey that she should attend your opening." After some time, the two men agreed that she could indeed attend if she were to receive a special tribute as one who had made outstanding contributions to the international cinema—this would be the beginning of a tradition, said Rogers.

Late that afternoon, Rogers departed for London. In his hotel room early next morning, he took a call from Audrey, who was sobbing: she had been up all night, she had not slept, she was miserable. "You know how much I care about you," she said, her voice choked with weeping, "and how much I value your friendship. I'm crying because I have decided that I don't want you to represent me anymore. I won't hire anyone else. I just can't stand any more of this. I just don't like what is happening to me, and my life and my friends."

Rogers had no idea what she meant.

"First you embarrassed me with Hubert. You and Mel made

such a thing about his taking advantage of me, and I told you—I don't care. He's my friend. And last night, after you left, it was terrible. I was embarrassed. I was ashamed. I started to cry and ran out of the room. Favre Le Bret told me you had tried to blackmail him, that you told him the only way I would go to the Cannes Film Festival would be if he gave me some kind of phony, trumped-up award. Henry, I don't want you to work for me anymore." There was a pause, but Rogers heard her weeping still—and then she said, "Henry, will you still be my friend?"

"Of course we will be friends," Rogers said gently, and he apologized profusely for causing her embarrassment when all he wished to do was to be a good publicist. "But before we finish this conversation, Audrey, you must understand one thing. You have known me for *many years*. You know how I work. You know very well that I never tried to blackmail Favre Le Bret. If he is stupid enough to interpret my proposal, which was good for him and good for you, in that way, then I never want anything to do with him again—and you shouldn't, either." Audrey did not attend the Cannes Film Festival.

"It was frustrating to do what I had felt was right for my client and then have it boomerang against me," Rogers reflected years later. Had he not met with Givenchy in Paris at Mel's behest, had he known beforehand that Audrey did not want to be compensated for her perfume endorsement, "and if I had merely told Le Bret, 'No, Audrey won't attend your opening night ceremonies,' [then] I would have still retained her as a client." He did not, however, lose her friendship.

BECAUSE AUDREY HAD accepted MGM's additional offer of *The Unforgiven* after *Green Mansions*, and because she had also gone to an independent company for *The Children's Hour*, she owed

Paramount another picture. The head of production, Martin Rackin (who had disliked "Moon River"), learned from his contracts department that William Holden had an identical obligation to the studio. A deal was made to put the two stars together in a movie Rackin and company believed could not miss: an American remake of a successful French romantic comedy, Julien Duvivier's *La fête à Henriette* (*Holiday for Henrietta*). George Axelrod, who had created the script for *Breakfast at Tiffany's*, was the writer, and Richard Quine, with some recent light comedies to his credits, was assigned to direct the satire, called *Paris—When It Sizzles*.

Audrey apparently agreed to the picture for three reasons: it would be made in Paris; Givenchy was to design her wardrobe; and Kurt Frings had negotiated her salary at $12,500 a week and an additional $5,000 a week for expenses—she was also given a car and driver for the entire time in Paris.

Paris—When It Sizzles began filming interior studio sequences and exterior location scenes in July 1962, after a month of preproduction chores. The story concerns an American writer in Paris (Holden) who has been paid a handsome sum to write a screenplay, but he has squandered his time in high living and—two days short of the deadline—he has not come up with a single page of script. In desperation, he engages a typist (Audrey), and together they invent possible scenarios. From this premise, Axelrod developed sequences in which the couple fantasize and even sometimes live their ideas, until the line between reality and imagination blurs. A predictably romantic ending ensues, but even that is mocked at the fade-out.

A few days into production, Audrey learned that there was a burglary at Villa Bethania: her Oscar for *Roman Holiday* had been stolen, along with a Picasso painting and some jewelry. Only the statuette was recovered, in a nearby forest. "The housebreakers must have decided that there just was not any place in the Swiss black market for it," Audrey wrote to columnist Hedda Hopper on July 27.

Except for the occasional chance meeting in Los Angeles, there had been no contact between Audrey and Bill Holden over the nine years since *Sabrina*. She did not want to resume a romance for which she had no nostalgia, but she thought they might at least have an enjoyable time working together. In this, she miscalculated by a wide margin.

The film was far more enjoyable for some audiences than it was for those in the production, which was plagued by Holden's advanced alcoholism. "I remember the day I arrived at Orly Airport for *Paris—When It Sizzles*," he recalled. "I could hear my footsteps echoing against the walls of the transit corridor, just like a condemned man walking the last mile. I realized that I had to face Audrey and I had to deal with my drinking. And I didn't think I could handle either situation."

He was far more apprehensive over the prospect of working with Audrey, and his escape was to drink more heavily. "Bill had always drunk during films," according to his biographer, "but never as he did on *Paris—When It Sizzles*. He started drinking early and continued through the day." Quine had once before directed Holden, and he was astonished. "Bill was like a punch-drunk fighter, walking on his heels, listing slightly, talking punchy. He didn't know he was drunk." More than once the actor arrived at the studio completely unable to work, and Quine had to send everyone home.

Throughout the filming, Audrey was concerned and considerate, but sometimes Bill took her kindness for something more. When he was disappointed, he drank more heavily, which made Audrey more solicitous, which in turn made Bill more unrealistic in his expectations, which made Audrey more sympathetic—and so it went, a roundel of missed cues that became more awkward and poignant each day over the four months of filming. None of this is revealed in the performances.

The situation quickly reached critical mass, and Quine convinced Holden to enter an alcoholic clinic. The production was at a standstill, losing cash daily, until Axelrod (in his capacity as co-producer) rang his friend Tony Curtis and asked him to rush to Paris and assume a guest role. Thus the company was kept busy while Curtis's scenes were hurriedly written and filmed; as it happens, they provide some of the movie's most amusing moments, for Curtis did a neat satire on a self-important, vainglorious and frivolous young actor. (Marlene Dietrich and Mel Ferrer also had roles in the picture: they are seen but not heard, and only for a few seconds.) After a week, Holden returned from treatment temporarily sober and refreshed.

By that time, however, Audrey had had time to review the scenes filmed thus far, and she did not like what she saw. In five of her films—*Roman Holiday, The Nun's Story, The Unforgiven, Breakfast at Tiffany's* and *The Children's Hour*—she had been photographed by the great Austrian cinematographer Franz Planer, who brought his genius to more than 150 motion pictures. Audrey had developed an almost fraternal rapport with "Frank" Planer, on whom she relied not merely for flattering lighting but also for a look that was right for each scene. But that autumn, Planer was ill with cancer (and died very soon after). With the influence that was hers by the time of *Paris—When It Sizzles,* Audrey asked that Claude Renoir, the cameraman on the picture, be replaced. Her wish was a command, and over the weekend, the man she recommended arrived—Charles Lang, who had photographed Audrey so rapturously in *Sabrina.*

Also by this time, Noël Coward had been cast in the role of the Hollywood producer who is Holden's boss; Coward worked on the picture for three days. "Audrey, unquestionably the nicest and most talented girl in the business, deluged me with praise and roses," Coward noted in his diary. "Bill Holden, *off* the bottle [as he was that week] and looking fifteen years younger, absolutely charming to work with . . . Audrey and Bill are enchanting. So is Tony Curtis." But Holden was very soon back *on* the bottle, and again he was shuffled off for a week while the production worked around him, shooting Audrey's close-ups.

During that week, the press reported that she had been elected to the Fashion Hall of Fame for the third consecutive year, and she agreed to a long interview. Her private wardrobe was very simple, she said—long straight shifts or plain pants with a jersey top. Her favorite earrings were simply small pearls, and her makeup took only a minute to apply. "But my coloring lacks definition. I therefore prefer to wear black, white or muted colors such as beige or soft pinks or greens. These colors tend to make my eyes and hair seem darker, whereas bright colors overpower me and wash me out." She was quite tall and angular, she added, "therefore I don't wear padded or squared shoulders, and I often cheat on my armholes and collars to give an illusion of narrow rather than wide shoulders. I wear low-heeled shoes to give the impression that I'm smaller than I am."

AUDREY WAS THIRTY-THREE that year, and before production began, she at last completed a long, gradual process of orthodontic work that had begun in 1956. The crooked and pointed bicuspids she so hated had been replaced, along with several others that she thought unflattering; in addition, her increasingly uncomfortable overbite had been corrected, and several teeth had been capped. There had not been much call for her to smile broadly in a picture since *Funny Face;* now, at last, she was ready to do so as much as possible, for directors, photographers and the public loved her ingenuous and broad grin, which is much in evidence in *Paris—When It Sizzles*.

The finished film had a strange and unfortunate history. When it was screened at Paramount, few executives understood Axelrod's satire on scriptwriting under pressure—or perhaps they comprehended it but did not much like it. Even fewer among them noted the dozens of references to Audrey's earlier movies and to classics like *Casablanca* and *High Noon*.

Although the last third of the movie lost its initial pace and dynamic verve, it is very much a Hollywood insider's joke book, and for those aware of the difficulty of screenwriting, it should have been seen at once for what it was: a spoof of moguls and money-grabbing. *Paris—When It Sizzles* was also a comic treatment of the damply romantic imagination, with an acerbic take on the foolishness of living as if one were in a movie. It was, in other words, far better and more intelligent than Paramount recognized. Modern audiences often think comedy should be unsubtle—direct and without much style or substance, merely a matter of quick laughs. This picture offered more; it was also in many ways the prototype for much in the later work of Mel Brooks.

But Holden's troubles and the concomitant inconvenience caused to the director, the crew and the budget had poisoned the project so far as the studio was concerned. With publicists in the dark before the film's self-referential clowning, unconventional structure and clever repartee, the decision was made to withhold it from release until the spring of 1964. Hence, critics knew well in advance that even those responsible were fearful, and their notices were, perhaps inevitably, negative. Seen forty years later, the film is in some ways superior to *Breakfast at Tiffany's*. Whereas she often seemed detached and discomfited by the shenanigans of that picture, here Audrey balanced farce with satire: as a typist falling in love with her highly strung boss, she was both girlish and savvy, and her comic pratfalls were executed with unflinching gusto.

Despite the awkward conditions at work, she demonstrated the infallible sign of a natural comedienne: she seemed to take everything and nothing seriously.

IN EARLY OCTOBER 1962, Audrey completed her scenes for *Paris—When It Sizzles.* Ordinarily, she would have rushed home, but although she missed Sean, she remained in Paris when it cooled down and immediately began work on another picture. Audrey was now free of her obligations to Paramount, and Stanley Donen (her director on *Funny Face*) offered her the leading role in an intricate romantic thriller with multiple identity-shifts and, as it turned out, a good deal of violence. The original screenplay was by Peter Stone.

Charade, set in the French Alps and Paris, was a stylish, colorful, occasionally witty and utterly implausible story of Regina Lampert, who is planning to divorce her wealthy husband and then learns that he has been murdered and has left no money. She meets Peter Joshua, a man of many identities and a multiplicity of names; as it turns out, he is interested in the husband's fortune. Also on the trail of the booty is a trio of unsavory thugs. As it turns out, the fortune was stolen by Lampert from a treasure that belonged to all the men during World War II. A suspicious American intelligence officer is also on the case. Everyone believes that Regina knows the whereabouts of the fortune, but one by one the murderous hunters are killed off—until the surprising, comic-romantic finale unites Regina and the man first known as Peter Joshua.*

Audrey read the script during Holden's first week-long absence in July and signaled her interest—on two conditions: Cary

---

* Two of Donen's sons were named Peter and Joshua—hence the character in *Charade.*

Grant must be her co-star, and Charles Lang her lighting camera-man. Lang was available even in time for preproduction, but Grant declined, citing another commitment; in addition, he was more nervous than ever about their ages—he would turn fifty-nine during production, and Audrey was thirty-three. Eventually, when the script he had been awaiting turned out to be dreadful, Grant agreed to do *Charade*, but he demanded certain changes that would make the relationship with Audrey more comic. Working with Holden and Quine, however sticky, had persuaded her that, introvert or not, she had a fair sense of comedic timing opposite the right leading man. More to the point, Stone's polished dialogue for *Charade* seemed actor-proof.

Despite the age difference, Cary Grant made the romance with Audrey believable, as Humphrey Bogart, Henry Fonda, Fred Astaire and Gary Cooper could not. Grant had, after all, been entirely convincing opposite Eva Marie Saint in Hitchcock's *North by Northwest*, filmed when she was thirty-four and he fifty-four. But Grant, entering his sixtieth year, did not want to appear ridiculous opposite Audrey, so he insisted on some touch-ups to the dialogue that would indicate it was the eager woman who was pursuing him, not the reverse:

REGGIE: Is there a Mrs. Joshua?

PETER: Yes, but we're divorced.

REGGIE: That wasn't a proposal—I was just curious.

PETER: Is your husband with you?

REGGIE: Oh, Charles is hardly ever with me. First it was separate rooms—now we're trying it with cities. What do people call you—Pete?

PETER: Mr. Joshua . . . Well, I've enjoyed talking with you.

REGGIE: Now you're angry.

PETER: No, I'm not—I've got some packing to do. I'm also going back to Paris today.

REGGIE: Oh. Well, wasn't it Shakespeare who said, "When strangers do meet, they should erelong see one another again"?

PETER: Shakespeare never said that.

REGGIE: How do you know?

PETER: It's terrible—you just made it up.

REGGIE: Well, the idea's right, anyway. Are you going to call me?

PETER: Are you in the book?

REGGIE: Charles is.

PETER: Is there only one Charles Lampert?

REGGIE: Lord, I hope so.

Donen arranged a restaurant dinner to introduce the two co-stars to each other. Audrey and the director arrived first, and when Cary joined them, Audrey stood up and said she was terribly nervous. "Don't be nervous, for goodness's sake," Grant said. "I'm thrilled to know you. Here, sit down. Put your hands on the table, put your head down and take a few deep breaths."

Audrey did just that—and promptly knocked over a bottle of red wine, which stained Grant's cream-colored suit. Audrey was mortified, everyone turned to stare and (thus Donen's recollection) "Cary took off his coat and comfortably sat through the whole meal just like that."

"I felt terrible and kept apologizing," Audrey said, "but Cary was so dear about it. The next day he sent me a box of caviar with a little note telling me not to feel bad." Donen decided to use the incident in the picture, and so in one sequence, along the banks of the Seine, Audrey's character accidentally tosses a scoop of ice cream onto Grant's shirt—and gets an identically suave reaction.

As the two stars began to work together in mid-October (just days after she completed the Quine film), there was a kind of benign, unstated competition. Always protective of his image and aware of both the value of good publicity and the danger of bad,

Grant monitored Paris newspapers and magazines to confirm that both his name and some flattering photos he had approved were regularly seen. Similarly, Audrey supervised the pictures of herself that were released: she did not, for example, generally agree to the publication of snapshot images captured on the fly: from the great still photographers (Richard Avedon, Bob Willoughby, Bud Fraker and Dennis Stock, for example) she had learned the value of meticulous studio lighting, careful cosmetics and the most advantageous pose. (Walter Matthau, who had an important role in *Charade*, acknowledged that Audrey taught him more about the camera than any director.)

For advance publicity and promotion, every film production unit has photographers present to document the actors and crew at work and between shots—but the photos they take are thoroughly reviewed before distribution. Grant and Hepburn had good reasons for a certain vanity, but in those days before there were omnipresent "handlers" to guard and guide actors, this attention to detail was simply part of their professional alertness. And whatever tacit jealousy the *Charade* company sensed between the pair—a low-grade jockeying for primacy in the press—it was soon offset by mutual respect and the sheer enjoyment of their collaboration.

Audrey saw that Grant was, in her words, "sensitive, reserved and quiet," and he recognized the same qualities in her. "Working with him was a joy," she added. "He was expressive and yet reserved. He led a very quiet life. I do, too. I think a lot of it has to do with shyness and wanting to be with people you're comfortable with, instead of having to always break new ground. I think because he was a vulnerable man, he recognized my vulnerability. We had that in common. He had more wisdom than I to help me with it. He said something very important to me one day when I was probably twitching and nervous. We were sitting next to each other waiting for the next shot. And he laid his hand on my two hands and said, 'You've got to learn to like yourself a little more.' I've often thought about that."

Here was a woman idolized and loved by millions worldwide, and admired for her beauty, talent and demeanor. But that Audrey ought indeed to have "liked herself a little more" is not surprising. Perhaps the most distressing aspect of movie stardom—especially for women—is the fact that they are pitched into a kind of constant self-criticism, the result of knowing that one is always being assessed by studios, directors, agents, colleagues, the press and the public. Only the most arrogant actor is convinced that his appearance is perfect, his talent unassailable and his love of self enough to withstand criticism in the present and anxiety about the future. Because Audrey was not arrogant but perhaps inordinately vulnerable, Grant was both correct and gently encouraging.

Like many seriocomic thrillers, *Charade* is perhaps remembered as better than it actually was—thanks to the smooth performances by Hepburn and Grant. Considered unnecessarily violent by many critics at the time (it was released two weeks after the assassination of President Kennedy), it had all the ingredients of a standard thriller: complicated plot shifts and changes of identity, an almost amusing but awfully sinister band of hooligans, unheroic war heroes and a buried treasure that is, of course, out in plain sight. These were mixed together in a story of wide and deep improbability with more holes than a wheel of Jarlsberg cheese. But never mind (and audiences did not): there were Hepburn, Grant and Paris, and they all looked terrific.

EARLY DURING THE filming of *Charade,* Audrey received far better news than that of her reelection to the Fashion Hall of Fame and her inclusion on the international lists of the best-dressed women. Since she had seen it on the New York stage in 1956, she had hoped to assume the role of Eliza in a movie version of the musical *My Fair Lady.* This was not a vain ambition, for the part was in many ways ideal for her—despite the fact that, in 1962, she was thirty-three, too old by at least a decade: Julie Andrews, who created the part in New York and then in London, had been twenty-one at the time of the premiere; she was even then a singer of surpassing distinction.

The story, based on George Bernard Shaw's *Pygmalion,* was another variation of the Cinderella story. Set in London in 1912, it concerns the coldly academic Professor Henry Higgins, who takes in a poor, bedraggled Cockney flower girl, wagering that he can in short order correct her speech and manners and pass her off in high society as an elegant lady. In this he succeeds so brilliantly that she is considered to be a princess. Shaw had based his play and the film of it on the ancient tale of Pygmalion and Galatea—hence his title.

Writer Alan Jay Lerner and composer Frederick Loewe, in *My Fair Lady,* made Eliza Doolittle a deeply sympathetic character that, as written, places exceptional demands on a singing actress. The Cockney flower girl must be credibly coarse but likable; as an apprentice under Higgins's stern tutelage she must touch the audience's sympathies and yet maintain a comic sense; and as the final idealized creation of Higgins's fantasy (and the audience's) she must convey the slight awkwardness of the "guttersnipe" transformed into a lady of shimmering elegance. And all this has to be achieved while the actress delivers no fewer than seven songs.

Finally, on October 30, 1962, Kurt Frings concluded the protracted negotiations for Audrey to star; her leading man would be the original Higgins of Broadway, Rex Harrison. Jack Warner had paid $5.5 million for the stage rights, and the movie was to have a budget of $17 million, by far the most expensive Hollywood product to date. According to the terms of her contract, Audrey was to receive $142,857.15, on the first of every July from 1963 through

1969; when bonuses were included, she eventually received a total of $1.1 million (exceeding even Elizabeth Taylor's million-dollar contract for *Cleopatra*, then in production).

While Frings was in the last stages of talks with Warner, *My Fair Lady* had closed in New York, after six and a half years and 2,717 performances. Julie Andrews had played the role for three and a half years on Broadway and in the West End, and her admirers were legion. After *My Fair Lady*, Lerner and Loewe had created another Broadway musical for her—*Camelot*. In 1962, she turned twenty-seven, and it was widely assumed that she would inherit the role in the movie.

But studios depended on international distribution for payoff and profit, and that meant the casting of internationally recognized movie stars. Warner was nervous about engaging someone like Andrews, who was known in New York and London, but could not (he believed) be counted on to sell tickets in Munich or Madrid. The producer also felt he was taking enough of a risk with Rex Harrison, who had been offered the part only when Cary Grant rejected it.

And so Jack Warner heard all the arguments in favor of Julie Andrews, whom he could have obtained for a far lower fee than he had to pay Kurt Frings. And then Warner confidently made his decision.

Chapter Thirteen

1963 – 1965

WHEN JACK WARNER signed Audrey Hepburn for *My Fair Lady,* a few journalists wondered why he had been willing to cast two major players from the theatrical version— Rex Harrison and Stanley Holloway (the latter as Eliza's father)— and not Julie Andrews, the original leading lady. But history was on Warner's side: replacement of stage actors with more widely known movie stars had been the rule rather than the exception for decades, especially in musicals. At a press luncheon at the studio on June 4, 1963, Warner introduced his pricey cast along with director George Cukor and costume designer Cecil Beaton, who had been on the original Broadway team and had first met Audrey in London in July 1953. Warner also fielded questions about the forthcoming production and talked with high-toned meaninglessness about the state of "film art" in America, even while he disparaged "the so-called art films" coming from Europe. That day, everyone engaged to work on this historically expensive production was content. Warm, friendly Hollywood had never seemed warmer or friendlier.

The research for *My Fair Lady* and the design of its sets and costumes were formidable enterprises. As much effort was expended, for example, on the style and execution of Audrey's shoes as on her outfits. "I pray every day to be as good as the role," she wrote in a note to Cukor that March, adding her request that the shoes be carefully measured, "because I have suffered ever since my ballet days."

Exterior and interior scenes for the picture were to be filmed within the Warner soundstages in Burbank, and Cukor, Beaton and art director Gene Allen had already traveled to London that spring for preproduction, scrutinizing everything from the dimensions of terrace houses and mansions to period photos of professors' home libraries; from the wall coverings to the furniture and furnishings of the turn of the century; from the clothing and hats worn by ser-vants to the wardrobes of the middle- and upper-class denizens of the Ascot race. The buildings in Covent Garden—the Royal Opera House, the portico of St. Paul's Church and the market—were to be carefully re-created, too, but in forced perspective.

Warner insisted that there be no appearance of the typical "in-door set" and nothing like a tourist's London in his picture, and none was delivered. In every visual detail, *My Fair Lady* will for-ever remain one of the great artistic achievements in popular entertainment. The brilliance of it is precisely the visual verisimi-litude of every scene (with the possible exception of the long shots in the Ascot sequence). This was a resoundingly difficult thing to achieve and was ironically one of the reasons why musicals even-tually fell out of favor with the American public.

In May, Audrey, Sean and the nanny arrived in Los Angeles, where a house had been rented for them. Audrey studied daily with singing coach Harper MacKay and diction teacher Peter Ladefoged, the former to help her with the intricacies of the score, the latter to work with her on the accuracies of both Cockney and Mayfair English. Mel occasionally dropped in and out of town while taking whatever roles he could land in movie comedies and historical melodramas.

"We keep hearing mild whisperings about their marriage," wrote Renée Zinnemann to Kathryn Hulme and Marie Louise Habets, adding that she and Fred were concerned about Audrey, for they "haven't heard anything from her." That entire year, in fact, Audrey was for the most part out of contact with her friends: not only was she preoccupied with her work on the film but she was also, as Renée surmised, desperately unhappy in her marriage.

George Cukor, Alan Jay Lerner and Cecil Beaton welcomed her. "Sean, her two-year-old son, was present, and it is obvious that this is the love affair of her life, and she of her son's." Over tea and apricot jam roll at Audrey's residence, she suddenly asked, "Are you going to use my voice for songs at all?" Well, her voice would be used for many of the songs, they said, "but certain notes might be interpolated from another voice." This set her mind at ease, for she was anxious that her own singing in the picture not be replaced on the soundtrack by a professional vocalist: the mix of voices would be jarring for the audience, and if they had an opera singer, it would be untrue to the role of Eliza.

In fact, Audrey's contract gave the studio the right to substitute another voice, but from the day a voice teacher was assigned to work with her, Warner and Cukor had told her they had no doubt that in the end, she would render the songs magnificently and her voice would be used (but for a few minor interpolations). Besides, her singing would of course be prerecorded, and she would lip-synch to the playback on the set, and so all kinds of corrections could be made in the recording studio afterward. "I'll work hard on my voice," Audrey said that May afternoon, adding that she would "have as many lessons as you like. It's all part of the business, to learn to sing and dance."

During costume fittings the following week, Beaton observed Audrey in a merry mood, "speaking in Eliza's Cockney accent, joking with all the adoring helpers." Two weeks later, she sat before a mirror in the makeup department. With her thick flower-girl wig of hair and a weathered hat—but without the usual mascara and eyeliner—Audrey's look was completely different from her appearance in any previous film or still photo. It was as Beaton observed: simply by artfully painting her brows and lashes, she was a modern beauty—but without that makeup, she emerged as the real manifestation of a young, sad, destitute girl from another era. According to Beaton, "Audrey was already very touching and real" from the first day of rehearsals.

By the end of June, Beaton believed that Audrey's concern about her singing was misplaced: "Having worked on it like a Trojan ever since her arrival, her voice has improved to such an extent that she will be singing most of Eliza's songs." So he had been told by George Cukor and by Jack Warner himself.

But this was an astonishing act of deliberate deception, and it would miscarry in a way that seriously diminished the effect of Eliza's character in the picture and the artistic success of the film itself.

On May 16, Cukor and Lerner had met privately with singer Marni Nixon, who had dubbed the singing of Deborah Kerr (in *The King and I* and *An Affair to Remember*) and of Natalie Wood (in *West Side Story*). After a brief audition, Nixon was engaged to do the same for Audrey; she was also asked to keep the matter strictly private. On May 20, a production memorandum marked "confidential," from Warner's executive assistant Steve Trilling, was distributed to a number of the *Fair Lady* company: "We must have the double voice for Eliza ready by June 24—fully rehearsed and ready to go." Audrey, who was still (thus Beaton) "engrossed in singing lessons," was unaware of this development. On July 9, she met with Cukor, music director André Previn, the orchestra and several executives for her first prerecording of songs for the film. "It was an ordeal for Audrey," Beaton noted in his diary.

After weeks of rehearsals, of costume and wig fittings, of makeup, lighting and film stock tests, the first day of shooting was scheduled for August 12. "Everyone's nerves are explosive," said Audrey to a few of her colleagues. "It's a difficult time for all of us." To her father and his wife, she wrote a hasty note: "The heat is on, [and there is] any amount of things to finish before we start, but then if we rehearsed for another three years, we still wouldn't feel ready, so we may as well start. I think so often of you both."

Beaton, among others, found her unruffled and "remarkably disciplined: her memory [is] never at fault, she appears on the set word perfect, and she can give exactly the same performance over and over again," despite the repeated takes that are customary in moviemaking.

Meanwhile, Marni Nixon was recording all Eliza's songs. "The decision had already been made to have Marni dub her voice," according to Harper MacKay, who was also Previn's assistant. No one conveyed that news to Audrey, who continued to lip-synchronize to her own music tracks and thus to believe that, except for an occasional high note from Nixon's recordings, her own voice would be heard in the picture. "Audrey dutifully worked on her vocalises for a half hour or so every morning, and the weeks went by," continued MacKay. To make matters worse, Cukor, Previn and Lerner listened to Audrey's singing and praised her lavishly, and (thus MacKay) "Audrey, unfortunately, began to believe them." And when she completed the scene in which she performed "Wouldn't It Be Loverly?" to a prerecorded track, the bit players and crew applauded loudly.

"Did you hear that?" Audrey asked Cukor excitedly at the end of the day. "They actually applauded!"

"Audrey," Cukor said gently, "they thought it was you."

Unknown to him, to Lerner and to Previn, the technician in charge of playback had indeed used her track instead of Nixon's. "George," Audrey replied, tears filling her eyes, "it *was* me."

But even for Audrey Hepburn's sake, the corporate decision was not to be revoked, Marni Nixon dubbed all her songs as filming continued, and the final disposition was the reverse of what Audrey had hoped: in the end, it was Nixon's singing, with but a few of Audrey's musical phrases interpolated here and there—apparently so that Warner could say something about Audrey's singing in the film and not be accused of outright mendacity. This was cold comfort to her: she had worked on her singing as on her diction and performance almost to exhaustion and under a deliberately false impression. When she learned the truth, she felt keenly let down, but after that day, she displayed no dejection or resentment—she simply proceeded with her assignment.

According to André Previn, Marni Nixon was hired because "Audrey Hepburn could not do her own singing . . . [and] the leading lady had to trill like a bird . . . since Rex Harrison was already firmly established as a master of *parlando,* a kind of half-spoken singing." But Previn—along with Cukor, Warner and the rest—had in fact supervised what was eventually a disastrous consequence.

Marni Nixon's singing, heard to this day in the picture, is brilliant, carefully prepared, finely realized and worthy of an accomplished recitalist—it is, in other words, entirely inappropriate for the role. Nixon was right for the songs in *The King and I,* in which Anna Leonowens (Deborah Kerr) is a genteel nineteenth-century British lady. Even Nixon's dubbing for Natalie Wood as Maria (a lovesick Puerto Rican girl in New York) in *West Side Story* was acceptable, since that picture combined dance and music drama in a way perhaps never intended to be realistic.

Two of Audrey's recorded tracks have survived—her renditions of "Wouldn't It Be Loverly?" and "Show Me"—and they banish all doubt as to how the matter should have been settled: audiences should indeed have heard Audrey's own singing voice.*

---

* The exquisitely restored and remastered digital video disk of *My Fair Lady,* released in 1994, made available Audrey's expert renditions of these two songs; the others were lost or destroyed.

To be sure, the songs would have been very different from what Julie Andrews and Marni Nixon delivered—but those songs would have had an added measure of credibility. When Eliza, the forlorn Cockney, indulges her fantasy about what would be "loverly," it is ludicrous to hear Audrey's touching middle-range voice, full of gentle pathos and youthful pluck, suddenly replaced by an operatic soprano.

Her singing in *Funny Face* and *Breakfast at Tiffany's* was apposite for the characters and would have been in this case, too. In this regard, Jack Warner's reasoning had to be supported with specious arguments put forth by musicians who forgot about larger issues and (we must surmise) a director who simply took the line of least resistance. Otherwise, the final judgment is impossible to understand. Why would Jack Warner have engaged Audrey for *My Fair Lady* if, from day one, he knew she could not sing and he would have to mandate the dubbing of her voice throughout the picture? Why pay an actress $1 million for a musical if her singing—absolutely central to her performance—will not be heard? And if he did believe, based on her previous pictures, that she could in fact sing, then why did he not make a picture that was also dramatically credible?

As it was released, the film provides a disagreeable jolt every time Eliza's speech segues to song. The disjunction, due to the obvious disparity in vocal styles, does for *My Fair Lady* precisely what ought never to happen: it makes the audience aware of the unreality of the sequences. At these junctures, Audrey Hepburn remains on the screen but Eliza vanishes from the picture.

Even a casual movie-watcher realizes that one voice blithely replaced another that fateful autumn of 1963. For "Show Me," Eliza is to be infuriated with men who talk instead of act. The song should have an edge, even a slight stridency to it—instead, the audience then and later heard a meticulously executed aria. Perched on a stool in the recording studio, the estimable Marni Nixon did not have to be a singing actress, and her interpolations suggest that this was not among her considerations or the studio's. Nixon's singing is both accurate and, alas, vacant.

And so audiences view Audrey Hepburn's nuanced and highly effective performance rudely interrupted because of an obtuse misreading of popular expectations. Previn's argument to the contrary notwithstanding, Audrey's natural voice would have been the perfect match for Rex Harrison's stylized combination of speaking and vocalizing: the picture would, in other words, have sustained its keen realism in both characters.

After the resounding success of *The Sound of Music* in 1965, audiences became impatient with the artifice of characters breaking into song (as if anything in movies were real to begin with). As for any prospect of an Academy Award for Audrey—who might indeed have won if her voice had been heard—that possibility was sabotaged the day Marni Nixon was hired. The situation was quite logical: it would perhaps have been unimaginable for her colleagues to cite her for a role in a major musical in which she did not sing.

"You could tell, couldn't you?" Audrey asked when a journalist brought up the subject a year later and mentioned the unfortunate difference between her speaking style and that of the singing. "There was Rex, recording all his songs as he acted. Next time . . ."—but she left her remark uncompleted. At that moment, she might well have sung another song from *My Fair Lady*—"Just You Wait."

THE PRESSURE OF working on a complex film and its concomitant frustration were aggravated by a fierce heat wave in Los Angeles that summer, even more relentlessly over the San Fernando Valley, where Warner's Burbank studio was located. "We are only just surviving a truly 'infernal' heat wave that has had us all gasping for air the last week," Audrey wrote to her father on September 28.

At the studio [it has been] 110–118 [degrees Fahrenheit, or 43 to 48 Celsius] every day . . . without any cool off during the night. We pant through the night on top of our beds only to find a yet hotter blast of desert air to greet us in the morning. Weekends are spent submerged in the pool and wet bathing suits are our survival dress—but there is little I can do about Eliza's heavy wool skirts and laced-up boots under the multi kilowatts of light. I just float away underneath.

She did not, however, report to her father the loss of her diamond wedding ring, stolen from a bag in her studio dressing room.

In this climate, Audrey had to appear at the studio each morning at five o'clock, to be dirtied up for her scenes as a poor flower girl. For an hour, experts pushed dirt behind her fingernails and ears, smudged her face and generally turned her into the bedraggled Eliza; the process required an hour in the morning and, for the reverse, again in the evening. The task was no easier for later scenes, in which her makeup had to be modified for each camera setup and for every costume and hairpiece. Audrey's only dispensation with realism was to spray L'Interdit liberally before the crew set to work on her appearance.

By November 19, she was on the verge of collapse and, under doctor's orders, had to withdraw for three days. She returned on Friday, November 22. Work that day proceeded cheerfully until late morning, when someone with a portable radio ran to George Cukor as he discussed a scene with Audrey. And then everyone learned of the assassination of President John F. Kennedy. "I was too shaken to make the announcement or to tell the crew," Cukor recalled. "No one else could do it, either. And Audrey said simply, 'I'll do it.' " She took a microphone and said, "The President of the United States is dead. Shall we have two minutes of silence to pray or do whatever you think is appropriate?"

As everywhere else, many stood weeping; others were simply stunned. A few moments later, Audrey said, "May God have mercy on us all." Then the production continued until six that evening, for the schedule was five days behind, three of them due to Audrey's indisposition. A year later, a journalist asked Audrey about that day. "It is a tradition in the theater in England and in America," she said, "for the leading lady or the leading man to make any special announcements to the company. I just did what had to be done."

Because the unseen participation of Marni Nixon was circulated in the press during the last weeks of production, reviewers invariably noted the fact when the film was released in the autumn of 1964. The London press was generally dismissive of the first half of the movie, most of all because of what was considered her inadequate Cockney accent—as if there were only one standard East End intonation by which those who assume it could be judged. No less an authority than John Gielgud was most enthusiastic: he went so far as to assert that Audrey was "much better than Julie Andrews."

Many American journalists felt such loyalty to Julie Andrews that they were unable to consider how distinctive a movie version of a role must be. But major critics were delighted. "Her wit is delivered with sure instinct," wrote one New York journalist, "and her volcanic and hilarious wrath is always smoldering." *The New York Times* praised her most zealously: "Miss Hepburn brings a fine sensitivity of feeling and a phenomenal histrionic skill [to the role] . . . She is dazzlingly beautiful and comic in the crisply satiric Ascot scene, stiffly serene and distant at the embassy ball, and almost unbearably poignant in the later scenes when she hungers for love." Even *The New Yorker* joined the report supporting Audrey: "Her qualities as an actress and as a personality turn her Eliza into an utterly different, though no less captivating, creature than that of Miss Andrews."

In every sequence, Audrey's performance is one of brightly natural calibration. As a flower girl, she is moving and funny in a way that Eliza Doolittle perhaps can never be on the stage, for the close-ups of her reactions to the overbearing professor are a precise balance of waiflike poignancy and sudden ambition. Later, as the brand-new creature presentable at embassy receptions, Audrey gave Eliza an almost imperceptible hint of gaucherie still remaining beneath all her stylish grace—the flicker of an eyelid here, the merest change in her smile there—that kept alive the girl she was, right alongside the woman she was becoming.

SHE MIGHT NOT have considered it in those terms, but Audrey had to deal with precisely that sense of transition when she completed her work on *My Fair Lady* in December 1963: she knew her marriage was beyond repair, yet she was not ready for divorce and was making valiant attempts to avoid the inevitable. "There was a lot of difficulty and some strain, because [Mel's] career had peaked and she was at the top of hers," said Sean later, speaking of this time in his parents' lives. "In an almost unrealistic way, she hoped real love would come in the form of flowers that are sent and not requested, and when that [hope] was disappointed, things started to come apart."

The emotional distance between the Ferrers matched the geographic. Mel had traveled to Spain for his role in *The Fall of the Roman Empire*, and then he had dashed back to Hollywood during the production of *My Fair Lady* for a part in *Sex and the Single Girl*. Now he was preparing to write and direct a Spanish film called *Cabriola* and to produce and star abroad in the life of the painter El Greco.

And so, despite the many offers she received in early 1964,

Audrey decided to be a sort of married camp follower: clinging to the hope of saving her marriage, she and Sean (who turned four that summer) spent most of the year traveling with Mel. "I split my time between Melchor and the boy," she wrote to George Cukor, who tried without success to interest her in a musical based on the stage production of *Oliver!* "How glorious if Mel and I could contribute together and not be separated for once," she replied as she declined the offer. She did not add that she and Mel had indeed briefly considered making a film together—the story of Ferdinand and Isabella of Spain—but they saw the unlikelihood of him directing her, and they soon abandoned the project.

In their brief visits, Cukor, the Zinnemanns, Kate and Lou sensed Audrey's almost desperate attempt to shore up the family as she endured a torrid summer while Mel completed his scenes in a Spanish film about the life of the French educator Jean-Baptiste de La Salle, founder of the Christian Brothers. About that time, the Ferrers bought a summer house on the Costa del Sol, near Marbella—"Santa Catalina," they named it, for Audrey Kathleen (Catalina, in Spanish). They intended to take advantage of it as a holiday refuge, but the place was not much used.

In the autumn, Audrey had to fulfill her contractual obligation to travel across America promoting the release of *My Fair Lady,* and so, without much enthusiasm, she left Mel with his projects and Sean with the nanny. "I long to get home to our own cozy cottage and the peace of our mountains," Audrey wrote to "Dearest Daddy and Fidelma" that autumn. "I went to the states for three weeks of *MFL* presentation. Mel was able to come to New York for the premiere, but he had to return to Rome and work next day. I had to complete the tour alone and came home." She mentioned the launch of the film only once but wrote five pages about her "splendid" Sean and his new dog, an Alsatian.

In Hollywood, on February 23, 1965, the Academy of Motion Picture Arts and Sciences released the names of those nominated for Oscars. In addition to *My Fair Lady,* some memorable movies had been released in 1964: *Dr. Strangelove, Becket, Zorba the Greek* and *Mary Poppins* among them. The nominees for best actress of the year were Julie Andrews (*Mary Poppins*), Anne Bancroft (*The Pumpkin Eater*), Sophia Loren (*Marriage Italian Style*), Debbie Reynolds (*The Unsinkable Molly Brown*) and Kim Stanley (*Séance on a Wet Afternoon*).

"As for the whole nomination mish-mash," Audrey wrote to George Cukor,

I think I am the only one who is not *in the dark. Everybody seems to search for an explanation. It seems to me it is all very simple—my performance was not up to snuff. I firmly believe that were it true that anyone had it in for [Jack Warner] or me, or wished to ensure Julie Andrews's Oscar, their sentiments would have been automatically cancelled out had my bravura been worthy. Because* My Fair Lady *meant so terribly much to me, I* had *sort of secretly hoped for a nomination but never never counted on the Oscar. Therefore, disappointed I is, but not astounded like my chums seem to be. What does amaze me is the hullabaloo which ensued and the constant pressure . . . to get me to come to California on the big night.*

Cukor replied to her letter, vainly protesting that she did not receive a nomination because Warner did not release the picture on enough screens in Los Angeles prior to the nominations. Audrey knew better: *My Fair Lady* had had sufficient exposure that it received twelve nominations, and she was the only player in the cast not nominated in one of the four top acting categories.*

On March 31, the British Film Academy named Audrey best

---

* The picture received nominations for best actor (Rex Harrison), supporting actor (Stanley Holloway), supporting actress (Gladys Cooper), art direction (Gene Allen, Cecil Beaton and George James Hopkins), cinematography (Harry Stradling), costume design

British actress of the year for her performance in *Charade*. That was not much remarked in Hollywood, however, where there was high tension for the rites of spring. Oscar statuettes were handed out on April 5, and Audrey was there, having gallantly agreed to travel from Europe to present the award for best actor—a task, in the circumstances, that might have been masterminded by a sadistic functionary. With obvious pleasure, she announced Rex Harrison's name; he then stepped up, embraced her and, to polite applause, said chivalrously, "I have to thank two fair ladies, I think." One of them was right there, and the other, as if on cue, then came up, as Julie Andrews received the award for best actress for *Mary Poppins*. Her opening remark brought the house down, as the saying goes: "First of all, I'd like to thank Jack Warner . . ."

FOR A DECADE, the Ferrers had lived in a German-speaking canton of Switzerland. By 1965, the family had outgrown the place, and Audrey wished Sean to attend a French-speaking school. They decided to purchase a two-hundred-year-old restored farmhouse near Morges, a half-hour from the Geneva airport. The eighteenth-century, nine-bedroom stone villa was called La Paisible—the peaceful place—and was situated in the village of Tolochenaz, part of the French-speaking canton of Vaud. Their neighbors were mostly orchard farmers, and the place was wonderfully quiet. At the same time, Mel learned of a new play that was to open on Broadway the following winter—*Wait Until Dark*, by Frederick Knott, the author of *Dial M for Murder*. Film rights were quickly negotiated for Audrey to star and Mel to produce, at Warner Bros. in Burbank.

(Beaton), directing (Cukor), editing (William Ziegler), music scoring (Previn), sound (George Groves), writing (Lerner, for material previously in another medium) and best picture (Jack Warner as producer).

The picture she first made, that August, was her fifth to be filmed partially or completely in Paris; it was also her third picture for William Wyler, and his first comedy since *Roman Holiday*. For *How to Steal a Million,* as it was titled, Audrey's leading man was three years her junior: Peter O'Toole, recently of *Lawrence of Arabia* and *Becket*. The screenplay by Harry Kurnitz, set and made entirely in Paris, was impossible to believe on any level, but the picture was so engagingly made, and with such stylish deadpan humor and appealing (but not exaggerated) glamour, that it was a commercial and popular hit.

Audrey was cast as the daughter of an art forger (Hugh Griffith) who makes his fortune brilliantly copying the works of the masters and selling them as genuine. This felonious occupation is suddenly threatened when a detective masquerading as a burglar (Peter O'Toole) joins with Audrey in a preposterous scheme—to steal one of papa's fakes, loaned to an art exhibit, so that he will not be revealed as a counterfeiter and be hauled off to prison. Romance is then added to comedy, with the predictable happy ending.

Kurt Frings had negotiated with Wyler and Twentieth Century–Fox to ensure that Audrey would be supported by her now customary and loyal allies: Givenchy clothed her (in no less than two dozen outfits); Grazia De Rossi styled her hair and Alberto De Rossi her makeup; and Charles Lang was the cinematographer—all of whom made it possible for Audrey to look considerably younger than her thirty-six years. This team, and the amiable, relaxed working style of O'Toole, made for an agreeable summer's employment, and Audrey's performance in the film—nothing so demanding as *My Fair Lady*—was impressively unfussy, which was exactly what the script required. Gregory Peck had been on the mark when he said that she should have done much more comedy during her career.

For Wyler and O'Toole, much of the pleasure of making *How to Steal a Million* was their casual punctuation of the dialogue with improvised jokes that reward the careful listener. At one point in their plot to steal a fake statue, O'Toole dresses Audrey in the drab garb of a museum cleaning servant. That will do just fine, he says, looking at the unflattering outfit. For what? Audrey wants to know—and O'Toole replies quietly, "Well, it gives Givenchy a night off." Delivered as a throwaway remark of no special significance, it was but one of several inside jokes relished by Audrey, the cast and the crew.

In September, Mel was laboring to secure the rights to the Knott play and to confirm a deal with Warner, and he visited Audrey in Paris for a weekend. She was not eager to plan a project to be undertaken two years in the future, but she wanted to support her husband's efforts. And so she agreed to play the difficult role of a blind woman terrorized by thugs who are hunting for a stash of heroin that she does not know is in her home. Weeks after Mel's visit, Audrey learned she was pregnant.

With two months left to work before *How to Steal a Million* was completed in December, Audrey was advised to ask Wyler for a slower working pace, but this she refused to do. "She had worked without letup," according to Mel, who took her home to Switzerland after the last day's work. There, the family celebrated their first Christmas at La Paisible, and Audrey decorated the house and wrote greetings to friends around the world. She sent a generous cash gift to her father, wrapped in a hand-drawn card depicting holiday bells, ribbons and wreaths. "I have decided," she wrote, "that you must know much better than I what you would best like for Christmas, and also to avoid customs [taxes] I send my gift this way. Forgive its prosaic appearance, but it is from a loving heart—and with a huge hug for both of you." Nor did she forget an equally lavish present to her mother, who had been living for several years in San Francisco after emigrating from London.

It was just after this holiday season that Audrey miscarried again. "She took it very, very hard," said her husband.

Chapter Fourteen

~

1966–1970

"SHE IS NOW beginning to feel much better," Mel wrote to Audrey's father in late January 1966. "She is on her feet again, and although we are not letting her do too much, her spirits and physical being are much improved. She is going to take four months' rest here."

Mel may have found her "much improved," but Audrey did not feel so. In a postcard to her father, she said she felt as if only "a thin layer" separated her from a complete breakdown. "There is much to go through still, and I pray God for strength and gentleness." She closed the short message "All my love, MP." (In Audrey's childhood, Ruston's nickname for her was Monkey Puzzle, a reference to what he thought was her odd face and her enigmatic personality.)

By late March, however, she was indeed stronger. "Having at last a real rest and sunny weather," she wrote to her father from an Alpine resort. "I walk every morning and swim in the afternoon, also take massages and sleep lots . . . am well again and not so sad anymore. I start work on May 1 in St. Tropez, then Paris—a wonderful script." It was indeed, but the circumstances of making the movie would have serious consequences on Audrey's personal life.

William Wyler had directed her in a trio of memorable performances, and now it was Stanley Donen's turn to complete his cycle of three Hepburn movies. He had sent her a script he had prepared with writer Frederic Raphael, whose screenplay for *Darling* had won the Academy Awards in Britain and America. *Two for the Road*, as it was called, would be a radical departure for Audrey.

The style with which Audrey Hepburn had been associated, and which (with few exceptions) defined not only her look but also the public's perception of her, was vanishing as rapidly from Hollywood as from ordinary life. The chic clothes, the exquisite diction, the European flavor of her movies and their literary tone, her choice of scripts and directors—all these were being rethought by Hollywood. The new kind of movie was represented by, among others, *Cat Ballou*, *The Pawnbroker*, *Darling*, *Who's Afraid of Virginia Woolf?*, *Alfie*, *Georgy Girl*, and *Help!* In 1966, Audrey turned thirty-seven, but popular taste was now dominated by the preferences of teenagers; the effect of the Beatles, and the upheaval in just about every area of youth culture, could not be minimized.

So it was that when Donen submitted the script for *Two for the Road* to Universal Studios, they were eager to finance and distribute it—until he mentioned that he wanted Audrey Hepburn as the leading lady; with that, Universal withdrew from the project. Twentieth Century–Fox, however, liked *How to Steal a Million* and gave Donen a green light and the cash he needed.

The screenplay covered a twelve-year period in a marriage threatened by routine, infidelity, remorse, mistaken cues, false hopes—and occasionally buoyed by shared satisfactions, warm memories and indelible moments of love, support and empathetic understanding. The story was not told in strict chronology, but rather by bending backward and forward in time, interlocking episodes as they are evoked by one or another event or recollection—all of it supporting the notion that relationships do indeed proceed along an uncertain road with unforeseen curves and turns. The road itself was in fact a character in the script, present in every sequence.

When she read the script, Audrey was wary of the content and protective of her image. The seriocomic dialogue was acerbic, often cynical, and the character of Joanna, the wife who changes and matures—not always admirably—was not at all prettified from Raphael's primary idea (as, earlier, Holly Golightly had been transformed from Capote's rougher original). Indeed, Joanna was nothing like a Hepburn character at all: she bore no similarity to any woman Audrey had impersonated, and so the actress feared losing both her image and her public. Joanna did, however, resemble some aspects of Audrey herself, and the recognition of this frightened her. Perhaps the most unsettling element for her was not the character's infidelity, or even the frank bedroom scenes, but rather the disturbing parallels of the couple to her own marriage, then in its twelfth year. No, she told Mel, she was not at all sure this project was right for her—which was her way of turning it down.

To his credit, Mel would not let the subject drop. He understood that, if her career was not to be a casualty of the new age in entertainment styles, Audrey had to rise to the moment. The princess of *Roman Holiday,* the child-woman of *Sabrina* and *Love in the Afternoon,* the romanticized party girl of *Breakfast at Tiffany's* and the clever lady of *Charade*—these characters were becoming commercially past tense. "Audrey usually makes up her own mind about what she's going to do," Mel said at the time. "But when I read the script of *Two for the Road,* I told her to make it—right away. I knew it would be good for her." Human motives are rarely undiluted, and Mel may have thought that if he was going to produce *Wait Until Dark,* which was very much a contemporary thriller, it would be prudent for Audrey to be seen in advance as still pertinent for a new audience.

There were arguments from the start, and in fact the deal was declared dead more than once. First, Donen was adamant that Givenchy was not to be part of the creative team. But his clothes gave her confidence, Audrey protested. The director was intransigent: her clothes were to be taken off the rack. She left the task to Mel and Stanley, but she was not happy. "She thought the bright colors and modish prints would take away from her face," recalled Ken Scott, part of the costume design team that included Hardy Amies, Mary Quant and Paco Rabanne, all of whose fabrics and patterns were chosen for their contemporary look.

Then there were heated discussions about Audrey's leading man. Now that she had the authority, she would no longer accept a replica of Holden, Bogart, Fonda, Cooper, Lancaster or even Grant. She might, she added, just as well have a co-star who was of the day, like Peter O'Toole. Names rose and fell, some were contacted, Paul Newman read the script and declined—and then someone suggested Albert Finney, six years younger than Audrey and a classically trained actor who had just had an international success in the uproarious *Tom Jones*.

Filming began in the South of France on May 3, the eve of Audrey's thirty-seventh birthday. Explaining to George Cukor why she had been out of touch for so long, Audrey wrote from St. Tropez:

I have drawn a complete blank in the whole period of Christmas and the two months that followed. I find even now hard to remember what I did and did not do, who and when and what I saw—perhaps [this is] nature's sometimes so charitable way of helping one to forget—in my case not so much the anguish but the joy I had felt.

Sean is now in school and God knows how I miss him . . . Albert Finney is a marvel, so easy and "cooperative," as they call it, that he makes even me *look "uncooperative"!!*

Our new house is a dream. As I left, the fruit trees were in bloom, the fresh spring grass stood high below them, filled *with buttercups and clover. All the tulips were out and the glycinia [was] blooming away on our walls.*

"My private life was not always happy," Audrey said, recalling the production of *Two for the Road*. "But with Stanley, I was always happy on the set. He made me laugh, and that, for me, was an enormous turn-on." She certainly had a friendly rapport with Donen, for whom she had respect and from whom she always claimed to have learned a great deal. He felt that Audrey was always reserved, even to the point of being aloof:

> I longed to get closer, to get behind whatever was the invisible, but decidedly present barrier between her and the rest of us, but I never got to the deepest part of Audrey. I don't mean to imply that I thought she was playing a game with me. But she always kept a little of herself in reserve, which was hers alone, and I couldn't ever find out what it was, let alone share it with her. She was the pot of gold at the end of the rainbow.

Jacqueline Bisset, also in the cast, recalled Audrey's extraordinary preparation for each scene, and the constant presence of her hair and makeup team, on whom Donen depended to clarify the chronology of each sequence. "Audrey was very pleasant to everyone on the production," according to Bisset,

> but there was a kind of distance there. When we first met, she gave me a very broad smile I'll never forget. It wasn't a smile with the eyes, but with her mouth only. Of course, she was the star of the film and had enormous responsibilities. And she could be very generous with us. A few times, on the weekends, she cooked dinner for several of us—very rich pastas, with all

sorts of wonderful cream sauces. But when we worked during the week, she went to her trailer and had lunch on her own—a bit of cheese with some tomato, or something like that—a very tiny meal, so that she could work at top form through the afternoon.

But there was a good reason why Audrey kept her distance from the other players and from her director—a greater distance during *Two for the Road* than perhaps at any other time in her career. For the four months of filming, she and Albert Finney pursued a frolicsome romance in the most discreet manner possible. They rehearsed in private, they went to beaches with no other company, they dined *à deux*. Her marriage, she had to accept, was merely legal, and Finney was divorced. More to the point, he had a keen sense of humor, he was highly intelligent, he took his craft with utmost gravity, and he had a personality that was enormously beneficial to Audrey at this point: he was entertaining and exuberant. The relationship was refreshingly uncomplicated and so perhaps unique in her romantic life.

"I didn't even know the Audrey of the last few weeks on this film," recalled Donen. "She overwhelmed me. She was so free, so happy. I never saw her like that—so young! I don't think *I* was responsible. I guess it was Albie."

"She and Albie had this wonderful thing together," recalled writer Irwin Shaw, a frequent visitor to the production that summer, "like a pair of kids with a perfect understanding and a shorthand of jokes and references that closed out everyone else. When Mel was there, it was funny: Audrey and Albie got rather formal and a little awkward, as if now they had to behave like grown-ups." As for Finney, he was discreet then and later: his relationship with Audrey, he said, was "one of the closest I've ever had." Audrey was typically equivocal. "I really love Albie," she said with a smile, and that was that. Meantime, columnists around the world reported the friendship that was blossoming between the two stars—with the usual innuendoes neatly appended.

Six-year-old Sean, meanwhile, was in the South of Spain with his father. "Mel splits his time between him, me and his work," Audrey wrote to her father on August 11. But as the production drew to a close early the following month, there was a development Audrey may not have foreseen. How Audrey and Albie parted may never be known, but in September, everyone around her noted a fearful expression and a nervous anxiety that even Finney was unable to alleviate. According to some who knew them both, Mel informed his wife that unless she ended the affair, he would bring suit for divorce and specify her adultery as the reason. This struck terror into her, for that would mean at least part-time separation from her son—if not the complete loss of him when she was proclaimed in court as an unfit mother. Sean, after all, was the single compelling reason for her to remain so long in an emotionally sterile marriage.

Even if Mel did not communicate his intention directly to her, Audrey could not be certain that he would, from afar, play the role of a complaisant husband regarding an affair that was noised about even in the press. If indeed he were to accuse his wife of infidelity—and there was no guarantee he would not—then Audrey could not anticipate a favorable judgment on her request to keep her son. Whatever might have been an analogous situation in Mel's private life, it was unreported by the press, and that made the difference. She was potentially the one to lose, and catastrophically.

"I remember there was a tension in my parents' marriage at that time," Sean said long after. "Only years later did I realize it was because she was having an affair with Finney during the making of that movie." The Finney-Hepburn romance ended precisely to save the child from a public humiliation; he could not, however, be saved from the experience of his parents' separation.

In a way, this chain of anxieties brought a depth of complex feelings to Audrey's performance in the movie, in which she progresses from a pensive young lady to a frisky young companion, then a happy wife, later a doubtful spouse and mother, then an adulteress and finally a woman who comes to terms with the ambiguities of her marriage. The audience can always mark the periods of transition, however disjointed in the narrative, by her different clothes and hairstyles, but Audrey also conveyed the evolution through expressions and voice modulations.

"The role required a depth of emotion, care, yearning and maturity that Audrey had never played before," according to Stanley Donen. "She gave what I think is her best performance." Critics worldwide agreed, but, as she had anticipated, the American public was resentful of the shift in Audrey's image. When the picture was first released in 1967 in America, at Radio City Music Hall, the theater did not sell enough tickets to cover even a minor portion of its usual lavish, live entertainment. Box-office receipts abroad were far healthier, perhaps because European audiences were accustomed to franker depictions of marriage in the movies.

AFTER CHRISTMAS AT Tolochenaz, the Ferrers traveled to Los Angeles, where, as planned, Mel was to produce and Audrey would star in *Wait Until Dark* at Warner Bros. studios. "We are both here," she wrote to her father from their suite at the Beverly Hills Hotel. "Sean we left (sob, sob) at home, as he hated to leave his new school and all his friends. [It was] the best decision for him although hard on us . . . I long to go home and stay there!"

Jack Warner introduced Mel and Audrey to the production company, to the crew and to her fellow actors (Richard Crenna, Alan Arkin, Jack Weston and Efrem Zimbalist, Jr.). The great pleasure for Audrey that January afternoon, however, was her reunion with the director—none other than Terence Young. He had been among the war-wounded at the Battle of Arnhem, a thirty-year-old British paratrooper nursed back to health by Audrey and her mother at a Dutch clinic in 1945. After his recovery, he had made a film about that battle and had then begun a successful career in commercial films. Young had in fact just directed the first two James Bond films, *Dr. No* and *From Russia with Love,* and he now had a deal with Warner. Every day during filming, Young and Audrey called an English-style tea break for the production team, promptly at four o'clock.

Preparing the difficult role of Susy Hendrix, the terrorized blind woman, Audrey immediately began painstaking research. She studied at a school for the blind, learned Braille, forced herself to stare widely at someone with a blank gaze that gave the impression she saw nothing, taught herself to negotiate around a room with a stick (her eyes shielded by a blindfold) and became adroit at dialing a telephone and applying makeup without a mirror. For even greater realism, Mel wanted his wife to wear milky, light-colored contact lenses. This she attempted, but they were extremely irritating to her eyes, and she did not believe they were necessary. In his capacity as producer, Mel then summoned Jack Warner and a few colleagues, and they pronounced their agreement; dutifully, Audrey wore the lenses.

In every way, the filming was exceedingly difficult, from the start date on January 16 to the conclusion on April 7. First of all, Audrey missed Sean to the point that she accumulated thousands of dollars in transatlantic telephone bills, calling every night from the Beverly Hills Hotel to Tolochenaz. Second, her collaboration with Mel was much constrained by his status as producer, for he tended to act more like her agent, manager and director. Third, Audrey had to endure almost constant bumps and bruises, especially those caused during the violent scene in which she is attacked. The climactic sequence, for example, had to be filmed mostly in very low lighting (it was a nighttime scene, enacted—for plot reasons—without lightbulbs), and it involved carefully orchestrated moves and leaps by Audrey and Alan Arkin, as the arch-villain; he recalled that the only thing he hated about *Wait Until Dark* was his obligation to terrorize Audrey Hepburn.

Despite the complicated emotional and physical circumstances, *Wait Until Dark* was a hugely effective picture. The characteristic critical reaction was that her performance was "superior . . . beautifully modulated without ever turning shrill." For it, Audrey received a salary of $900,000 plus ten percent of the gross proceeds, which brought her eventual profit to more than $3 million; she also earned a fifth Academy Award nomination.*

Within days of completing her work, she returned to Tolochenaz and Sean. Mel remained at the Burbank Studios to supervise the editing of the picture, and in July he proceeded to Paris and Madrid to discuss future projects. "It will be a long time before I make another film," Audrey said. "I promised my son at least two thousand hours of my time." From this time, she visited America only rarely over the next two decades. She did, however, return to New York as early as April 1968, to receive a special Tony Award (perhaps inexplicably) for contributions to the theater. Speaking of her American stage debut in 1951, she said that she had been "a rather thin girl with a rather thin talent."

Otherwise, she kept her word on both counts. "I really quit when my son Sean became of age to go to school," she added later. "I had always wanted children so badly that I was miserable when I went off and did [*Wait Until Dark*] . . . I could not bear to be separated from him, so I stopped working."

That was certainly her primary reason for what was eventually an eight-year retreat from her career. But she also coolly assessed

---

* The other nominees were Anne Bancroft *(The Graduate)*, Faye Dunaway *(Bonnie and Clyde)*, Dame Edith Evans *(The Whisperers)* and the winner, Katharine Hepburn *(Guess Who's Coming to Dinner)*.

recent developments in popular entertainment and saw how ill suited she was for most of it by both temperament and image. Audiences in 1968 were buying tickets to see new kinds of pictures— among them, *Bonnie and Clyde, In the Heat of the Night, The Graduate, Cool Hand Luke, The Dirty Dozen, In Cold Blood* and *The Valley of the Dolls.* Neither the sexual frankness nor the violence, neither the tone nor the design of the new Hollywood much appealed to her. At the same time, there were very few roles for someone of Audrey's type and age: she was too fixed in the public mind, even after *Two for the Road,* to undertake something like Mrs. Robinson in *The Graduate* (which she was not offered in any case), and she very likely could not have projected the voracious and pathetic hunger of characters like that.

Grace Kelly, born the same year as Audrey, withdrew from screen acting in 1956, when she was twenty-six. She, too, had appeared twice on Broadway and, like Audrey, had received an award for her stage work. Like Audrey, she then went to Hollywood, where she appeared in only eleven films during her five years there, and won a best actress Oscar the year after Audrey. Just so, Grace worked with several first-rate directors; the best were Alfred Hitchcock (three times), Fred Zinnemann and John Ford. Like Audrey, Grace acted opposite leading men who were old enough to be her father (Clark Gable, Gary Cooper, Ray Milland, James Stewart, Cary Grant and—twice—Bing Crosby) and with men who simply looked considerably older (Stewart Granger, William Holden and Alec Guinness).

Grace was also like Audrey in her earnest desire to be a good actress, in her classic elegance, her photogenic beauty and the admiration and affection she earned from colleagues. And Grace made a decision in 1956, at the age of twenty-six: wanting to be a wife and mother, she exchanged what she knew to be the ephemeral life of a movie queen for the lifetime role of Princess of

Monaco. Audrey spoke of her to friends several times after *Wait Until Dark*.

And so in 1967, Audrey Hepburn, international movie star, undertook the role of Audrey Hepburn, full-time mother. "She liked things plain and simple," according to Sean, who recalled that his mother loved to tend the roses, hydrangeas and dahlias in her garden, that she shared the kitchen chores with their cook, and that she supervised her son's schoolwork. Never an unduly severe parent, she nevertheless permitted Sean only a half-hour of television-watching daily and, to encourage good eating habits, only one Coca-Cola a week. As for her own menus, she maintained a healthy vigilance over her diet but was not obsessive about her weight or lack of it. She ate pasta and steak, allowed herself a piece of chocolate every afternoon, drank a scotch or bourbon before dinner—but, unfortunately, she was also a heavy smoker.

DURING THE SUMMER of 1967, Audrey and Mel separated at last, and she filed for divorce; that season, he left La Paisible. "The breakup between my mother and my father was hard," Sean recalled. "My parents never argued in front of me, but I was aware from quite a young age that something just wasn't right. She came and told me that she and Dad were going to divorce, but explained that none of it was my fault—children often believe they are in some way to blame. When she told me, I was very upset, naturally, because I loved them both, but I was also relieved in a way, because it explained why things didn't feel quite right at home."

"I still don't know what the difficulties were," said Mel, perhaps somewhat disingenuously, years later. "Audrey's the one who asked for the divorce." That year, he was photographed at this or that Hollywood spot with this or that attractive woman, some famous and some not.

Addressing the charge that he had been Svengali to her Trilby, Mel insisted: "I had a great deal to do with her career, and I'm delighted I was able to contribute." So much was true until he added: "But I didn't benefit from it, I was not competitive, nor was I controlling . . . I don't think anybody could compete with Audrey. I don't think there was any sense in trying to."

Very soon, Audrey was quoted in the European press, speaking of her marriage as if it had been an illness: "I am completely recovered—now I am free and at peace." But this sounded very much like whistling in the dark.

"She never spoke badly of Monsieur Ferrer," Givenchy recalled, "even when things went badly with them and she was making enormous concessions for the sake of their marriage." At home, too, she did not openly disparage Mel to Sean, but the boy had the impression "and the underlying feeling [from her] that he was the only responsible party. On the surface, it appeared that way, because he was more difficult . . . He wasn't an easy man, by any stretch of the imagination. He was extremely talented, well read, educated, [and] certainly played a very important role in the choices that she made and the standards that she kept . . . But she stayed too long in the marriage, and it had a toxic effect [on her]—she kept reacting over and over [to the failure of] the marriage."

Audrey indeed felt that Mel was accountable, but simultaneously she felt that she was to blame. The paradox is easy to untangle, as Sean did: "They were both responsible for the failed marriage," he claimed, "she for projecting [onto it] something that wasn't, and he for not being able to get over himself at some level."

Sean was right. For years, Audrey had worked so hard to present an image of the perfect marriage that she began to believe it was. From the start, there had been a disparity in their goals and ambitions, and the gulf widened after the birth of Sean. "Success isn't so important for a woman," she said, "and with the baby I felt that I had everything a wife could wish for. But it's not enough for a man. It was not enough for Mel. He couldn't live with himself, just being Audrey Hepburn's husband." For far too long, the Ferrers did not want to remain together, yet in some ways, they wanted precisely that.

After *Ondine*, Mel had wanted them to collaborate more and more, on stage, screen and television, and he saw himself as her mentor and guide to achieving that. For a time, when they worked together on *War and Peace* and *Mayerling*, it seemed possible. On her side, Audrey certainly wanted to work, but at a more leisurely pace so that she could be a mother; multiple miscarriages did not deter her from that intention. Nor, indeed, did the gradual unraveling of their commitment to each other: parenthood, she may have thought, would unite them more deeply.

Even up to 1965, Audrey was still willing to have Mel as the father of another child. By this time, as her son Sean later observed, she had projected something onto the marriage that did not exist—even while Mel could not "get over" the fact that he was never going to achieve his ambition to be an internationally acknowledged actor, producer and director. Eventually, for the remainder of his career, he was offered only mediocre roles in forgettable films and television episodes—enough for him to provide a comfortable life for himself and his fifth wife (whom he married in 1971), but not, perhaps, sufficient to gratify his earlier dreams of what might have been.

By the beginning of 1968, Audrey was firmly established as the chatelaine of La Paisible—a single mother, supervising house, garden and son, but the freedom and peace of which she had spoken so warmly soon began to seem illusory and purposeless. For almost fourteen years, she had been able to rely on someone to look after things—to run interference with directors, agents, managers, publicists, the press; someone with whom she could discuss things, and on whose intelligence she relied to advise her. Hence, despite the fact that there were incidents of Mel's intervention that were embarrassing or downright infuriating, Audrey was now, at thirty-nine, completely on her own, and lonely.

She may have thought of herself as simply a mother, maintaining a home and devoting herself to her son, but she was still Audrey Hepburn, the Oscar-winning actress, a worldwide celebrity and international fashion plate—virtually unacknowledged royalty. It had been comforting to talk of full-time motherhood and to anticipate withdrawal from the demands of moviemaking, but suddenly she was alone, caring for an eight-year-old son who could not supply what had enriched her in a gratifying public life.

Nor were there friends with whom to collaborate on projects: no Wyler or Wilder, no Donen or Zinnemann, no Alberto and Grazia De Rossi or Charles Lang. Everything about her public life, to which she was long accustomed, suddenly came to a halt. She was the private person she said she wanted to be—but now she began to realize that she did not want to be just a private person. Two maids, a cook and a gardener-chauffeur certainly lightened her chores, but these helpers were hardly to be regarded as proper companions in whom she could confide. She smoked more than ever, and her weight again dropped to eighty pounds, far too little for her five-foot-seven frame. She was, as Givenchy said, "miserable"; in fact, she was again close to a full-scale collapse.

Audrey and Sean frequently traveled to Italy on weekends and school holidays: she had maintained friendships in and around Rome since the time of her work there, and so they could be part of a family rather than hotel clients—with, most notably, the Lovatellis, who, long contrary to Italian law and custom, relished using their aristocratic titles. La Contessa Lovatelli, sister of one of Henry Fonda's former wives, took it on herself to introduce her famous guest at lavish dinners, sporting events and beach outings.

That season, a curious period of *la dolce vita* began in the life of Audrey Hepburn. There was, after all, no serious occupation in her life, and whatever the joys of motherhood, they could not entirely compensate for the radical difference in her days. She craved the company of grown-ups, and by default she accepted facsimiles thereof.

Indeed, La Contessa was rather like the Italian Dolly Levi, arranging romantic *appuntamenti* for her friend from spring to early autumn 1968. During those months, Audrey was seen in the company of, for example, the dashing matador Antonio Ordoñez. He claimed that classical dance was the controlling metaphor for his promenade in the ring, and he had enjoyed the friendship of Ernest Hemingway and Orson Welles. Ordoñez had a knowledge of ballet and film that enabled him to speak with Audrey about much more than corridas, and for a brief time, La Contessa thought she had succeeded on the first throw. But for some reason, that liaison ended. Next, Audrey briefly dated Prince Alfonso de Bourbon, seven years her junior, a champion sportsman and ski fanatic. That, too, was a short-lived business. Presently, she was photographed leaving a restaurant and then a concert hall with Prince Marino Torlonia, who traced his lineage back to a wayward pope, and whose family still advised the Vatican on financial matters. *Il principe* was strike three.

Audrey returned to Switzerland in the autumn of 1968 for her final divorce decree. "My parents didn't talk for twenty-five years," said Sean. "Well, they did once, at my graduation, and then fifteen years later, at my first wedding." Audrey remained on good terms with several of her ex-husband's relatives. "She maintained a warm and sturdy bond with my mother," said Joe Ferrer, Mel's nephew. The legal details of the divorce thus settled, Audrey hastened back to Rome—not because the Countess had found another candidate, but because Audrey had already met a man who very much attracted her.

Andrea Dotti was not a prince, but he was nominally a count. Son of the Count and Countess Domenico Dotti, he was born in Naples, where titles are even more plentiful than pizzas. Andrea had taken a medical degree and had then built a respectable career as a practicing psychiatrist and faculty member at the University of Rome.

Five foot nine and boyishly handsome, with light brown hair and gentle, dark brown eyes, he turned thirty in 1968 and was therefore almost a decade younger than Audrey. They had met as guests aboard the yacht of a mutual friend, a twenty-four-year-old princess with the operatic name of Olimpia Torlonia dei Principi de Civitella-Cesi. She was married to a wealthy French oil magnate and was none other than the sister of the investment banker politely turned away by Audrey. During an indolent cruise to Greece, Andrea had swiftly charmed Audrey out of depression; indeed, the so-called depressive personality in women was his clinical specialty.

That encounter took place on the *principessa*'s schooner in June, and shortly thereafter, Audrey rang Givenchy. "I'm in love and happy again," she confided. "I never believed it would happen to me. I had almost given up." She saw her designer in Paris that autumn. "After she met Monsieur Dotti," he recalled, "she began to perk up—oh, not full-cheeked, of course, that's not Audrey. But [she was] happy, and her body began to show it."

When did the relationship become serious? "Somewhere between Ephesus and Athens," Andrea said—on Olimpia's love boat. "It was not, however, that the Signora Hepburn came to cry on my shoulder about the breakup of her marriage, or that I gave her comfort as a psychiatrist. It was none of this. We were playmates [!] on a cruise ship with other friends, and slowly, day by day, our relationship grew into what it is."

What it was, was a whirlwind courtship. They met several times in Rome, and once or twice Andrea came to La Paisible to meet Sean, but the lovers' customary weekend hideaway was a friend's cottage on the island of Giglio. On Christmas Eve, Andrea presented Audrey with a solitaire diamond ring from Bulgari. She accepted his proposal on the spot.

To Audrey's closest friends, everything happened with alarming rapidity—especially when the couple wed, on January 5, 1969, just six weeks after she signed her final divorce decree. Givenchy designed a short-skirted pink jersey dress for her, with a cowl collar and a matching foulard tied under her chin. "I have married a man whose culture is unlimited and whose conversation is endlessly fascinating," said the bride after the ceremony, held in the town hall of Morges, near La Paisible.

It was the first marriage for Andrea, who had enjoyed a busy bachelorhood, often escorting wealthy, titled or merely good-looking women. Officially, Audrey was now La Contessa Dotti, but using that title was no more a consideration than her title of baroness.

Andrea's mother was just fourteen years older than Audrey. She helped train the bride in the fine points of Italian cooking and introduced her to the large Dotti family. "Andrea," said his mother ominously, "has two distinct personalities. He's very serious and very social. I used to call him Dr. Jekyll, because he shut himself off for hours to study. Then, when his work was done, he was very witty and social and dying to go out. I always encouraged my boys to have a good time when young. If you start life too late, it's awkward, and you never have good manners." This was not merely the amusing, somewhat paralogical repartee of an up-to-date Italian mamma—it was also something of a cautionary comment, for Andrea was long accustomed to "having a good time."

"OF COURSE WE will all live together," the doctor told a journalist that winter. "I will try to be a good companion to Sean. I will play with him. I will teach him things he doesn't know and above all I will love him. We will be a happy family."

At first, Andrea's mother offered two floors of her own house, a cozy palazzo. Wisely and with thanks, Audrey and Andrea declined, and soon they found a penthouse with a wide view over Rome. Audrey delivered Sean to the Lycée Chateaubriand in the mornings and met him in the afternoons, and for a time the three lived together in what seemed an easy rapport.

But to Audrey's astonishment, Andrea began to grant an occasional press interview, and he did not discourage the ubiquitous paparazzi who were never far from their door and even popped up outside Sean's school. Audrey loathed those moments, but Andrea thought it was all very amusing and glamorous. Alas, he went further: of course his wife would return to films, he told journalists: "She is a great actress, and it would be criminal to deprive her of something she loves." Indeed, Dotti had captured a star for a wife, and he expected that she would continue to be his trophy as one of the world's most alluring celebrities.

She was in training to be an Italian housewife and, she hoped, eventually a mother to Andrea's son. "I worked nonstop from when I was twelve until I was thirty-eight," she said. "I feel a need to relax, sleep in the morning, take care of my child. Why should I resume the work and life I rejected?"

Why, indeed—especially when she learned of her pregnancy in June of that year?

Audrey kept the house in Tolochenaz, which was hers according to the divorce terms, and where she and Sean spent many weekends and school holidays in retreat from the constant pursuit of photographers. At first, Andrea regularly accompanied them to Switzerland, but professional obligations required him to remain in Rome, even on weekends. To avoid yet another mishap, Audrey spent the last ten weeks confined mostly to bed at La Paisible. In Lausanne, on February 8, 1970, she underwent a cesarean operation and gave birth to a boy she and Andrea named Luca, after his younger brother.

The Dottis were, for the present, the picture of a happy couple with their two children, and Audrey said she would be glad to have more. But her doctors, considering her age and history, advised against that. Said Andrea: "You shouldn't tempt the devil."

But it wasn't Audrey who was assailed by temptation. While she spent a quiet life with her boys at La Paisible and waited for her husband's weekend or monthly visit, he continued to work in Rome by day and to frolic by night, often in the company of glamorous women. These were colleagues, he protested—or former patients, or advanced students. In any case, Audrey thought it better to return to Rome in May with the two boys and to devote herself to family life. This seemed, for a time, to temper her husband's schedule. Exhausted after the cesarean delivery and the Swiss winter, she was glad to have their household staff. And with no financial or psychological incentive to work, she did not. Scripts were duly forwarded by her agent, she read them, and dutifully they were returned.

In the autumn of 1970, Audrey was approached by a European representative of UNICEF, the United Nations Children's Fund. Would she be willing to appear in a special Christmas television program? Audrey would have simply to be seen briefly with a group of youngsters, singing with them and greeting the hosts of the program in New York. The program was to be called *A World of Love.*

She readily agreed, and on December 22, 1970, she was seen in America for the first time in three years. She sang and spoke in flawless Italian with the children—many of them rescued from dire poverty—and then she led them in song. The filmed record of that brief appearance shows the children crowding around her, competing for the chance to hold her hand, while Audrey reaches out and gathers them into her capacious embrace.

Part Four

ENCHANTMENT
[1971–1993]

Chapter Fifteen

⁓

1971–1986

"I'M AFRAID I may have nothing to express in a movie, since I'm much fulfilled at home," Audrey said in 1971.

Home was the Dottis' penthouse, a busy spot in the center of Rome. Once a cardinal's residence, it measured about fifteen thousand square feet and had soaring ceilings and painted frescoes. The place easily accommodated the parents, two boys, a live-in staff and vast company for dinners—which were frequent, as Andrea loved to entertain colleagues while stepping into the limelight to exhibit his famous wife. They eventually sold the penthouse and relocated to a smaller but no less sumptuous apartment in a neighborhood that had more abundant parks and trees nearby. For herself, Audrey preferred less exhausting social events like small dinners for old friends visiting Rome—the Pecks, the Wylers, the Zinnemanns and Kate and Lou, for example.

Among Audrey's closest confidantes was the beautiful but ill-fated movie star known as Capucine. Born Germaine Lefebvre, she had been briefly married as a teenager and then went on to bedazzle a legion of men—most notably, William Holden, with whom she made two movies. Audrey and Capucine had more in common than a past lover: they were both prone to bouts of serious depression, and at such times they offered each other a sympathetic listening. While Audrey found that either work or love (or loving duties) was an effective remedy, Capucine was often close to suicide and counted very much on Audrey's empathetic friendship. From the 1960s, she lived in Lausanne, not far from La Paisible, and when she was in good spirits, she, too, was a sensible and compassionate companion on whom Audrey could rely.

Audrey doted on her sons. "She did all the things that mothers do," according to Sean: she awakened them in the morning, helped with their schoolwork, read to them, took them to the movies and arranged for them to visit friends. "She used to surprise my friends with how casual she was," recalled Luca. "They expected something incredible, and instead they found just a nice person." According to Sean, "she was also clear about what she expected of us . . . [and she] was as gentle as she was strong—the velvet glove and the iron hand." For the boys' sake, she refused, for the moment, to resume her career. But she did accept a lucrative offer to make four one-minute commercials in a Rome studio for Exlan, a Tokyo wig manufacturer: she received more than $1 million for a half-day's work. That was the only time she was paid to appear before cameras in the eight years between April 1967 and May 1975.

BY 1974, AUDREY's life had all the appearances of an enviably comfortable routine. She had enough money to satisfy both her needs and her caprices; her sons were healthy and well mannered; and she was the respected Signora la Contessa, the celebrated actress who had married an esteemed physician. If the paparazzi would just leave her and the boys in peace, she said . . .

That year, Italy was traumatized by a kind of political unrest that often turned vicious and even homicidal. A wave of thefts and assaults affected many wealthy and politically active families, and many children of celebrities were besieged by kidnappings and subsequent calls for ransom. Andrea was very nearly abducted at gunpoint near his office, but he was quickly saved by nearby *carabinieri*. Thereafter, the Dottis were always accompanied by a bodyguard or two.

Audrey felt that life in Italy was starting to resemble wartime Holland, and she did not want her boys to be in jeopardy or to live amid violence. Thus fourteen-year-old Sean followed Audrey and Mel's suggestion that he attend a Swiss boarding school. Luca was only four and of course was not to be sent away to school, but the brutalities in Rome were increasing as the so-called Red Brigade swung into action. With that, the Dottis agreed that the boy would be safer with Audrey in Tolochenaz, which she essentially made her primary residence. This decision was both logical and reasonable at the time, and for a while, Andrea traveled back and forth on weekends. That summer, at age forty-five, Audrey was again pregnant—and for the fifth time, she miscarried.

Simultaneously, the formidable Baroness van Heemstra gave up her home in San Francisco and came to live with Audrey. For over a decade, she had worked raising funds to help train Vietnam veterans in peacetime jobs. For a brief time, Ella was her daughter's de facto chief of staff at La Paisible, assuming the role of manager and putting to good use her experience as a London concierge. But she was, as Sean said, "a grande dame," and while Audrey made a comfortable life for her mother, "their personalities were not well suited." Ella turned seventy-four that year, and soon her health began to fail; over the next decade, she required ever more medical attention.

"I am incredibly busy," Audrey told a journalist early in 1975. "People always ask me if I'm not bored just being a wife and mother. I'm not—not at all . . . I think you need time to live, to invest in the things you care for the most. For me, that is raising my boys. Children grow up by themselves, of course, but they do need to be given love. That they can't do by themselves."

In January 1975, Frings sent yet another screenplay for her to consider, and this time, Audrey was not so quick to reject the project. James Goldman had written a witty and touching script about the middle-aged Robin Hood and Maid Marian, years after their colorful youth. He has returned from the Crusades, battered and weary, to find that she has become a nun and the abbess of a community in the English countryside. The wicked sheriff of Nottingham still scours Sherwood Forest in search of revenge against Robin and his merry men, for Little John has survived, along with Friar Tuck and Will Scarlett.

Goldman had written the award-winning play and film *The Lion in Winter*, about Henry II; his wife, Eleanor of Aquitaine; and their sons, all pretenders to the English throne in the twelfth century. Among the distinctive achievements of *Lion* was its fidelity to history and medieval life, on the one hand; and the bold use of modern English diction and humor, on the other. Goldman had brilliantly brought Henry and Eleanor to life as figures who were larger than life and altered the course of history, yet who bickered, bargained and plotted like any family caught in the fierce throes of politics. In contrast, the main characters of *Robin and Marian*, for all their verisimilitude, were legendary. History itself was at stake in the earlier film; only the resumption of romance mattered in the new film. However sincere its charm and its understanding of the poignant impossibility of recapturing youthful passion, the new script was mostly a star vehicle.

Goldman's screenplay appealed to Audrey perhaps because she saw Marian as a woman like herself. Each had given up one life for another that was radically different, and each had found that, however introverted, she still hankered for romance. She also liked the idea of the fee that was offered—$1 million for thirty-six days of work. "It's not that she was destitute," said Robert Wolders, who was later her companion, "but she had to replenish her coffers." There were, after all, the expenses of La Paisible and of her mother; and Audrey decided to buy another property, a small chalet in Gstaad.

The director of *Robin and Marian* was to be Richard Lester, who was especially skilled with stories that required a delicate blend of comedy and swift action and famous for two films starring the Beatles. Her leading man was Sean Connery, and the cast included Robert Shaw, Nicol Williamson, Denholm Elliott and Kenneth Haigh—all of them dependable British players. The film was scheduled to be made in Spain between late May and early July, which seemed to Audrey an astoundingly quick plan. "Because my husband encouraged me to do it," she packed for Spain—accompanied by Luca and his nanny; her personal hairdresser; her makeup artist; and an assistant. She also went with "stomach aches and clammy hands, because after all those years, I didn't know what to expect."

The press, of course, buzzed with news of the so-called comeback of Audrey Hepburn. "I never said that I was going to quit acting, to retire," she said defensively. "Retirement means that if you do another picture, that's a 'comeback.' I'm not having a comeback. I may never make another movie!" One of the reasons she had enjoyed the long hiatus, she added, was that she always found acting before the cameras a nerve-wracking business. "I'm always nervous when I start a picture. You take an awful chance every time you make a film. You never know how it's going to come out."

That must have occurred to her many times during the brief but trying weeks in the forest and fields near Navarre. For one thing, she did not like the rapidity of it all—one or two takes, and that was it for Lester, who knew what he wanted and was not at all interested in protracting the romantic elements of the story. Audrey had been accustomed to a longer time for shooting multiple takes and for discussions with the cameraman as to what might be her best look in a particular scene. None of that seemed to matter here.

Nor was she amused or impressed when, during a sequence in which she was to drive a wagon through a shallow river, the horse and cart turned over, and she and three other actors were plunged into knee-deep water. Recognizing a superb bit of comedy that he could never have planned and implemented, Lester kept the camera rolling, sent Connery in to improvise dialogue, and included the scene in the picture to great comic effect—and to Audrey's outspoken dismay. "It was actually very frightening even though the water wasn't deep," she recalled. "With those heavy nuns' habits getting waterlogged and pulling us down, it made things difficult."

She was equally frustrated when she had a bout of laryngitis one day and could manage only a gravelly rasp. No matter, said Lester: much if not most of the picture would have to be postsynchronized in a recording studio in any case. But when he heard the scene as recorded, he felt her hoarseness was right for the tender scene with Nicol Williamson. The director's biographer documented the production: "Down to the smallest detail, like having to make do with an aluminum chair from her trailer instead of the canvas variety normally provided, Hepburn let it be known, albeit in her supremely ladylike manner, that she was used to better things."

Richard Shepherd, who had produced *Breakfast at Tiffany's* and who now had the same function for *Robin and Marian,* said at the time, "Audrey could get along with Hitler, but Lester is not in her scrapbook of unforgettable characters." If this was the new wave of filmmaking, she did not like it. "I've never made a film so fast, and I would like to have had more time"—perhaps especially since the circumstances of the thirty-six-day shoot made her "petrified the first day," as she said, and "still shivering and shaking before each take."

When released in 1976, the film had mixed reactions from the critics, but Audrey's return was heartily welcomed. She was forty-six when she acted in the picture, and her smooth-skinned loveliness and remarkably youthful features were widely noted.

WHILE IN SPAIN, Audrey caught sight of some European tabloids that featured color photos of her husband, cavorting in this or that nightclub with this or that slinky young woman. They are just friends, said Andrea, who affected shock when she expressed her suspicions after her return to Rome.

For the present, she did not pursue a divorce. "I hung on to both marriages as long as I could, for the children's sake. You always hope that if you love somebody enough, everything will be all right—but it isn't always true." As the summer heat enveloped Rome, she and Luca repaired to La Paisible. "I think she knew from the beginning who [Dotti] was," said Sean, "yet I think she dreamed and hoped that somehow she could change that. And I think she was gravely disappointed when she realized she couldn't." As Audrey later admitted ruefully, "Dotti was not much of an improvement on Ferrer."

According to Sean, Audrey loved both her husbands dearly and sustained her marriages as long as she was able. "What she didn't do was to speak up and be heard when she needed to, and she didn't put up healthy boundaries." He was referring, of course, to Dotti's blatant infidelities: "My stepfather was a brilliant and funny psychiatrist—but he was a hound dog. He just didn't know how to be faithful. Not a good choice of husband if what you are looking for is security."

Audrey was, according to Robert Wolders, "humiliated" by all this. "It was especially painful for her to have a second marriage fail." As for Dotti, he was frank but defensive: "I was no angel. Italian husbands have never been famous for being faithful."

Security was not to be found in her second marriage, but she was not yet prepared to terminate it. Audrey allowed very few friends and no journalists to the Dotti apartment, and when she had to submit to an interview, she went to the home of a friend like Arabella Ungaro. There she met a few reporters when she was promoting *Robin and Marian* early in 1976, telling them, "There's not one drop of tap water in my house today. From June to November, I had no hot water! I had to bathe at my husband's studio. You might say I went to Spain last summer to make *Robin and Marian* just so I could take a bath!"

Audrey agreed to travel to the United States for publicity surrounding *Robin and Marian,* and Andrea accompanied her. In New York, she was scheduled to appear on the *Today* show, but she canceled because she was unfamiliar with the interviewer, Barbara Walters, and no one would promise that her private life would not be discussed. "She must have matters under her control," said Dotti, "and she's afraid of surprises." He was quite right, and when Audrey felt she had lost that control, her anxieties multiplied. Asked to field questions at a press breakfast, she was visibly tense. "Her hands shook noticeably and she smoked without letup," one reporter noted.

That March of 1976, the Dottis proceeded to Los Angeles for the Oscar ceremony, at which she announced the statuette for best picture. "On camera, she was all serene elegance," according to the same reporter, "but backstage, she was so nervous that she lost her purse and then refused to go to the press room after the telecast."

Audrey was happier to attend the American Film Institute's Salute to William Wyler, to whom she paid a gracious tribute. "I'm not trying to be coy," she told a journalist, speaking of Wyler, Wilder, Cukor, Donen and Zinnemann, but I really am a product of those [directors]. I'm no Laurence Olivier, no virtuoso talent. I'm basically rather inhibited and I find it difficult to do things in front of people. What my directors have had in common is that they've made me feel secure, made me feel loved. I depend terribly on them. I was a dancer, and they managed to do something with me as an actress that was pleasing to the public.

By the spring of 1978, Audrey's life with Andrea was effectively over, although she continued to tell the press that she was happily married; the divorce decree would not be final until 1981. She took a small house with a garden, which she loved, according to Sean, "and regarded it as a working garden, cultivating the plants and then using the flowers in our house." The final revelation precipitating her commencement of legal action had been her discovery that, in her absences, Andrea conducted his romantic trysts in their home. "In her mind, this was the greatest failure of her life," according to Robert Wolders. Refusing to believe that she could not change her husband's habits by some sublime force of love, she simply blamed herself. And with that, her depression became so profound that, for perhaps the first time in her life, she seriously considered suicide.

As if on cue to alleviate her deepening despair, a script then came to Audrey's door. At once, she agreed to appear in a movie called *Bloodline* because, she said later, the director was her old friend Terence Young.* That could have been the only reason she accepted a script that was utterly without merit. The immediate catalyst for her quick affirmative reply was twofold: she needed to act like a survivor, and she would be paid over a million dollars.

---

* The film was based on a novel by the popular writer Sidney Sheldon. Evidently he and Paramount believed that his own name in the title would sell tickets, and so it was released as *Sidney Sheldon's Bloodline*. The movie did nothing for the career of the author or anyone in the movie.

The story, filmed between November 1978 and February 1979, took her to New York, Paris, Rome and Sardinia. Luca was enrolled in Rome's Lycée Français and Sean was at a Swiss university, so Audrey agreed to work on location—but for no longer than three weeks at a time, so that she could return home for visits.

At forty-nine, Audrey portrayed a character originally written in Sheldon's novel as a twenty-three-year-old heroine; with a few adjustments, the role was forthwith reshaped for her—that of a woman who inherits a family-owned pharmaceutical house and who is threatened by people with a variety of motives to kill her. No amount of rewriting remedied the witless story and script ("Why would anyone want to do this to you?"). Like Audrey, the other players could not resist the hefty fees offered; her co-stars included Ben Gazzara, James Mason, Irene Papas, Michelle Phillips, Omar Sharif and Beatrice Straight (Audrey's old friend from the cast of *The Nun's Story*).

In addition to the monumentally dreadful story and script, there were multiple problems as filming began. "There was Irene Papas, who kept saying she'd forgotten how to act," recalled Straight, listing the troubles; "and James Mason, muttering he never again wanted to make a film he wasn't also producing and directing; and Audrey, who had come with her own bodyguard but decided that on balance she'd rather be kidnapped by the Mafia than have to complete the picture—so all in all, it wasn't one of the best." Anxious throughout the production, Audrey smoked almost nonstop—on camera as well as off.

She arrived in New York for the first scenes, only to discover that many younger crew members were not quite sure who she was. But her co-stars did, of course—most emphatically, Ben Gazzara, who thought that "something was already happening" at their first casual meeting.

The filming proceeded to a lush spot on the island of Sardinia, where Audrey, almost desperate for affection, was remarkably bold in approaching Gazzara, then still married to the actress Janice Rule. Awaiting his call to the set, he was reading a book when he noticed Audrey standing in front of him. The book, he said, had been good company the previous night, when he could not sleep. She had had trouble sleeping, too, she said, adding: "When it happens to you again, feel free to call me. We'll keep each other company." For the moment, that was that.

Then, in Paris, Audrey and Ben had a kissing scene that was (in his words) "no movie kiss." In Munich, they had lunch together one afternoon, and Audrey confided not only that Andrea had been unfaithful in her absences, but that he had chosen their home for his trysts. She was, she admitted, so distraught that she had seriously contemplated suicide. The relationship was consummated very soon after. "No promises were made," he recalled. "For us it was going to be an 'on-location romance.'" Or so Ben Gazzara intended it to be—"end of movie, end of romance," which, he admitted, was his custom.

Much of the dialogue between Audrey and Ben had to be dubbed in Paris, where the affair continued at the Hôtel Crillon, "a night filled with far more feeling than any other we'd had together." The picture was completed, in early 1979.

When *Bloodline* was released that June, the critics were appalled and the public bored by a movie of remarkable absurdity that might have been better directed by a first-year film student. "Faceless chic . . . bloodless, ludicrous and clumsy" were among the quieter journalistic dismissals. But the best verdict on the picture was delivered in character by the stalwart James Mason: "I can't take any more of it!"

By that time, Terence Young had already signed for his next job, which was to direct a film in Korea; Gazzara was to have a starring role, and none other than Sean was engaged as a production assistant. Hence for Audrey, there were two reasons to visit Korea.

But after Gazzara began his work abroad, he discouraged

Audrey from visiting: by this time, he was involved with a woman named Elke Stuckmann, who would become his third wife. There was no contact between him and Audrey until late that year, when she learned that they were in Rome. "I want to see you," she told him, calling his hotel suite. He replied that he was busy. According to Gazzara, he rang later to offer an explanation. "She answered, but I said nothing. A very long time passed with neither of us saying a word. She didn't say my name. She simply whispered 'Good-bye.' "

"Obviously I wasn't in love," Gazzara explained later. "I was flattered that someone like that would be in love with me. But I didn't know how deeply she was in love with me until I left her. She told others, not me, that I had broken her heart. She was so kind and sweet. And I hurt her."

About this time, director Peter Bogdanovich sent to Ben (with whom he had already collaborated) the first draft of his new script, called *They All Laughed*. In considerable detail, Gazzara told Bogdanovich about his affair with Audrey. "I took note of it all," said the director, "and used this for the character she eventually played opposite Gazzara in *They All Laughed* . . . Her real life became the inspiration for the character I [re]wrote for her in our picture: a woman devoted to her young son, braving a jealous, philandering husband on the boy's behalf, finds respite in a brief but intense love affair."

Meanwhile, when Audrey learned that Ben would be in the picture, she signed on at once, unwilling to abandon hope of some sort of continuing liaison with him—and perhaps not paying much attention to the script then being rewritten. But as the new pages arrived, she agreed to participate, Gazzara said, "to play out our romance on the screen." Perhaps she assented to perform (in what was now so obviously a template of her own life) for the salary: $1 million for six weeks of work, plus a generous account for expenses. With her presence guaranteed, *They All Laughed* was scheduled for production in late spring and early summer 1980. Bogdanovich also hired Sean as his personal assistant and gave him a small role in the film, a gesture that of course pleased Audrey.

In early 1980, as filming approached, a brief meeting between Audrey and Ben convinced her that the relationship was over. At once, she reneged on her promise to participate in *They All Laughed*. That seriously threatened the film's prospects—no Audrey, no film, many unemployed people, Sean out of a job and a lot for her to justify publicly, as she would have to defend an action unprecedented in her career. After some thought, she recanted her withdrawal and made the picture, which was shot in New York between April and July 1980. "Audrey showed a lot of courage," according to Ben Gazzara. That was as it may have been, but at that point he did not know that another man had replaced him in Audrey's affections, and that she could now, with more equanimity, perform her unusually explicit love scenes with Ben.

"AGEING DOESN'T BOTHER ME, but loneliness does," she had said in the autumn of 1979, when she was fifty and working with Ben, for whom her love had been unrequited.

After the divorce from Mel Ferrer, Audrey had been, as Givenchy said, "miserable." In 1968, not yet forty and no longer being offered sympathetic roles, she had embarked on a somewhat frantic period of nervous socializing in Rome. Then, in little more than a whirl of quixotic and ill-advised romance the following year, Audrey had married a much younger man with style and professional credentials—a man who flattered her ego, to be sure, but who eventually could not conform to her idea of a proper husband.

Benighted William Holden, who was often overwhelmed by his demons, could not have given her the children she so desired—nor could Robert Anderson, who in any case was steeped in grief over his wife's recent death. The affair with Albert Finney ended over the strong likelihood of a threat to her relationship with Sean. And then there was Ben Gazzara, who saw his time with Audrey as a pleasant, short-term escapade with no further responsibility. Reviewing her passionate life, she might have thought that she had not been, as the saying goes, lucky in love.

But just after Christmas 1979, Audrey was introduced at a dinner party to a man named Robert Wolders. Born Robertus Jacobus Godefridus Wolders in Rotterdam, the Netherlands, in 1936, he had acted in a few television programs and movies before he met Merle Oberon, the leading lady in his last picture. Six feet tall and attractive, with expressive green eyes, subtle humor and a keen mind, Wolders was an asset at any Hollywood gathering and enormously appealing to Oberon, who was twenty-five years his senior. In 1975, after their joint work on a picture, they were married and lived at her home in Malibu until her death at the age of sixty-eight in November 1979.

Of the evening Audrey and Wolders met, she said, "I was charmed with him, but he didn't register much. We were both very unhappy: he was getting over the death of Merle, and I was in one of the worst periods of my life, the low ebb of divorce. So we both cried into our beers." Fortunately for them, they could communicate in their native Dutch as well as their expressive English, and their shared national background was no small element in the formation of a bond.

"I got a kick out of exchanging a few words with her in Dutch," Wolders recalled. "But I thought that would be it."

In the spring of 1980, Audrey was in New York, in residence at the Hotel Pierre during the production of *They All Laughed;* Wolders was in Los Angeles. She rang Rob, after which he told himself, "That's it—I have to go to New York." He did so. "We had to be very discreet. She was still married, even though unhappily, to Andrea. Eventually, we realized the only thing to do was for me to move to Europe and live in Switzerland."

THEY ALL LAUGHED did not find much favor with critics or audiences, who were confused by the bittersweet and not very interesting stories of several not very interesting couples. The action was badly paced, frenetic one moment and languid the next, and it was difficult for audiences to know just how they were to feel about anyone. Those aware of Audrey's real-life affair with Ben Gazzara—politely alleged by gossip columnists at the time—may well have felt a sort of winking guilt, especially during the embarrassing and awkward bedroom sequence.

But the real crime of the picture was that it gave Audrey no chance to appear anything other than bored. She trotted around the streets of Manhattan in a state of blank bemusement, wearing a black jacket, very tight jeans, stiletto-heeled leather boots and huge dark glasses—a Manhattan disco denizen aiming for the high life but reaching into low dives and bedrooms with the private detective hired to pursue her. "Mr. Bogdanovich treats Audrey Hepburn so shabbily," wrote the *New York Times* movie critic, "that if this were a marriage instead of a movie, she'd have grounds for divorce." As for the male lead: "Mr. Gazzara can't even smile convincingly." Evidently, the critic did not know why.

A tragic corollary of the production was also the most unhelpful element in the film's unfortunate destiny. Bogdanovich, then forty-one, had met and fallen in love with a twenty-year-old *Playboy* model named Dorothy Stratten, whom he cast in his picture. At the time, she was married to an unbalanced hustler named Paul Snider. Two weeks after Bogdanovich completed filming, she moved into the director's home and told Snider she was leaving him. On August 14, he lured her to their former apartment, assaulted her and then shot her to death and turned the rifle on himself. Despite Audrey's name, this negative publicity made it impossible for the director to find a distributor until late the following year.

In July, just after Audrey returned from filming in New York, Ella suffered a third stroke. "I have just brought her back from the hospital," Audrey wrote to her father's wife, Fidelma. "I have been nursing her day and night, her heart is very bad and she has just had a third stroke . . . I have been struggling to find a way to come to see Daddy—but everything always happens at once! . . . Added to all this, my marriage is in bad shape so am suffering on all sides . . . I am very torn about all this, but I can only do the best I can."

To Audrey's relief, the infirm Ella liked Rob when he arrived. "There was some tension between Audrey and her mother," he recalled, "because her mother was very strict and severe and had difficulty showing all the affection she felt—and she felt a great deal for Audrey, but she couldn't express it. So she would use me as a conduit because she knew I would convey all that she felt to Audrey, plus she was very tickled by the fact that we could speak Dutch."

The life Audrey and Rob shared had a quiet, almost elegiac routine. They rose early, took a light breakfast, walked their Jack Russell terriers, puttered in the garden, read the mail and newspapers and shopped for meals at the local market. After a light lunch, they had an afternoon siesta, and then Audrey allowed herself a piece of chocolate, took a stroll through nearby vineyards and returned to the house. She did a few household chores, strolling about with her pack of cigarettes and her nightly drink of scotch before dinner. In the evening, she and Rob watched tapes of favorite television shows, and they retired early. This was not the madcap life of jet-set celebrities but the serene style of retired country gentlefolk. Only rarely did a special event lure them to Paris, Rome, New York or Los Angeles—an awards ceremony for her or a close colleague (William Wyler and Fred Astaire, for example), or a few days of work that paid handsomely.* Almost always, she traveled with her dogs, and when airline attendants objected, she prevailed. "It's the only time I act like Audrey Hepburn the movie star," she said.

In 1981, a sad episode brought them to Dublin, where Audrey's father, then ninety-two, was also failing. Since 1959, they had met only once, when he and Fidelma accepted her invitation to visit La Paisible. His withdrawn, remote attitude was unchanged even in his last days, and doctors said they had no idea how long he would linger. Audrey and Rob departed after two days, during which Ruston (like Ella) could admit his regrets and proclaim his pride in her only by speaking these sentiments to others. He died within the week.

In the summer of 1982, at the time her final divorce decree from Andrea was announced, Audrey's dear friend Cathleen Nesbitt died at ninety-three. Ella finally succumbed in August 1984, after ten years of devoted care by Audrey and her staff. All during her adulthood, Audrey had sent gifts of cash to her parents and paid for extraordinary care when necessary.

"I was lost without my mother," Audrey said later. "She had been my sounding board, my conscience. She was not the most affectionate person—in fact there were times when I thought she was cold—but she loved me in her heart, and I knew that all along. I never got that feeling from my father, unfortunately."

There were other losses, too, and they affected Audrey very deeply. William Wyler and Kathryn Hulme died in 1981, George Cukor in 1983 and Marie Louise Habets in 1986. Each of them had

---

* Between 1968 and 1992, she received no less than nineteen tributes and awards, five of them for her humanitarian work.

grown closer to her during the years after their collaborations; each was in a way a parent figure; each had cherished and encouraged Audrey. Her memories of them were indelible, and their names were often in her conversations.

In 1986, AUDREY took a role in her only movie made for television—*Love Among Thieves*, directed by Roger Young. He arrived at La Paisible late one afternoon to discuss the production, and his hosts offered him a drink. He thought he should decline—but not after Audrey piped up, "Well, *I'm* having a drink!" Over glasses of Glenlivet, they talked about the shooting schedule in Arizona and California.

Later, in Los Angeles, the cast gathered for a script reading at the home of Robert Wagner, who was starring with Audrey. Everyone seemed pleased, but during a break in the reading, she motioned to Roger Young to step outside for a moment. "Listen, Roger," she whispered, "R. J. [Wagner's nickname among close friends and colleagues] is really a big television star. You've got to help me—I can't let him down!" He calmed her nerves and insisted that she would, of course, be splendid in the production. Later that afternoon, R. J. motioned to Roger to step outside for a moment: "Roger, you've got to help me! That is Audrey Hepburn in there— she's a major movie star, and I don't want to let her down!"

According to Young, neither one let the other down. "The script [by Stephen Black and Henry Stern] was written with the Audrey of *Breakfast at Tiffany's* in mind—and this impossible anachronism was what the producer demanded."

The early scenes were appropriately filmed with Audrey's character as her own age, which was fifty-eight in 1987—and that is what she preferred to play. But despite Audrey and Roger's disagreement with him, the producer saw the first scenes and insisted on turning back the clock. "She said she would try to please him,"

Young recalled, "but she understandably became more and more uncomfortable with the project. And she was proven right by the critics, who were incensed that the movie had taken away the mature Audrey Hepburn and made her dance on the end of a string as a younger version of herself." The film was not what it should have been, said Young, and he assumed full responsibility for it; years later, he said, "I let her down, and it pains me to this day." Audrey felt, quite rightly, that the blame was not Young's but the producer's.

As for Robert Wagner, an actor held in high and affectionate regard, he very much enjoyed reviving a friendship with Audrey that had begun years earlier, when they were young players at Paramount. "She was not merely wonderful to work with," he recalled, adding memories of his visits to her and Rob at La Paisible. "Everything about her that was so good was reflected in her home, her furniture, the art, the flowers—even her dogs. And her kindness was extraordinary, not just to me but to everyone on the production. And of course she was so good, always a loyal friend staying in touch with Capucine, who was going through so many bad times. She raised the bar for everyone, and I felt so blessed to visit her at home in the years after our movie, and to have her friendship."

After *Love Among Thieves* was broadcast on February 23, 1987, it vanished from the network's library, and no viewing copy was available in any television archive as late as 2005. As for Capucine, she later committed suicide at her home in Lausanne at the age of fifty-nine.

Chapter Sixteen

1987–1990

IN THE AUTUMN of 1987, Audrey and Rob took a holiday trip to the Far East. One of her cousins, working in the diplomatic corps at Macao, on the Chinese coast, had invited her to be an honored guest at the International Music Festival held there, which had scheduled a concert benefiting the United Nations Children's Fund. She and Rob gladly agreed to include the event in their schedule.

Founded in 1946, UNICEF works to save, protect and improve the lives of children in more than 160 countries by making available immunization, education, health care, nutrition, sanitation and clean water. Funded entirely by voluntary contributions from individuals, foundations, businesses and governments, it has always been nonpartisan and nonprofit and has, since its inception, worked free of discrimination and without political agenda. UNICEF's priority has always been to meet the needs of the most disadvantaged children in the neediest places of the world; in this regard, it has responded to the results of natural disasters as well as civil and international strife.

"Due to my own early experiences, I can testify to what UNICEF means to children," Audrey told the audience at the festival. "I have kept a long-lasting gratitude to them and a trust in what they can do." Her remarks were brief but deeply felt, and she was besieged by the press to elaborate.

From Macao, she and Rob proceeded to Tokyo, where Audrey had also agreed to be mistress of ceremonies for a concert by the World Philharmonic Orchestra, again because they were performing a benefit for UNICEF. Christa Roth, who was special events coordinator for UNICEF and its goodwill ambassadors, met them in Tokyo, arranged the details and very quickly became Audrey's close friend and confidante. "She was so natural, relaxed and beautiful," Christa recalled. "It seemed inevitable that everyone would pay attention to her, and they did. She started by putting me at ease—there was nothing of the prima donna, nothing of the great movie star or fashion icon about her. She was just there to help a cause she believed in."

Christa had arranged a press conference at the hotel, where Audrey, who had done her homework, introduced the orchestra members and discussed the work of UNICEF. "We had picked a room that accommodated about twenty-five or thirty members of the press," Christa recalled. "But we looked outside and saw a line around the corner, so we had to move to the ballroom. Her effect on people in Japan was phenomenal. She had always been a fashion idol for Japanese girls, and now the international press discovered that she was also a serious woman with serious concerns." That day, according to Christa, was like a national event.

"I guess everyone reaches a point in his life where he wants to find out who he is and what he wants his life to be," Audrey said. Back at La Paisible for Christmas, she reached that point. Was there not something more she could do for UNICEF? In her own estimation, her career had begun to fade in her mind like a watercolor exposed to the sun—perhaps especially in the harsh light of the essential silliness of her recent movies. She was paid exceedingly well for them, and so there was no anxiety for her own and her family's future. But now that Sean was twenty-seven and Luca seventeen and she seemed comfortably settled with Rob, what would attract her energy, and what was the deepest need of her nature? She was fifty-eight, and she wanted—indeed, needed—a new and deeper purpose in her life. She was, as Kate Hulme had said, hungry for something more.

Her visits to Macao and Tokyo guided her in the right direction. As she had said so often since her own childhood, she was drawn to care for children when she was little more than one herself; she had longed to be a mother and would, had she been able, have borne several more. "I've been given an enormous privilege," she said as she began to alter her entire life that season. "It's to speak for those children who can't speak for themselves. It's an easy task, because children have no enemies. To save a child would be such a blessing."

"And so she came to us," Christa said. "She said that if she could give her name and her fame to UNICEF in such a way that it would help our work, she wanted to do that. That was how it began."

At first, UNICEF officials in New York and Geneva said they would be pleased if Audrey would be a kind of media symbol, making public statements, being mistress of ceremonies at fund-raising dinners or gala benefits or appearing in television or radio announcements asking for donations.

But that was not her way. She insisted on taking her cue from the actor Danny Kaye, UNICEF's first goodwill ambassador: from 1954 almost to his death in 1987, he had traveled the world on behalf of suffering children. Her fame, Audrey reasoned, had a clear benefit she could now exploit. She could attract attention—and so she would focus the eyes of the world on what was necessary to save the poor, the starving, the uneducated, the abused children everywhere. She could speak for those who had no forum; she could approach those in power and beg—even demand—that whatever hostilities engaged men running powerful nations, children everywhere must not be blithely permitted to suffer for the sins of the elders.

ON MARCH 1, 1988, Audrey wrote her formal application to be accepted as a goodwill ambassador for UNICEF. Answering the pages of questions, she gave a summary of her background and early life, her dance studies, her witness to the German invasion of Holland, the tragedies of her family, the deprivations of wartime, the Battle of Arnhem—and her clear memory of the relief provided in 1945 by the Red Cross and UNRRA. She informed UNICEF that she was a citizen of the United Kingdom, that she traveled on a British passport and that she was fluent in English, Dutch, French and Italian.

On the application form, she was asked to reply to the question "Why do you come to UNICEF?" Her answer sealed her acceptance: "I have always accepted opportunities to help whenever offered [to] me, such as Christmas-card sales, Christmas TV fundraising in Rome, the Macao Music Festival and the 'Music and Peace' Concert by the World Philharmonic Orchestra in Tokyo— all benefiting UNICEF." She concluded: "I have been offered by UNICEF an opportunity to assist with any project on which I might be useful—this is for me an immense privilege and an answer to my longing to help *children* in whatever small way I can." That might have been Sister Luke's reply to the question "Why do you want to go to the children of the Congo?"

A week later, she received word of her appointment as a goodwill ambassador for UNICEF, for which she would receive the compensation of one American dollar per year. Her travel expenses would be paid by the organization and its contributors, but they would be at nothing like celebrity status, because the funds were supervised by the United Nations itself. Often, the lowest fares and accommodations had to be sought, which meant many stops before reaching a destination.

Eight days after her acceptance and a series of immunization injections, Audrey and Rob set off to visit the east African nation of Ethiopia, then the poorest nation in the world. The degree of personal risk here was very high, as there were epidemics of bacterial diarrhea, hepatitis, typhoid fever, malaria, rabies and meningitis. "She and Rob traveled in military planes, sitting on sacks of rice," recalled Christa Roth. "She asked for no special considerations, and she got none." The goal of the trip was to call attention to the severe drought conditions there, and, according to UNICEF archives, Audrey received more media coverage than any goodwill ambassador in its history.

She visited the Ouiha Health Center and, with an interpreter's help, spoke with mothers and children as well as the doctor of the makeshift clinic. She walked through a refugee camp, where people attempted to loosen the dried soil for planting; she took parched and hungry children in her arms; she discussed with people the construction methods they used when they had cash gifts for water projects. "I'm very impressed by the people of Ethiopia," she said at a press conference that evening,

> and by their beauty, by their dignity, by their patience and by their enormous desire and will to help themselves—not simply to sit there waiting . . . They deserve help not only because they are the poorest people in the world and are receiving the least aid, but because they are a brave people and they do so much for themselves.

And then she told the press about UNICEF: "There aren't any banners saying, 'This is a UNICEF project.' The important thing is that, given the spade that UNICEF can give them, they will dig a well. What we have to make sure is that they don't use the spade to dig graves for their children."

Next day, Audrey again met with the press.

Surely caring is better than killing. We care for our own children when they go through a crisis, when they have an accident or are stricken by disease—not only during that moment, but also through what may be a fairly long convalescence. If we can do that for our own children, I certainly think we can do it for all those silent children that I saw yesterday and today at the refugee camp. And I firmly believe that those children are our sacred charge.

As she said to a reporter from *Time* magazine, "It is a menacing emergency here now [in Ethiopia]. As Gandhi said, 'Wars cannot be won by bullets, but only by bleeding hearts.' I think we can help all these beautiful, silent children."

Her colleagues at UNICEF were at once impressed by a major difference between Audrey's work for them and that of other volunteers. It is standard procedure that celebrities, like politicians and others, read speeches prepared and written by experts. But Audrey researched and wrote her own texts, preparing and rewriting her remarks both for the press and for her UNICEF reports. At home, she read books and journals about the country she was to visit, studying like a scholar preparing for an important examination—and then, after her research, she put questions, in writing or by telephone, to her colleagues at UNICEF headquarters. "You can't just get up and say, 'Oh, I'm happy to be here, and I love children,'" Audrey said of her homework. "No, it's not enough to know that there's been a flood in Bangladesh and seven thousand people lost their lives. *Why* the flood? What is their history? Why are they one of the poorest countries today? How are they going to survive? Are they getting enough help? What are the statistics? What are their problems?"

Christa Roth recalled Audrey's method in preparing her talks and remarks for press conferences and fund-raisers. "Sometimes the New York office sent rough speeches for her, or an outline, and then she wrote a new one in longhand—and in large print, because she preferred not to use her glasses when she glanced at her remarks."

The organization's central archives contain an enormous cache of material relevant to Audrey Hepburn's voluntary tenure with UNICEF—hundreds of pages in her clear handwriting, speeches written and rewritten, notes added and removed, books and articles noted and referenced, questions put to UNICEF staff. "When I visit sick children and then report to their community leaders or to the press," she noted in one report, "they know that I'm with UNICEF, and that thrills them more than *Breakfast at Tiffany's*."

When someone objected that there have always been suffering children and there always will be—and that perhaps one merely prolonged that suffering by treating them, Audrey had a quick response: "Okay, let's start with your grandchild. Don't buy antibiotics if he gets pneumonia; don't take him to the hospital if he has an accident. It's against life, against humanity, to think that way!"

That year, Audrey began to travel on a United Nations passport, as "Audrey K. Hepburn." And to Horst Cerni, a UNICEF photographer, she wrote after her first four trips: "I am tickled pink by my little red U.N. passport!!!! It's a sore temptation not to 'show off' with it . . . UNICEF is keeping me going—and young!"

Over the next five years, her schedule never spared her energies, and 1988 provides an example of the actions she undertook on behalf of UNICEF—work that filled seven to eight months of every year. "I auditioned for this job for forty-five years," she said, "and finally I got it. I always felt very powerless when I saw the terrible pictures on television. But I was offered a wonderful opportunity to do something."

Early in her travels, some former colleagues were astonished. "Never in a million years would I have predicted that Audrey would give so much, so selflessly and at such personal cost to a cause like UNICEF," said Stanley Donen. "In the years we made movies together, Audrey was much more concentrated on her own work and its gratifications. So this is a true evolution. Audrey's really grown up; she's come of age and entered another stage of life where her concern for others extends beyond her concern for herself."

"No," countered Rex Harrison, "it's just the sort of thing she would do. She was brought up in Holland during the war, remember. That's a very different sort of background from American kids. She understands the urgency of hunger and deprivation in a personal, immediate way."

Leaving Ethiopia on March 18, she and Rob spent a week at home, where Audrey prepared for a trip to New York. On March 23, she gave a press conference at UNICEF's Manhattan headquarters. Thirty-five journalists were present, and after their questions were answered, she gave three individual interviews. The same day, she appeared on two network television programs to discuss the needs of the Ethiopian people, and on the twenty-fourth, she was driven to the two major morning programs for the same purpose. Four more television appearances were on the schedule that day, and between interviews, she recorded television appeals for UNICEF, attended an advocacy luncheon and went to an evening reception for major contributors. The workday lasted twenty hours.

This schedule would have wearied even an ambitious political candidate, but Audrey did not stop. The next day, March 25, she attended a congressional breakfast in Washington, met with members of the Foreign Affairs Committee and fielded questions from the Washington press corps; she also gave interviews on no less than six radio shows. On Saturday morning, March 26, she and Rob flew to Toronto, where reporters were at first more interested in her career than in humanitarian endeavors. She smiled graciously and deflected those questions, instead going straight to the issue of Ethiopia's desperate need for water. "Miss Hepburn was fully forthcoming with answers—even to tough political questions," reported George Kassis of UNICEF's Canadian Committee. After the press conference, she granted nine interviews and made three media appearances.

On the twenty-seventh, she flew to London for an eight-day fund-raising tour and the next day was seen on nine British television programs.

"I was a little cynical about the set-up at first," wrote one British journalist who trailed her around London,

but as soon as Ms. Hepburn began speaking, all doubts fell away. Her commitment is passionate and sincere. She seemed near tears as she talked about "the heart-rending and also heart-warming" sights she had seen in Ethiopia. Someone asked a rather hostile question about the Ethiopian government's controversial resettlement policy, but Ms. Hepburn fielded it intelligently, admitting that the government had panicked in the famine of 1985, but that conditions were now improving.

Later that afternoon, during an interview at her hotel, Audrey welcomed the same journalist, while gratefully accepting a large scotch whiskey from Rob. "I'm not a lush," she said, "but I've been up since four and I need a pick-me-up." The reporter noted that she "chain-smoked, too, [and was] clearly ragged with exhaustion."

That day, Audrey spoke of Rob's participation in her new vocation: "We've done all this together. He's just as passionate about it as I am, and so supportive." The following year, he was engaged by UNICEF as Audrey's manager—"to coordinate/facilitate field missions, advocacy appearances, media interviews and participation and meetings and conferences of Goodwill Ambassador Audrey Hepburn, and [to] assist Miss Hepburn in the preparation and execution of these activities on behalf of UNICEF." She could not have managed this important work without him, and UNICEF recognized this. In 1989, Rob was paid $2,200, and from September to December 1991 another $1,500—token compensation for the countless details he supervised and the interference he ran on Audrey's behalf. "Audrey wanted Rob to travel with her," according to Christa. "I arranged the basics for the programs in each place, and Rob protected her from unreasonable demands and kept her on schedule, too. She wanted things properly prepared, and he was a great help in that regard."

"Each time [we traveled]," he recalled, "she deliberated carefully over whether she could make a difference. She studied endlessly and became extremely knowledgeable. But she was not trying to be Mother Teresa or vying for sainthood."

After a brief return to Tolochenaz, Audrey gave an international press conference in Geneva on April 6, and then she and Rob hurried to Turkey for three days, where there was a massive UNICEF effort to immunize children against measles, tuberculosis, tetanus, whooping cough, diphtheria and polio. She visited clinics and helped with injections before speaking to reporters about epidemics that unnecessarily kill hundreds of millions of children annually. A whirlwind journey to Los Angeles for the Oscar telecast followed; she and Gregory Peck gave awards, and she insisted on making time for more than fifteen interviews to bring UNICEF's work to greater public awareness in California.

Readers of *Vogue* saw her photo in an advertisement for Revlon that year. For this, Audrey received a fee of $50,000—to which she added another $10,000 and donated the entire sum to the victims of the Armenian earthquake.

For the remainder of 1988, she was on field missions to the poor of Venezuela and Ecuador, and she spearheaded fund-raising events in Austria, Finland, Germany, the Netherlands, Switzerland, Italy, Ireland and America. By Christmas, she had visited fourteen countries and raised more than $22 million. In the days of movie promotions, she had agreed to only three or four interviews in a day; for UNICEF, she did no less than fifteen daily in New York and Washington and at least ten elsewhere. When someone expressed admiration for the sacrifices she was making, her response was swift: "It's not a sacrifice! A sacrifice means you give up something you want for something you don't want. This is no sacrifice, it's a gift I am receiving."

During these five busy years, she was no less anxious in front of crowds than before. "I get very nervous, you know, when I have to speak at these conferences." Those who were with her took note of her anxiety, her shaking hands, her dry mouth. "The whole thing terrified me, and still does. Acting is something quite different from getting up in front of people over and over again in so many countries. Speaking is something that is terribly important."

Audrey was no less anxious about television interviews. Karen Cadle, a successful independent producer, booked stars on the *Hour Magazine* television program from 1980 to 1988. At the beginning of Audrey's work for UNICEF, and just before the show ended its run, Karen approached Audrey about appearing. "We met at a Los Angeles hotel," Karen recalled. "I thought she was a remarkable woman, but I also found her shy, introverted, quiet and a bit scared about the idea of coming on the program." But because it would benefit UNICEF's cause, Audrey agreed. "Of all the stars and all the notable persons we booked over eight years," Karen continued, "she was the most anticipated person of all."

When Audrey arrived at the studio for the taping, she said to Karen, "I just need two things: a cup of coffee and—do you have any bourbon?"

"I realized then just how nervous she was. But we came up with what she wanted, and Audrey felt better. Still, she needed a lot of reassurance before she went on the show. I was happy to give her that, and I told her that the audience would love her—which of course they did. I then told the host of the show to begin the conversation gently, to talk about Audrey's two grown sons and then move on briefly to her movies before spending the majority of the time speaking about UNICEF.

"But it was plain to see that Audrey was never comfortable before an audience. She did relax for one moment, however. She had to smile at the host's first question, which was 'Tell me about your two daughters.' " After the first segment of the show had been taped and there was an interval, Audrey came to Karen and asked, "Did I do anything wrong?"

AUDREY OFTEN REMINDED listeners that the specific problems that caused children so much suffering came from greater causes than famine, drought, floods or any natural disaster. "We are dealing with a far more ominous threat than sickness and death," she said in April 1989.

We are dealing with the dark side of humanity—selfishness, avarice, aggression. All this has already polluted our skies, emptied our oceans, destroyed our forests and extinguished thousands of beautiful animals. Are our children next? . . . It is no longer enough to vaccinate them or give them food and water and only cure the symptoms of man's tendency to destroy everything we hold dear.

Audrey's voice broke, and she brushed away a tear before continuing: "Whether it be famine in Ethiopia, excruciating poverty in Guatemala and Honduras, civil strife in El Salvador or ethnic massacre in the Sudan, I saw but one glaring truth: these are not natural disasters but man-made tragedies for which there is only one man-made solution—*peace*." She never lost sight of the larger issue: even UNICEF's programs would be threatened as long as nation continued to lift sword against nation.

In February 1989, Audrey visited Guatemala, Honduras, El Salvador and Mexico, supervising the openings of new drinking water systems in slum areas and surveying rural health centers. She also met with the vice president of Guatemala, the president of Honduras and the president of El Salvador and offered specific programs to benefit the children of Central America. In April, she appeared before the House Foreign Operations Sub-Committee and the House Select Sub-Committee on World Hunger. "There is no deficit in human resources," she said in a strong voice. "There is only a deficit in human will."

That same month, she spent five days in the Sudan, where she found a malnourished boy of fourteen lying on an earthen floor. "He had acute anemia, respiratory problems and edema—swelling of the limbs," she said later. "And that was exactly the same way I finished the war." Audrey also supervised deliveries of food and medical supplies from Khartoum to Kosti. According to UNICEF archives, "she also traveled the difficult roads to the rebel-held Southern Sudan, where she met with rebel leaders." She then visited camps for refugees.

There was one final role she accepted in a commercial film. Just after her sixtieth birthday, in early summer 1989, Audrey received her usual fee of $1 million for a few days of work in Steven Spielberg's romantic fantasy *Always*. Dressed in a plain white sweater and white pants, she portrayed Hap, an angelic guide to a young pilot (Richard Dreyfuss) who has just died in an airplane accident.

"You've had your life, and anything you do just for yourself is a waste of spirit," she says, urging him to return unseen to earthly life to help others and to free himself from painful memories. Without heavy makeup to cover the lines of character and age around her eyes and mouth, and with her chestnut hair drawn back and tied at the neck, Audrey was a figure of radiant simplicity in a film candied with the usual Hollywood brand of bogus mysticism. Speaking almost in a whisper, and with the accent of wisdom instead of large gestures or expressions, she was quietly credible as a guide to a mysterious life beyond expectations.

At the same time, she was looking for a text that could be set to music—as in Macao and Tokyo, that had been a way to raise substantial funds for UNICEF. She wanted something that would not require her to attend a gala dinner and, wearing a stunning Givenchy gown, solicit large donations from wealthy patrons. Instead, at her suggestion, UNICEF offered to commission the composer and conductor Michael Tilson Thomas to create a concert piece. Audrey suggested that they might somehow use *The Diary of Anne Frank*. "I was exactly the same age as Anne Frank," she said. "We were both ten when war broke out and fifteen when the war finished. I was given the book in Dutch. I read it, and it destroyed me. This was my life."

"We both reread *The Diary of Anne Frank* and highlighted our favorite passages," he recalled, "and then we sent them to each other." On February 28, 1990, Audrey wrote out forty pages of excerpts from the diary and posted them to Michael; she then made a tape recording. "I listened to her reading," Tilson Thomas added, "and I developed the idea of composing the kind of music that could be a counterpart to her voice and intonation."

They met several times during the late summer and early autumn of 1989, mostly in Miami Beach, where Tilson Thomas resided during the months of his annual commitment as director of the New World Symphony, which he founded in 1987. "After I began to organize the text, Audrey and I discussed how much the libretto would refer to the Holocaust. It had to make that connection, of course, but we wanted to stress the overall hopefulness of the book." The piece was, after all, to be used for a UNICEF benefit, and they worked each day to emphasize the theme of the optimism of childhood. "The Anne Frank spirit was forgiving," said Tilson Thomas. "This is not a grim, horrific piece, although it is sad and disturbing. Anne is a special person, a wonderful spirit, even though we know she had an unhappy ending." For Audrey, "She is certainly a symbol of the child in very difficult circumstances, which is what I devote all my time to now. She transcends her death."

Once his composition was complete, Tilson Thomas played a piano version for Audrey, who liked it enormously—"but she was afraid of it at the same time," he added, "because at last it dawned on her that she would have to do this in performance. Some parts were very intricate for her vocal entrance and exit, even though I had tried to write so that there was some leeway for her. Nevertheless, it was tricky, especially for people who don't read music. But we worked hard and finally got it together." Above all, Audrey appreciated that the composition was musically dramatic and evocative, and she would not be required to act it. "She was very firm about that," the composer recalled. "She did not want to try to be—or to sound like—Anne Frank, but rather to read it sympathetically."

During her working sessions and rehearsals with Michael Tilson Thomas, Audrey confided her thoughts about working for UNICEF. "I was so lucky in my career, from the very start," she said. "I didn't know much of anything when I began, but I got parts in which I could pretty much just be myself. Then all this stardom and celebrity took off. But what is the purpose of all that if you don't do something constructive with it?"

They presented the world premiere of his composition *From*

the Diary of Anne Frank on March 12, 1990, in Philadelphia and then performed the work in Chicago, Houston, New York and London. Reviews of both the work and the performance were most enthusiastic, and music critics everywhere declared it an important composition that belonged in the standard catalog.

That year, Audrey was asked to be the host for a documentary series of television programs about the great gardens of the world, and so she traveled from April to June for the filming—in England, France, the United States, Japan, the Netherlands, Italy and the Dominican Republic. The producers at Public Broadcasting presumed that she would require a team of people accompanying her: a personal assistant, a hairdresser, a makeup artist, a wardrobe mistress. They also knew that those people would of course add several hundred thousand dollars to the budget.

But as they were trying to raise the money, producer Janis Blackschleger had a phone call from Audrey: "You know, I was thinking—if you could get me a hair dryer every fourth day wherever we are, and an ironing board and an iron, I'll do my own hair and I'll do my own makeup and I'll do my own wardrobe." Blackschleger protested, but Audrey laughed: "No, no—I like to iron!"

And that was how she saved the company an enormous amount of money—doing all her own chores while she traveled with the crew for three months. "She was always on time and ready to work," recalled Blackschleger. "She could give lessons on celebrity behavior." *Gardens of the World* was a miniseries aimed at television release in 1991, but then it was decided to expand it to eight segments. By that time, Audrey was unable to do additional commentary, nor to introduce viewers to the lush gardens. The series was finally broadcast after she died.

To no one's surprise, it was then learned that Audrey had donated her fee to UNICEF. She had loved walking among the great gardens for this series, which brought back memories of her summer when she had toured gardens on the English coast with her mother—and of course, she loved her gardens at La Paisible. Careful not to upstage the flowers, she wore only the simplest outfits, and her delivery of the text was both natural and full of quiet enthusiasm.

A FUND-RAISING CONFERENCE and musical gala brought her to Oslo, on August 29, 1990. After addressing the Elie Wiesel Foundation for Humanity, Audrey was asked to present the great mezzo-soprano Frederica von Stade to the audience at a benefit concert.

"How would you like to be introduced?" she asked the singer.

"As Flicka," she replied, using the nickname known to all her friends and fans. "Backstage, Audrey and I spoke mostly about our children," she recalled years later. "And it was great fun for me to tell her that, when I was about eighteen or nineteen and working as a salesgirl at Tiffany's in New York, she came in to pick up an order of printed stationery, and I waited on her. That was a day I never forgot!"

Before, during and after these engagements, Audrey continued her travels—most remarkably, to the provinces of Vietnam and to the slums of Thailand and Bangladesh, where she discussed programs for homeless children, for the eradication of slums and for women's rights. "My task is to inform, to create awareness," she told a journalist who challenged her effectiveness. "It would be nice to be an expert on education, economics, politics, religion, traditions and culture. I'm none of those. But I am a mother, and I will travel." When she saw a need somewhere in the world, she telephoned Christa Roth in Geneva, or their colleagues in New York: "Why not send me?"

For Audrey, the matter was simple: "Giving is living. If you stop wanting to give, there's nothing more to live for."

Chapter Seventeen

1991–1993

ON APRIL 22, 1991, the Film Society of Lincoln Center, New York, paid tribute to Audrey Hepburn. Excerpts from her films were screened, and there were laudatory comments from some of her co-stars and directors. "I think it's quite wonderful," she said when she rose to speak after the prolonged applause, "that this skinny broad could be turned into a marketable commodity."

"I never thought of myself as beautiful," the skinny broad told an interviewer at the time. "I'd like not to be so flat-chested. I'd like not to have such angular shoulders, such big feet, and such a big nose." But then she seemed embarrassed and said, "When you see what is happening in the world, it's so trivial to talk about looks. Actually, I'm very grateful for what God has given me. And there's a lot more—so much more—that I must do!" Asked if she would like to make more movies, she replied, "It was fun once—but it wouldn't be fun now." That season, as the tributes and award citations accumulated, Audrey was hailed as one of the finest actresses in American film history.

But she was not an American actress. She never took American citizenship, she never owned a home in the United States, she was never a member of the American movie community. Like some of the great European stars—perhaps most notably Greta Garbo, Marlene Dietrich and Ingrid Bergman—she worked for American companies. Garbo and Bergman had made films in Sweden before coming to America, and Dietrich was well established in the German cinema, but Audrey was not known to American audiences before *Roman Holiday*.

Although her accent was less pronounced than those European women, she had a similar kind of understated European elegance and a slight air of detachment, which she used as an effectively alluring quality. Garbo and Dietrich, whatever their talents, carefully calculated their public personae and doled them out in morsels of meticulously controlled photographic and cinematic images: everything was for effect, and their stardom was perhaps very much a matter of lighting. Both women eventually retreated into a kind of eremitical privacy, sad most of all because they deprived themselves of any real human communion for a long time. Having presented themselves as if they had the motto "Nothing is as attractive as indifference," they became the ultimate casualties of the remote illusions with which they so fully cooperated.

Bergman, on the other hand, was far more involved in the world and never relied on her beauty or her reputation to determine the variety of her roles. She had a more realistic approach to age, a far broader talent and a much greater range than Garbo or Dietrich, and her career extended so far that in fifty years she mastered five languages (Swedish, German, English, French and Italian) on stage, screen and television.

Garbo, Dietrich and Bergman were always and obviously European stars. Audrey, on the other hand, did not seem entirely European to Continental audiences; nor did she seem quite English to the British; in fact, she did not seem entirely anything, which may have been why writers relied on words like *elf*, *gazelle*, *nymph*, *gamine*, *sprite* and *doe* for their descriptions. Obviously she was a woman, or a girl-woman, but her sensuality was neither flagrant nor exploited by herself or by her employers, and when at last she got to make something like love on screen, some viewers shifted a trifle uneasily in their places. In a way, she was like Tinker Bell (James Barrie's, not Walt Disney's): her origins were shrouded in a kind of ethereal glow.

If her admirers considered Audrey's career, they could count only eleven films made partly or completely in Hollywood—the remaining eighteen were produced in Europe, where she always felt more at home; she came to the United States only when she had to. That did not make her a European actress or a European woman in the eyes of most American critics and moviegoers, who (whether they admitted it or not) wanted Audrey to be American. But in life, if not always in art, she was in every way a European woman.

FOR EIGHTEEN MONTHS beginning in early 1991, Audrey's work for UNICEF was primarily European fund-raising, but in September 1992, after repeated requests, she was finally permitted to visit Somalia—a country on the East African coast that was torn apart by civil war, drought, famine and political anarchy. Audrey, Rob and a small team from UNICEF landed in Mogadishu without visas, because there was no government. Nor were there roads, nor any guarantee of safe passage, since killings for the smallest materials were daily experiences. They found that the country had no electricity, no postal service, no telephones—and almost no sustenance. "She insisted on seeing the worst of the worst," according to Madeline Eisner, who was on that mission.

"The country is in total anarchy," she said after her return. "There is no infrastructure, and there have been four years of the most atrocious civil war. I thought I was prepared for what I saw, because I read the articles and saw pictures on television. But nothing can prepare you for the reality. What is an abstraction on the written page becomes a horrifying reality in person. Flying in to Somalia, I saw hundreds and hundreds of graves around every settlement and every village. Along the roads are dead animals, people like walking phantoms—and children, thousands and tens of thousands of them, who are only just barely alive. They have little shacks made of a few twigs. Children are being snuffed out every day by starvation. They disappear slowly, with no energy to swat the flies that cluster on their faces and eyelids. There were huge trucks being loaded up with the bodies of children who had died the night before."

Audrey, Rob and a small team from UNICEF went to a feeding center in Kismayo, then north to Mokomani and back to Mogadishu. From there, they went across the southern border into Kenya.

"It was a living nightmare: there were these thin, thin, thin children of all ages—small and just a little bit bigger—who to me seemed to have gone already. And their eyes were like enormous pools of—of questioning. They look at you with such—I don't quite know how to say this—as if they are asking, 'Why?' Some of the children have no light in their eyes. Most of them refuse food, because they are beyond wanting to eat or being able to eat. It is unacceptable to see children die right in front of your eyes. There were fifty-five thousand people in one refugee camp—half of them children, starving to death right before your eyes."

She then spoke more frankly and with greater passion than ever, and she opened her heart about the political situation.

"I am becoming more raw, more hurt, more angry, feeling the pain more deeply. It's really not to be believed how these people live, away from their homes in Somalia, and who knows when they can go back. The cattle are dead, the crops are gone. Families have lost their villages, their little homes. Most of all, they are losing their children every day."

Asked to comment on the political situation, she was clear:

"Politics by definition is supposed to be about people, for the welfare of people. I don't believe in collective guilt, but I do believe in collective responsibility. Somalia is our responsibility. It's certainly Britain's responsibility and the Italians' responsibility, because they colonized the country. And they should be doing more—they have an obligation to those people from whom they benefited for so many years.

"Humanitarian means human welfare and responding to human suffering—and that's what politics should be, ideally. That's what I dream about. Think about it—four hundred thousand Somalis are in refugee camps. They fled the war and hunger. And here— it's as if they came here only to die—this is really hell."

She resumed her contact with the refugees, embracing babies and their parents, encouraging children to take a little food that was available—but the children could no longer eat. "I saw a little boy, rail-thin, just sitting with a bit of cloth around him—he was just bones and eyes, and he was struggling for breath. He obviously had a respiratory infection. I just wished I could breathe for him, but while I was there, he lay down—and then he was gone."

And with that description of just one child's death, Audrey could no longer report the awfulness of it all. She broke down and wept.

"She generated hope and goodwill with dignity and compassion," said Martha Hyer Wallis, her friend from the time of *Sabrina*. "She gave so much of herself to so many people."

RETURNING TO TOLOCHENAZ in mid-October after press conferences in London to discuss their African journey, Audrey and Rob hoped for a few weeks of rest before proceeding for UNICEF activities in California, but she was feeling unwell, with stomach pains, indigestion and a colicky abdominal tenderness. Local doctors could not determine a specific cause, and Audrey presumed her indisposition was due to a virus or bacteria she had contracted in Africa. She was put on a regimen of metronidazole, an antibiotic that is often effective against parasitic infections; unfortunately, this powerful medication can have unpleasant side effects, and Audrey suffered badly from them—nausea, violent diarrhea and peripheral neuropathy, or tingling in the hands and feet.

Her condition worsened, despite the drugs. She then decided to have tests in Los Angeles before resuming her work there. "Etiology unknown" was the first report: the source of her infirmity could not be determined. One of her physicians recommended that Audrey enter Cedars-Sinai Medical Center for a laparoscopy, a surgical examination of the interior of the abdomen and pelvis. The procedure was performed on November 1, and it revealed a widespread cancer that had begun in the appendix and enveloped her colon. A partial colectomy was performed, and Audrey was placed on intravenous feedings, with no normal ingestion of food or drink permitted. When her elder son informed her of the diagnosis and procedure, she was not surprised and remarkably calm.

In the last week of November, Audrey began the first round of chemotherapy, which she tolerated well. Recovering at the home of a friend in Beverly Hills, she was briefly optimistic—until she was overcome by sudden and severe abdominal pain, the sign of a bowel obstruction. Frightened but composed, she returned to Cedars-Sinai. On December 1, a second surgery was performed, but her disease had spread so widely that it was beyond remedy.

When she emerged from anesthesia, Sean told his mother that the interior incisions were too "irritated" from the previous surgery to operate again. "Neither the boys nor I could acknowledge that she was dying," Robert Wolders said later with admirable candor. "We perhaps made a mistake in not telling her how ill she was. I think that was very unfair to her, because Audrey was as realistic about death as she was about life. When she began to sense that she was dying, she made us promise that we would let her go when it was time. We promised, but I don't think we followed through."

She wanted desperately to go home to Tolochenaz for Christmas, but doctors warned that a routine commercial flight could be disastrous in her frail condition; still fed intravenously, she now required a morphine pump to control the agonizing pain. When he heard the details, Givenchy arranged for a private jet to collect Audrey, Sean, Rob, a nurse and the dogs and to bring them to Switzerland. They departed Los Angeles on December 19 and arrived home next afternoon. Still unable to take anything by mouth, Audrey remained in bed for most of the holiday. For all that, she insisted it was the best Christmas in her life, for she was surrounded by undiluted love.

"My one wish for Christmas would be peace," she had said. "Peace especially for the children of the world. Only then will the water we provide quench their thirst, the food nourish their bodies, the medicine make them well—and only then will they live to play and learn, and their parents will live to love them."

A few close friends were invited for the holiday, Christa Roth among them. "Frail though she was," Christa recalled, "she took a basket and distributed little presents to everyone, personal mementos. She gave me a black-and-white Givenchy scarf." Givenchy arrived, too, and Audrey asked Rob to take down a coat from a closet. "Take the blue one, Hubert," she said in a barely audible voice, "because blue's your color." She took the coat, kissed it and held it out to her friend. "I hope you will keep this coat all your life." On his flight to Paris that evening, Hubert de Givenchy, wiping away tears, kept the coat around his shoulders.

The days at La Paisible were cold but sunny. Despite the intrusive paparazzi, buzzing in their helicopters above La Paisible like vultures, Audrey insisted on trying to walk a bit each day around her beloved gardens, pointing out to Sean or Rob or the housekeeper which plants or trees would require special care. Wrapped in a sweater and down coat, she sat and inhaled the winter air, raising her head toward the sunlight and whispering, "Mmmm—delicious."

On Sunday, January 17, 1993, she made her last effort. "Oh," she whispered, "I am just so tired."

Over the following two days, Audrey slept intermittently. As she slipped in and out of consciousness, she said several times, to whomever was at her bedside, "They are expecting me . . . the Amish people . . . the angels . . . they are waiting for me . . . working in the fields." To Luca, she said, "I'm sorry, but I'm ready to go."

"My life has been so much more than a fairy tale," Audrey had said a dozen years earlier. "I've had my share of difficult moments, but it's as if there was always a *light* at the end of the tunnel."

On Wednesday, January 20, the minister who had officiated at Audrey's marriage to Mel was summoned; later, Mel arrived, too, as did Andrea. Luca was there with Sean, and the house staff, and a nurse. After some quiet prayers at Audrey's bedside, everyone left the room. Christa Roth then arrived for a brief visit and remained with her. Audrey was dozing, apparently without pain.

EXCEPT FOR TWO SCRIPTS and her Oscar statuette, Audrey Hepburn kept no relics from her career, but she did have boxes and albums full of photos that told the story of a remarkable life.

There was the seven-year-old Audrey Ruston, gazing serenely in her first passport photo, her dark hair cut short and straight, with a stylish swatch of bangs strategically combed by her mother. And there she was at nine, with the cool and elegant baroness. Her father's photo, yellowed and creased, showed him holding her hand tentatively, a distracted look clouding his features.

In other snapshots, she could be recognized as a rambunctious teenager, suddenly reed tall and lean, an apprentice dancer waiting to leap into any story—and then she was a leggy chorine, high-stepping onto the London musical stage. There was a tender image of her leaning on the ample bosom of Colette, who was reading aloud from Jacques Porel's *Fils de Réjane*. And of course, there were photos of Audrey as Gigi, wide-eyed and innocent, but determined that she could not be bought, thank you. Photos of Princess Ann, variously elegant and playful during her Roman holiday, were neatly arranged with production stills from *Sabrina*, in which she had worn her first Givenchy wardrobe. In her working script for *Funny Face*, there were snaps of Audrey, all in black but for the dramatic white socks, bounding joyfully in her mod-expressive dance. And in the pages of her *My Fair Lady* script were her notes: how to make the character come to life, how to make everything better.

There, too, were the first wedding photos—the golden girl, with the chaplet of flowers, and her handsome, protective groom. And there was the great cache of glossies of her boys, albums that documented their lives from the cradle . . . and Audrey with Andrea, both of them trying against all odds . . .

But most of all, there were the dozens of still photos from *The Nun's Story*, the role and the film that gave her a lifetime of precious friendships and that forever altered something in her life—precisely what that was, she could not say at the time, but as she had written to Marie Louise Habets and Kathryn Hulme, the experience of making that film had thrust down very deep roots that might take years to flourish:

"All I can tell you is that any resemblance between the present Hepburn and the former one is purely accidental. I have seen and learned so much and have been so enriched by a milliard experiences that I am and feel a different person." In that letter, written twenty-five years before she lay dying, Audrey had written of the hardships of working in Africa, which provided her with memories from which she hoped to be enriched for years to come. "Delving into the heart and mind of Sister Luke, I have also had to dig deep down in myself . . . The seeds of all I have experienced have fallen on neatly prepared ground, and I hope will result in harvesting a better Audrey."

Years later, those who worked with her at UNICEF, and those who felt the breadth of her caring, her compassion and her effective work in Africa and around the world, knew firsthand the result of that harvest. The circle had closed; art had been enfolded into the core of her being. As she once exclaimed about her garden in full flower, so it could now at last be said of her own life: "It is all so impossibly—so wonderfully—exquisite."

INSIDE LA PAISIBLE, all was quiet as Audrey's sons, Robert Wolders and a few others tried valiantly to maintain their composure. They were about to go back upstairs, to bid a last farewell to Audrey as she lay sleeping. Then Christa summoned them, and when they entered the room, everything was still and peaceful. All traces of suffering had vanished and there was, as everyone recalled, the same indelible smile on her lips that they had known so well over the years. As Audrey had said, she was ready, and the others were waiting for her.

Audrey in 1959.

Notes

The following abbreviations have been used for certain archival sources:
Herrick Library/AMPAS: The Margaret Herrick Library at the Academy
of Motion Picture Arts and Sciences, Beverly Hills, Calif.
Hulme—Beinecke/Yale: The Kathryn C. Hulme Papers, Yale Collection
of American Literature, Beinecke Rare Book and Manuscript Library at
Yale University, New Haven, Conn.
Warner/USC: The USC Warner Bros. Archives, School of Cinema—
Television, University of Southern California, Los Angeles

CHAPTER ONE: 1929–1939

7   *On Ruston's birth:* Joseph Ruston always claimed London as his birth-
place (and so it is stated on the registration of Audrey's birth in Brussels). But he was in fact born in Bohemia of a British father. Cf. *The
British Overseas: A Guide to Records of Their Births, Baptisms, Marriages, Deaths and Burials,* 3rd ed. (London: Guildhall Library, 1994).

7   *the sad truth is:* Sean Hepburn Ferrer, *Audrey Hepburn—An Elegant
Spirit* (New York: Atria Books, 2003), p. 10.

11   *And we were sometimes:* Ian Quarles van Ufford, in *Audrey Hepburn Remembered* (television documentary), written by Suzette Winter, produced by Gene Feldman (1993).

12   *As a child:* AH, at the gala tribute to her by the New York Film Society
at Lincoln Center, Apr. 22, 1991.

13   *I became a rather moody:* The journalist Jane Wilkie, who wrote many
carefully researched articles and conducted interviews for Hollywood

movie magazines over three decades, sat down with Audrey for a long conversation sometime in 1954 or 1955. From her notes, Wilkie drafted an unpaginated essay that seems never to have been published. The Constance McCormick Papers at the University of Southern California contain the typescript of this Wilkie essay, titled "Audrey Hepburn."

13 *I didn't care for dolls:* "Princess Apparent," *Time* 62, no. 10 (Sept. 7, 1953), p. 61.

13 *I myself was born:* Alan Riding, "25 Years Later, Honor for Audrey Hepburn," *New York Times,* Apr. 22, 1991, p. C13; see also Janet Maslin, "Audrey Hepburn: Farewell to the Swan," *New York Times,* Jan. 31, 1993, p. H11.

13 *When I was little: Audrey Hepburn: In Her Own Words,* a UNICEF documentary tribute (1993).

14 *My mother had great love:* "A Tribute to Audrey Hepburn," *People Extra,* Winter 1993, p. 10.

14 *Of necessity:* Sidney Fields, "Audrey Hepburn—Success Is Not Security," *McCall's,* July 1954, p. 62.

14 *I worshiped my father:* "Tribute to Hepburn," p. 10.

14 *Leaving us:* Winter and Feldman, *Audrey Hepburn Remembered.*

14 *the most traumatic event:* Edward Klein, "You Can't Love Without the Fear of Losing," *Parade,* Mar. 5, 1989, pp. 4–6.

14 *was a wound:* Ferrer, *Elegant Spirit,* p. 32.

14 *very insecure:* "Tribute to Hepburn," p. 36.

14 *has stayed with me:* Pamela Clarke Keogh, *Audrey Style* (New York: HarperCollins, 1999), p. 53.

15 *Other kids had:* Dunne, "Hepburn Heart," p. 197.

15 *spent the war:* Ferrer, *Elegant Spirit,* p. 10.

16 *If I could just have seen him:* "Tribute to Hepburn," p. 10.

16 *On Tester, Mosley and Ruston:* See Pauline Henri, "Verge of Treason," *Searchlight* (UK), no. 171 (Sept. 1989), pp. 9–12; and articles by David Turner and John Hope in the same periodical—no. 236 (Feb. 1995), pp. 12–13, and no. 237 (Mar. 1995), pp. 14–15. See also David Pryce-Jones, *Unity Mitford: A Quest* (London: Weidenfeld & Nicolson, 1976), p. 107.

17 *On Ruston as Tester's partner:* See "The Curious Case of Dr. Tester" on David Turner's website (www.canterbury.u-net.com/page4.html). Turner is a respected historian whose specialty is the history of far-left and far-right political movements in Britain during the twentieth century.

17 *terrified:* Martin Abramson, "Audrey Hepburn," *Cosmopolitan* 139, no. 26 (Oct. 1955), p. 30.

17 *I liked the children:* Wilkie, "Audrey Hepburn."

CHAPTER TWO: 1939–1946

19   *In no way:* Sean Hepburn Ferrer, *Audrey Hepburn—An Elegant Spirit* (New York: Atria Books, 2003), p. 8.

20   *For the occasion:* Dominick Dunne, "Hepburn Heart," *Vanity Fair* 54, no. 5 (May 1991), p. 198.

20   *I saw German trucks: Audrey Hepburn Remembered,* written by Suzette Winter, produced by Gene Feldman (1993).

20   *The occupation:* Lou Pollock, "Audrey Hepburn: I Was a Woman at 13," *Photoplay,* Nov. 1956, p. 57.

21   *My real name:* AH to Leo van de Pas, Jan. 2, 1990.

21   *For eight formative years:* Lydia Lane, "Real Life Experiences Teach Audrey Hepburn Diet Values," *Los Angeles Times,* Sept. 12, 1954.

23   *Families with babies:* Quoted in Sheridan Morley, *Audrey Hepburn: A Celebration* (London: Pavilion, 1993), p. 18.

23   *I didn't know:* Pollock, "Woman at 13," p. 57.

23   *The Dutch have a gift:* E.N. Van Kleffens, *The Rape of the Netherlands* (London: Hodder & Stoughton, 1940), pp. 230, 236, 252.

25   *Don't discount:* Jane Wilkie, "Audrey Hepburn," Constance McCormick Papers, University of Southern California.

25   *Once I started:* Ibid.

26   *I designed the dances:* Ibid.

26   *The best audience:* "Audrey Hepburn," *Coronet* 35, no. 3 (Jan. 1954), p. 46.

26   *They didn't give the support:* Pollock, "Woman at 13," p. 57.

27   *But there is probably:* Ibid.

27   *The only thing I remember:* Variously told—e.g., in ibid.

27   *I remember hearing:* Ibid., p. 58.

27   *unknown to the Germans:* The account of Audrey, the paratrooper, and the Resistance street-sweeper has been variously documented—e.g., in Pollock, "Woman at 13," p. 57.

29   *We really had nothing:* Major Tony Hibbert, quoted in Mark Fielder, "The Battle of Arnhem" (2001), www.bbc.co.uk/history/war/wwtwo/battle_arnhem_01.shtml

30   *Veterans and historians:* Richard Holmes, in the introduction to A. D. Harvey, *Arnhem* (London: Cassell, 2001), pp. 8–9.

30   *After the battle of Arnhem:* During the 1951 Broadway run of the play *Gigi,* Audrey spoke from her dressing room at the Fulton Theatre about Christmas 1944. The film of this talk has been preserved by the Museum of Television and Radio in Beverly Hills, Calif.

30   *We lived in a vacuum:* Quoted in *Motion Picture,* Dec. 1967, p. 77.

31   *We kept going:* Lane, "Real Life Experiences."

31   *If you went on:* Pollock, "Woman at 13," p. 59.

31   *We lost everything:* Pauline Swanson, "Knee-Deep in Stardust," *Photoplay,* Apr. 1954, p. 102.

31   *I ran to the window:* Martin Abramson, "Audrey Hepburn," *Cosmopolitan* 139, no. 26 (Oct. 1955), p. 30.

32   *All the schools:* Natalie Gittelson, "Personalities: Audrey Hepburn," *McCall's* 116, no. 11 (Aug. 1989), p. 36.

32   *It was that wonderful:* James Roberts, "Envoy for the Starving: Audrey Hepburn," *Independent on Sunday,* Oct. 4, 1992, p. 23.

34   *I've often been depressed:* Abramson, "Audrey Hepburn," p. 30.

35   *I read the diary:* AH, on *Larry King Live* (CNN), Oct. 1991. The Amsterdam publisher Uitgeverij Contact first published the diary of Anne Frank as *Het Achterhuis* (*The Attic,* or *The Secret Annex*) in 1947; publication in many languages followed. Audrey claimed to have read galley pages in 1946. Later in life, she was offered the role of Anne Frank on stage and in film, but she found herself "emotionally incapable" of the task (John Corr, "Mindful of Her Past, Hepburn Travels the World for UNICEF," *Philadelphia Inquirer,* Feb. 8, 1990, p. F12). Susan Strasberg memorably created the part of Anne Frank on Broadway, and Millie Perkins assumed the role in a 1959 film.

35   *I had gone through:* Abramson, "Audrey Hepburn," p. 30.

Chapter Three: 1947–1951

38   Nederlands in 7 lessen: See Ellen Cheshire, *The Pocket Essential Audrey Hepburn* (Harpenden, UK: Pocket Essentials, 2004), p. 11. There were two released versions—one of seventy-nine minutes, for Holland; and another at thirty-eight minutes, for England, where it was shown as *Dutch at the Double* and in which only Audrey's last moment is preserved.

39   *dull and conventional: Today's Cinema* (UK) 74, no. 5946 (Mar. 3, 1950), p. 6.

39   *always short . . . My first class:* Mike Connolly, "Who Needs Beauty!" *Photoplay,* Jan. 1954, p. 73.

39   *the most completely exhausting:* Henry Hewes, "Broadway Postscript: Stars Who Danced," *Saturday Review of Literature,* Nov. 15, 1952, p. 28.

39   *folding our arms:* Ibid., 29.

39   *my dream was:* Alan Riding, "25 Years Later, Honor for Audrey Hepburn," *New York Times,* Apr. 22, 1991, p. C18.

40   *My technique:* William Hawkins, "Interview with Audrey Hepburn," *Dance,* Oct. 1956, pp. 17–19, 61.

41   *When I was chosen:* Lydia Lane, "Find Your Best Weight and Stick to It, Counsels Audrey Hepburn," *Los Angeles Times,* Mar. 29, 1953, p. C8.

41   *one of the maddest:* George W. Bishop, "Christmas Shows: Early Films Burlesqued—Musical from America," *Daily Telegraph,* Dec. 23, 1948.

42   *Everyone in the company:* *Times* (London), May 19, 1949.

42   *tropical forests:* Ibid.

42   *stood out:* Eric Braun, "The Hepburn Quality Re-visited," *Films* (UK) 1, no. 9 (Aug. 1981), p. 20.

42   *We all noticed:* Ibid., p. 21.

42   *I have the biggest:* "J'ai les plus beaux nichons sur scène, et tout le monde n'a d'yeux que pour cette fille qui n'en a même pas!" Cited on the French website Audrey.hepburn.free.fr/theatre/sauce_tartare/sauce_tartare.htm (trans. DS).

42   *had the feeling:* ". . . la sensation d'avoir fait une véritable découverte quand j'ai trouvé Audrey. Elle était d'une telle fraîcheur, d'une beauté immatérielle." Ibid.

43   *As far as the dancing:* Ibid.

45   *I worked like an idiot:* Dominick Dunne, "Hepburn Heart," *Vanity Fair* 54, no. 5 (May 1991), p. 198.

47   *He taught me:* Gene Ringgold, "Audrey Hepburn," *Films in Review* 22, no. 10 (Dec. 1971), p. 587.

47   *What's most important:* "Princess Apparent," *Time* 62, no. 10 (Sept. 7, 1953), p. 62.

48   *For three months:* Mervyn LeRoy (as told to Dick Kleiner), *Take One* (New York: Hawthorne Books, 1974), p. 171.

48   *Associated British Pictures Corporation:* On its history, see Vincent Porter, "All Change at Elstree: Warner Bros., ABPC and British Film Policy, 1945–1961," *Historical Journal of Film, Radio and Television* 21, no. 1 (2001), pp. 5–35.

49   *There's a girl:* Stanley Holloway, *Wiv a Little Bit o' Luck* (London: Leslie Frewin, 1967), p. 161.

50   *If you add them all up:* Sidney Fields, "Audrey Hepburn—Success Is Not Security," *McCall's,* July 1954, p. 62.

50   *He had it in:* *Audrey Hepburn Remembered,* written by Suzette Winter, produced by Gene Feldman (1993).

51   *including that pretty:* *New York Times,* Nov. 4, 1952, p. 33.

51   *the rest of the cast:* Lindsay Anderson, ed., *Making a Film: The Story of "Secret People"* (London: Allen & Unwin, 1952), p. 21.

53   *No, it's my job:* Ibid., p. 81.

53   *If an actress:* Ibid.

54   *get sick:* Ibid.

54   *Audrey Hepburn combines:* *Variety,* Feb. 13, 1952.

55   *more interested in being:* Roger Cowe, "Wheeler-dealer Who Rose to Greater Fortune in the Thatcher Years," *Guardian* (UK), Nov. 3, 2004.

CHAPTER FOUR: 1951

59   *Witless . . . frenetic: New York Times,* May 29, 1954, p. 13; see also *Variety,* Feb. 12, 1952; and *Monthly Film Bulletin* 21, no. 243 (Apr. 1954), p. 58.

61   *delighted and told her:* Gilbert Miller, "The Search for Gigi," *Theatre Arts* 36, no. 7 (Jul. 1952), p. 50.

61   *losing himself in:* Anita Loos, *A Cast of Thousands* (New York: Grosset & Dunlap, 1977), p. 161.

62   DO NOT CAST: Ibid.

62   *Colette and I:* Miller, "Search for Gigi," pp. 50–51.

63   *and asked me:* AH to Hedda Hopper, Sept. 11, 1953 (published in Hopper's syndicated column—e.g., *Los Angeles Herald-Examiner*).

63   *I started walking:* Sidney Fields, "Audrey Hepburn—Success Is Not Security," July 1954, p. 62.

63   *I tried to explain:* "Princess Apparent," *Time,* vol. 62, no. 10 (Sept. 7, 1953), p. 61.

66   *very alert:* Pamela Clarke Keogh, *Audrey Style* (New York: HarperCollins, 1999), p. 65.

66   *I came back:* Ibid., p. 66.

67   *The Hepburn test:* William Wyler to Richard Mealand, Oct. 12, 1951, William Wyler Collection, Herrick Library/AMPAS.

67   *We were fascinated:* Paul Holt, "Audrey Hepburn—The Star in Our Lifetime," *Picturegoer* 26, no. 961 (Oct. 3, 1953), p. 8.

67   *On the ABPC/Paramount deal:* See Vincent Porter, "All Change at Elstree: Warner Bros., ABPC and British Film Policy, 1945–1961," *Historical Journal of Film, Radio and Television* 21, no. 1 (2001), p. 12.

68   *When Gilbert saw her:* Loos, *Cast,* p. 162.

68   *I can't say just how:* Martin Abramson, "Audrey Hepburn," *Cosmopolitan* 139, no. 26 (Oct. 1955), p. 29.

70   *I'm frightened:* Sidney Fields, "Audrey Hepburn—Success Is Not Security," *McCall's,* July 1954, p. 61.

70   *The role of Gigi:* Loos, *Cast,* p. 164.

70   *Audrey was terribly frightened:* "Princess Apparent," p. 62.

71   *On the suicide at the Blackstone Hotel and AH's introduction to David Niven:* See Graham Lord, *Niv: The Authorised Biography of David Niven* (London: Orion, 2003), pp. 219–20.

72   *a young actress: New York Times,* Nov. 26, 1951, p. 20.

72   *a candid innocence:* New York Herald-Tribune, Nov. 26, 1951.

72   *unquestionable beauty:* New York World-Telegram and Sun, Nov. 26, 1951.

72   *an orgy:* Graham Payn and Sheridan Morley, eds., The Noël Coward Diaries (London: Weidenfeld & Nicolson, 1989), p. 192.

72   *She was basically:* Sean Hepburn Ferrer, Audrey Hepburn—An Elegant Spirit (New York: Atria Books, 2003), p. 209.

72   *a star who:* Ibid., p. xiii.

73   *Oh, dear:* "Princess Apparent," p. 62; see also Helen Markel Herrmann, "Half Nymph, Half Wunderkind," New York Times Sunday Magazine, Feb. 14, 1954.

CHAPTER FIVE: 1952

76   *My career:* "A Tribute to Audrey Hepburn," People Extra, Winter 1993, p. 21.

76   *Audrey Is a Hit:* Life 31, no. 103 (Dec. 10, 1951), pp. 103–107.

76   *Audrey Hepburn—Her Star:* Look, Feb. 12, 1952.

80   *The picture was kind of:* Gary Fishgall, Gregory Peck: A Biography (New York: Scribner's, 2002), p. 172.

81   *This was a girl way ahead:* Edith Head and Jane Kesner Ardmore, The Dress Doctor (Boston: Little, Brown, 1959), p. 118.

81   *But what impressed me:* Edith Head and Paddy Calistro, Edith Head's Hollywood (New York: Dutton, 1983), p. 102.

82   *First apply:* Wally Westmore, memorandum on makeup requirements for AH for Roman Holiday, May 31, 1952, production files, Herrick Library/AMPAS.

83   *I went to work:* AH, on Larry King Live (CNN), Apr. 19, 1989.

84   *She is that:* Helen Markel Herrmann, "Half Nymph, Half Wunderkind," New York Times Sunday Magazine, Feb. 14, 1954, p. 26.

84   *nothing mean or petty:* Pamela Clarke Keogh, Audrey Style (New York: HarperCollins, 1999), p. 69.

84   *always put me at ease:* Gene Ringgold, "Audrey Hepburn," Films in Review 22, no. 10 (Dec. 1971), p. 590.

85   *as regal:* "Tribute to Hepburn," p. 74.

85   *The Audrey Hepburn credit:* Sam Frey (Paramount Pictures) to Maurice Lodi Fe (Rome office), Jan. 14, 1953, production files, Herrick Library/AMPAS.

87   *That was fine:* Eddie Albert, at the American Film Institute Tribute to William Wyler, Mar. 14, 1976.

89   *We are not drawing:* Wyler to Richard Mealand, Oct. 12, 1951, Roman Holiday production files, Herrick Library/AMPAS.

91   *When we got to the last scene:* Often cited; here, a conflation of Speck, p. 41, and Stephanie Mansfield, "Audrey Hepburn, Will of the Wisp," *Washington Post,* Aug. 5, 1985, p. B2.

92   *It appears to be possible:* James Hanson to Henry Henigson, July 8, 1952, *Roman Holiday* production files, Herrick Library/AMPAS.

93   *Our present plan:* James Hanson to Henry Henigson, Aug. 12, 1952, Herrick Library/AMPAS.

94   *We decided it was:* Mike Connolly, "Who Needs Beauty!" *Photoplay,* Jan. 1954, p. 73.

CHAPTER SIX: 1953

95   *We were there:* Arthur Wilde to DS, Nov. 15, 2004.

96   *I couldn't possibly play:* Joshua Logan, *Movie Stars, Real People, and Me* (New York: Delacorte, 1978), p. 97.

99   *Hepburn now realized:* Edith Head and Paddy Calistro, *Edith Head's Hollywood* (New York: Dutton, 1983), p. 104.

100   *the biggest thing:* Richard Buckle, ed., *Self-Portrait with Friends: The Selected Diaries of Cecil Beaton, 1926–1974* (London: Weidenfeld & Nicolson, 1979), p. 262.

100   *At last the daughter appeared:* Ibid.

101   *Melchor Gaston Ferrer:* The trajectory of Mel Ferrer's career has been succinctly documented by, e.g., Gene Ringgold, "Audrey Hepburn," *Films in Review* 22, no. 10 (Dec. 1971), pp. 590–92. Ferrer wrote with touching (if unrealistic) pride about the La Jolla Players in *Theatre Arts,* Aug. 1951, p. 4.

102   *It was fascinating:* Radie Harris, *Radie's World: The Memoirs of Radie Harris* (London: W. H. Allen, 1975), p. 58.

103   *like a very fragile animal:* Quoted in Pamela Clarke Keogh, *Audrey Style* (New York: HarperCollins, 1999), p. 16.

104   *There are few people I love more:* Gloria Emerson, "Co-Stars Again: Audrey Hepburn and Givenchy," *New York Times,* Sept. 8, 1965, p. 54.

104   *she always knew:* Quoted in Stefania Ricci, ed., *Audrey Hepburn: Una donna, lo stile* (Milan: Mondadori, 1999), p. 159.

105   *A remarkable young actress: New York Herald Tribune,* Aug. 28, 1953.

105   *Paramount's new star:* "Princess Apparent," *Time* 62, no. 10 (Sept. 7, 1953), p. 63.

105   *Through some private magic: New Yorker,* Aug. 29, 1953.

105   *Miss Hepburn is an actress:* Ibid.

105   *I have to try:* "David Lewin's Spotlight," *Daily Express* (London), July 29, 1953.

106 *This is the most trying time:* Paul Holt, "Audrey Hepburn—The Star in Our Lifetime," *Picturegoer* 26, no. 961 (Oct. 3, 1953), p. 9.

106 *I can't do it:* Ibid.

106 *When I get married:* Sidney Fields, "Audrey Hepburn—Success Is Not Security," *McCall's,* July 1957, p. 63.

107 *I had to:* Ibid.

108 *I quickly became aware:* Martha Hyer Wallis to DS, Nov. 2, 2004. See also Wallis, *Finding My Way: A Hollywood Memoir* (HarperSanFrancisco, 1990), pp. 49–50.

108 *Bogart thought:* Maurice Zolotow, *Billy Wilder in Hollywood* (New York: G. P. Putnam's Sons, 1977), p. 252.

110 *Audrey embodied everything:* Bob Thomas, *Golden Boy: The Untold Story of William Holden* (New York: St. Martin's Press, 1983), p. 103.

111 *I really fell in love:* Ibid., pp. 104, 176.

111 *They had great careers:* Charlotte Chandler, *Nobody's Perfect: Billy Wilder, A Personal Biography* (New York: Simon & Schuster, 2002), p. 174.

111 *How old is your daughter:* Cameron Crowe, *Conversations with Wilder* (New York: Knopf, 1999), p. 10.

111 *a Nazi son of a bitch:* A. M. Sperber and Eric Lax, *Bogart* (New York: William Morrow, 1997), p. 493.

111 *Maybe you should:* Thomas, *Golden Boy,* p. 85.

111 *I hated:* Jeffrey Meyers, *Bogart: A Life in Hollywood* (Boston: Houghton Mifflin, 1997), p. 284.

112 *but to do it discreetly:* Crowe, *Conversations,* p. 10.

112 *On the problem of photographing Audrey's neck and shoulders:* "Remind Charles Lang about watching the bony structure in Hepburn's neck." Production manager Frank Caffey, memorandum to unit production manager Harry Caplan, Sept. 25, 1953, Paramount Studios, *Sabrina* archives, Herrick Library/AMPAS.

112 *It was still being written:* Crowe, *Conversations,* p. 52.

113 *They showed the film:* Amy Fine Collins, "When Hubert Met Audrey," *Vanity Fair,* no. 424 (Dec. 1995), p. 181.

113 *Edith always thought:* Ibid., p. 182.

CHAPTER SEVEN: 1954

115 *Ondine:* A good history and summary of *Ondine* appears in Joseph T. Shipley, *The Crown Guide to the World's Great Plays from Ancient Greece to Modern Times* (New York: Crown, 1984), pp. 268–70.

116 *almost in a panic:* Sidney Fields, "Audrey Hepburn—Success Is Not Security," *McCall's,* July 1954, p. 63.

117 *I think Hepburn:* Jared Brown, *The Fabulous Lunts: A Biography of Alfred Lunt and Lynn Fontanne* (New York: Atheneum, 1986), p. 385.

117 *We had the chance:* Robert Anderson to DS, several letters in 1995.

118 *I am able:* Margot Peters, *Design for Living: Alfred Lunt and Lynn Fontanne—A Biography* (New York: Knopf, 2003), p. 253.

118 *He did not respond:* Marian Seldes, *The Bright Lights* (Boston: Houghton Mifflin, 1978), p. 127.

118 *Mel had done:* Marian Seldes to DS, May 4, 2005.

119 *That wasn't jealousy:* Ibid., p. 254.

119 *On Audrey's meeting with Sherwood in New York:* See Brown, *Fabulous Lunts*, p. 389.

120 *Audrey Hepburn gives:* Brooks Atkinson, "First Night at the Theatre," *New York Times*, Feb. 19, 1954, p. 23.

120 *Miss Hepburn's gift: New Yorker*, Feb. 27, 1954.

120 *His playing is: New York Post*, Feb. 19, 1954.

121 *Miss Hepburn gives:* Brooks Atkinson, "Magical Ondine," *New York Times*, Feb. 28, 1954, p. XI.

121 *philosophical debris:* Walter F. Kerr, in *Los Angeles Times*, Feb. 28, 1954, p. D2.

121 *Of course people:* Brown, *Fabulous Lunts*, p. 391.

121 *Yes, Madam:* Ibid., p. 390.

122 *I can't allow:* Martin Abramson, "Audrey Hepburn," *Cosmopolitan* 139, no. 26 (Oct. 1955), p. 29.

122 *It's like when:* Sergio Viotti, "Britain's Hepburn," *Films and Filming* 1, no. 2 (Nov. 1954), p. 7.

122 *I wouldn't say:* Fields, "Success," p. 61.

124 *Marriage is like:* Helen Markel Herrmann, "Half Nymph, Half Wunderkind," *New York Times Sunday Magazine*, Feb. 14, 1954, p. 24.

125 *a complete breakdown in New York: London Daily Mail*, Sept. 26, 1954.

126 *This is our marriage: Los Angeles Mirror*, Sept. 29, 1954.

126 *She was whole-hearted:* Michael Powell, *Million-Dollar Movie* (London: Heinemann, 1992), p. 144.

127 *When Jouvet paused:* Ibid., p. 276.

127 *We talked, wrote:* Ibid., pp. 252ff.

129 *We realized that Mel:* Ibid., p. 276.

130 *That was the closest:* Sean Hepburn Ferrer, *Audrey Hepburn—An Elegant Spirit* (New York: Atria Books, 2003), p. 140.

CHAPTER EIGHT: 1955–1956

132 *Audrey's career always:* Henry C. Rogers, *Walking the Tightrope: The Private Confessions of a Public Relations Man* (New York: William Morrow, 1980), pp. 216–17.

133 *I had the feeling:* King Vidor, quoted in Thomas Wiseman, "Show Talk," *London Evening Standard,* Aug. 18, 1956.

134 *I'm not worth it:* Amy Fine Collins, "When Hubert Met Audrey," *Vanity Fair,* no. 424 (Dec. 1995), p. 181.

137 *Oddly mechanical:* Bosley Crowther, in *New York Times,* Aug. 22, 1956, p. 26.

137 *She goes from smiling:* Penelope Houston, in *Sight and Sound* (UK) 26, no. 3 (Winter 1956–57), p. 152.

137 *It was of course inconceivable:* Charles Higham and Joel Greenberg, *The Celluloid Muse: Hollywood Directors Speak* (London: Angus & Robertson, 1969), p. 242.

137 *She has a rhythmic grace:* King Vidor, *King Vidor on Filmmaking* (New York: David McKay Co., 1972), p. 53.

138 *She really had no breasts:* Cardiff, p. 133.

140 *On Fred Astaire's agreement to do the picture:* See Fred Astaire, *Steps in Time* (New York: Harper, 1959), pp. 314–16.

142 *Absolutely not:* Stanley Donen, in "A Tribute to Audrey Hepburn;" *People Extra,* Winter 1993.

142 *Audrey was very serious:* Astaire, *Steps,* pp. 235–36.

144 *Audrey is a lady:* Ibid., p. 315.

145 *What do you want me:* Steven M. Silverman, *Dancing on the Ceiling: Stanley Donen and His Movies* (New York: Knopf, 1996), p. 238.

146 *She had great humor:* Pamela Clarke Keogh, *Audrey Style* (New York: HarperCollins, 1999), p. 189.

147 *What Audrey is hoping:* Edwin Schallert, "Audrey Hepburn Aims at *My Fair Lady,*" *Los Angeles Times,* Aug. 8, 1956, p. 25.

148 *On Cooper's discomfiture in* Love in the Afternoon: See Hector Arce, *Gary Cooper: An Intimate Biography* (New York: William Morrow, 1979), p. 259.

149 *He and Billy Wilder:* Charlotte Chandler, *Nobody's Perfect: Billy Wilder, A Personal Biography* (New York: Simon & Schuster, 2002), p. 190.

CHAPTER NINE: 1957

156 *A more pallid:* Jack Gould, "TV: $620,000 Isn't All," *New York Times,* Feb. 5, 1957, p. 51.

156 *they never really came close:* Jay Nelson Tuck, in *New York Post*, Feb. 5, 1957.

157 *Those are marvelous:* AH to Roger Edens, April 10, 1957.

159 *Christ will not abandon me:* Kathryn Hulme, *The Nun's Story* (Boston: Atlantic Monthly Press/Little, Brown, 1956), pp. 309–10.

160 *On the meeting of Hulme and Habets:* For background I am grateful to Debra Campbell for letting me read the text of her excellent paper, "The Nun and the Crocodile: The Stories Within *The Nun's Story*," delivered at the "Women and Religion" section of the annual meeting of the American Academy of Religion on Nov. 21, 2004.

161 *because it might do some good:* Kathryn Hulme, *Undiscovered Country: A Spiritual Adventure* (Boston: Atlantic Monthly Press/Little Brown, 1966), pp. 305–306.

161 *My neighbors say:* Marie Louise Habets to DS, from her home in Kauai, Hawaii. letter dated Feb. 9, 1984.

163 *I think you belong:* Robert Anderson to DS, Apr. 13, 1996.

164 *I realized very quickly:* Ingrid Bergman and Alan Burgess, *My Story* (New York: Delacorte, 1980), p. 350.

164 *I want you:* Cited in Donald Spoto, *Notorious: The Life of Ingrid Bergman* (New York: HarperCollins, 1997), p. 334.

166 *My novel* After: The story of Robert Anderson's affair with Hepburn and his transformation of it into fiction was told to by him to DS many times from 1974 to 2166, when he began to suffer a debilitating illness.

166 *The first thing you noticed:* Robert Anderson, *After* (New York: Random House, 1973), pp. 111, 263.

166 *She had changed:* Ibid., p. 117.

166 *I didn't think:* Ibid., p. 144.

167 *She was a very tidy:* Ibid., p. 149.

167 *she was sad:* Ibid., p. 251.

167 *the inner sadness:* Sean Hepburn Ferrer, *Audrey Hepburn—An Elegant Spirit* (New York: Atria Books, 2003), p. 210.

167 *There's not a great deal that I want:* Anderson, *After*, pp. 224–25.

167 *What I want:* Ibid., p. 228.

168 *I adored her:* Ibid., p. 251.

168 *a red bike:* Ibid., p. 174.

168 *We mustn't be apart:* Ibid., p. 253.

170 *Trying to shape:* Robert Anderson to Kathryn Hulme [n.d.] 1957, Hulme—Beinecke/Yale.

171 *She didn't really want:* David Zeitlin, "A Lovely Audrey in Religious Role," *Life* 46, no. 23 (Jun. 8, 1959), p. 144.

171 *I think we have:* AH to Fred Zinnemann, Nov. 19, 1957.

CHAPTER TEN: JANUARY–JUNE 1958

173   *We got together:* Miller, pp. 127–28. The Zinnemann interview was conducted by Arthur Nolletti Jr. and originally appeared in *Film Criticism,* no. 18–19 (Spring/Fall 1994), pp. 7–29.

174   *Eventually:* Fred Zinnemann, *Fred Zinnemann: An Autobiography* (London: Bloomsbury, 1992), p. 158.

174   *I rarely accepted:* Peggy Ashcroft (1907–91) to DS, Jan. 20, 1990.

175   *Twenty dancers:* Zinnemann, *Autobiography,* p. 162.

175   *You should do better:* Hedda Hopper, "Audrey in Belgium for 'Nun's Story,' " *Los Angeles Times,* June 23, 1958, p. C8.

175   *Fred Zinnemann arranged:* Patricia Bosworth to DS, May 10, 2005.

175   *One of the French:* Zinnemann, *Autobiography,* pp. 158, 162; see also Gabriel Miller, ed., *Fred Zinnemann: Interviews* (Jackson: University Press of Mississippi, 2005), p. 125.

176   *It was very hard:* George Haddad-Garcia, "Audrey Hepburn—Privacy Is Precious to Me," *Photoplay* 30, no. 10 (Oct. 1979), p. 58.

177   *The girls:* Renée Zinnemann (in Stanleyville, Belgian Congo) to Kathryn Hulme and Marie Louise Habets, Feb. 2, 1958, Hulme—Beinecke/Yale.

177   *After more than:* Zinnemann, *Autobiography,* p. 163.

178   *If you hear from Audrey:* Robert Anderson (in New York) to Marie Louise Habets and Kathryn Hulme, July 1, 1958.

179   *The discipline of postulants:* Mother Marie-Edmond (in Paris) to Fred Zinnemann, Apr. 30, 1959, production files for *The Nun's Story,* Warner/USC.

180   *The idea of the cloister:* Stanley Kauffmann, *A World on Film: Criticism and Comment* (New York: Harper & Row, 1966), p. 51.

181   *My mother had always impressed:* AH, in *Audrey Hepburn Remembered,* written by Suzette Winter, produced by Gene Feldman (1993).

181   *Audrey has reached:* Fred Zinnemann to Kurt Frings, May 19, 1958, production files for *The Nun's Story,* Warner/USC.

182   *Audrey is in almost:* Fred Zinnemann to Steve Trilling, May 13, 1958, production files for *The Nun's Story,* Warner/USC.

182   *I have never seen:* Zinnemann, *Autobiography,* p. 166.

183   *hungry for something more:* Hulme, *Undiscovered Country,* passim, esp. p. 306.

183   *The part:* Murray Schumach, "Audrey Hepburn Is Wary on Roles," *New York Times,* Jun. 16, 1961, p. 27.

183   *the marvelous serenity:* Zinnemann, *Autobiography,* p. 171.

183   *After looking:* Susan Schindehette, "Our Fair Lady," *People* 39, no. 4 (Feb. 1, 1993), p. 6off.

183 *All I can tell you:* AH (in Rome) to Kathryn Hulme and Marie Louise Habets, Apr. 7, 1958, in Hulme—Beinecke/Yale.

184 *Joyous happy Easter:* AH (in Rome) to Kathryn Hulme and Marie Louise Habets, April 5, 1958.

184 *forever silence:* Henry Hart, in *Films in Review* 10, no. 6 (Jun./Jul. 1959), p. 353.

184 *soaring and luminous: Variety,* May 6, 1959.

186 *I think the film: Intimate Portrait: Audrey Hepburn,* written by Suzie Galler and Ray McDonald, produced by Suzie Galler, a Galler/West Production for Lifetime Television (1996).

186 *I think my mother:* "Forever Audrey," *Town & Country* 157 (May 2003), pp. 142ff.

CHAPTER ELEVEN: JULY 1958–DECEMBER 1960

190 *I have become greatly dependent:* "A Tribute to Audrey Hepburn," *People Extra* (Winter 1993), p. 50.

191 *Many friends asked me:* Gene Ringgold, "Audrey Hepburn," *Films in Review* 22, no. 10 (Dec. 1971), p. 598.

193 *There was plenty of excitement:* Robert Anderson to Kathryn Hulme and Marie Louise Habets, July 19, 1959, Hulme—Beinecke, Yale.

196 *I'll ride that horse:* Thomas M. Pryor, "Audrey Hepburn Home to Recover," *New York Times,* Feb. 3, 1959, p. 36.

196 *in the end:* John Huston, *An Open Book* (New York: Knopf, 1980), p. 284.

196 *Ludicrous:* Stanley Kauffmann, *A World on Film: Criticism and Comment* (New York: Harper & Row, 1966), p. 147.

196 *portentousness:* Penelope Houston, in *Sight and Sound* 29, no. 3 (Summer 1960), p. 142.

196 *just a little less incongruous:* Gordon Gow, in *Films and Filming* 6, no. 10 (July 1960), p. 22.

196 *But the horses:* Bosley Crowther, in *New York Times,* Apr. 7, 1960, p. 46.

198 *comply with:* Kurt Frings to Y. Frank Freeman, May 11, 1959, Paramount Studios files on *No Bail for the Judge,* Herrick Library/AMPAS.

198 *When she read it:* Herbert Coleman to DS, Jul. 31, 1981.

199 *I still must spend:* AH to Hedda Hopper, Jun. [n.d.] 1959, Hedda Hopper Collection, School of Cinema–Television (Doheny Library), University of Southern California.

199 *Audrey looked:* Renée Zinnemann (in London) to Hulme and Habets, July 28, 1959, Hulme—Beinecke/Yale.

200 *totally disconnected:* Sean Hepburn Ferrer, *Audrey Hepburn—An Elegant Spirit* (New York: Atria Books, 2003), pp. 9–10.

200   *she realized:* Sean Hepburn Ferrer, in Fisheye Films, *My Best Friend . . . Audrey Hepburn,* BBC Television (2005).

201   *Audrey looks superb:* Kathryn Hulme (in Los Angeles) to Fred and Renée Zinnemann, Nov. 10, 1959, Hulme—Beinecke/Yale.

201   *Dearest most precious Lou:* AH (in Bürgenstock) to Marie Louise Habets, Apr. 4, 1960, Hulme—Beinecke/Yale. The two telegrams subsequently cited are in the same repository.

202   *On a brilliant Sunday: Daily Mail* (London), Oct. 23, 1964.

202   *Even when I was:* "Tribute to Hepburn," pp. 36, 38.

202   *My miscarriages:* Sheridan Morley, *Audrey Hepburn: A Celebration* (London: Pavilion, 1993), p. 103.

203   *My image will:* "Tribute to Hepburn," p. 56.

204   *I read the book:* Murray Schumach, "Audrey Hepburn Is Wary on Roles," *New York Times,* Jun. 16, 1961, p. 27.

204   *Despite her obvious: Audrey Hepburn Remembered,* written by Suzette Winter, produced by Gene Feldman (1993).

205   *I knew what to write:* Henry Mancini, production notes to *Breakfast at Tiffany's,* printed in the limited edition of the published score (1961).

206   *A movie without music:* AH to Henry Mancini [n.d.], reproduced at http://www-personal.umich.edu/~bcash/music.html.

206   *I remember our supper:* Patricia Neal, with Richard Deneut, *As I Am: An Autobiography* (New York: Simon & Schuster/London: Century Hutchinson, 1988), p. 213.

206   *The book was really:* M. Thomas Inge, ed., *Truman Capote: Conversations* (Jackson: University Press of Mississippi, 1987), pp. 159, 317.

CHAPTER TWELVE: 1961–1962

209   *It was not easy for Mel:* Joseph Barry, "Audrey Hepburn at 40," *McCall's,* July 1969, p. 125.

209   *Of course it's a problem:* Ibid.

209   *work acting:* Mel Ferrer (in Switzerland) to Kathryn Hulme and Marie Louise Habets, Mar. 7, 1961, Hulme—Beinecke/Yale.

210   *Pretense:* Ibid.

211   *I conceived:* Shirley MacLaine, *My Lucky Stars: A Hollywood Memoir* (New York: Bantam, 1995), p. 354.

214   *is about the effects of a lie:* Bernard F. Dick to DS, Aug. 17, 2005.

215   *just to tell you:* Hulme—Beinecke/Yale.

216   *She was always reluctant:* Henry C. Rogers, *Walking the Tightrope: The Private Confessions of a Public Relations Man* (New York: William Morrow, 1980), p. 217.

216 *For Christ's sake:* Ibid.

217 *Le Bret is very:* Ibid., p. 218.

217 *You know how much:* Ibid., p. 219.

218 *It was frustrating:* Ibid., p. 220.

219 *The housebreakers:* AH (in Paris) to Hedda Hopper, July 27, 1962, Hopper Collection, Herrick Library/AMPAS.

220 *I remember the day:* Bob Thomas, *Golden Boy: The Untold Story of William Holden* (New York: St. Martin's Press, 1983), p. 143.

220 *Bill had always drunk:* Ibid., p. 144.

220 *Bill was like:* Ibid.

222 *Audrey, unquestionably:* Graham Payn and Sheridan Morley, eds., *The Nöel Coward Diaries* (London: Weidenfeld & Nicolson, 1982), p. 514.

222 *But my coloring:* Joan Rattner, "Audrey Hepburn's Fashion Formula," *This Week,* syndicated in e.g. *Los Angeles Times,* Nov. 11, 1962, pp. TW14ff.

226 *Don't be nervous:* Steven M. Silverman, *Dancing on the Ceiling: Stanley Donen and His Movies* (New York: Knopf, 1996), p. 244.

227 *sensitive, reserved and quiet:* AH, in *Audrey Hepburn Remembered,* written by Suzette Winter, produced by Gene Feldman (1993).

227 Working with him: Nancy Nelson, *Evenings with Cary Grant: Recollections in His Own Words and by Those Who Knew Him Best* (New York: Morrow, 1991), p. 247.

CHAPTER THIRTEEN: 1963–1965

232 *I pray every day:* AH to Cukor, March [n.d.] 1963, George Cukor Collection, Herrick Library/AMPAS.

233 *We keep hearing:* Renée Zinnemann to Kathryn C. Hulme, Feb. 13, 1963, Hulme—Beinecke/Yale.

233 *Sean, her two-year-old:* Cecil Beaton, *Cecil Beaton's Fair Lady* (New York: Henry Holt, 1964), p. 50.

233 *speaking in Eliza's:* Ibid., p. 52.

234 *Audrey was already:* Ibid., p. 55.

234 *Having worked:* Ibid., p. 62.

234 *We must have:* Production files for *My Fair Lady,* Warner/USC.

234 *It was an ordeal:* Beaton, *Fair Lady,* p. 65.

235 *Everyone's nerves:* Ibid., p. 69.

235 *The heat is on:* AH (in Los Angeles) to Joseph Hepburn-Ruston and Fidelma Walshe Hepburn-Ruston, Aug. 9, 1963, quoted in Wendy Moonan, "To Daddy Dearest, From Audrey," *New York Times,* Aug. 22, 2003.

235   *remarkably disciplined:* Beaton, p. 74.

235   *The decision had already:* Harper MacKay, "On the Double," *Opera News* 59, no. 4 (Oct. 1994), p. 18.

236   *Audrey Hepburn could not:* André Previn, *No Minor Chords: My Days in Hollywood* (New York: Doubleday, 1991), p. 105.

238   *You could tell:* Eugene Archer, "Audrey the Fair Scales the Summit," *New York Times*, Nov. 1, 1964, p. X9.

238   *We are only just surviving:* Moonan, "To Daddy Dearest."

239   *I was too shaken:* David Lewin, "The Most Exciting Girl in the World," *Daily Mail* (London), Oct. 24, 1964.

240   *much better than:* John Gielgud to Paul Anstee, Nov. 22, 1964, in Richard Mangan, ed., *Sir John Gielgud—A Life in Letters* (New York: Arcade Publishing, 2004), p. 317.

240   *Her wit is:* Alton Cook, in *New York World-Telegram and Sun,* Oct. 22, 1964.

240   *Miss Hepburn brings:* Bosley Crowther, in *New York Times,* Oct. 22, 1964.

240   *Her qualities: New Yorker,* Oct. 31, 1964.

241   *There was a lot of difficulty:* Sean Hepburn Ferrer, in Fisheye Films, *My Best Friend . . . Audrey Hepburn*, BBC Television (2005).

242   *I split my time:* AH (in Villa Suvretta, St. Moritz) to George Cukor, Feb. 16, 1964, George Cukor Collection, Herrick Library / AMPAS.

242   *I long to get home:* Jane Warren, "The Daily News," www.thefairest-lady.com/audrey/article1.html.

243   *As for the whole:* AH (in Madrid) to George Cukor, March 8, 1964, George Cukor Collection, Herrick Library / AMPAS.

246   *She had worked without:* Michael Pearse, "Does Audrey Hepburn Still Love Her Husband?" *Modern Screen,* Dec. 1967.

246   *I have decided:* Warren, "Daily News."

CHAPTER FOURTEEN: 1966–1970

247   *She is now:* Mel Ferrer to Joseph Ruston, Jan. [n.d.] 1966, in Jane Warren "The Daily News," www.thefairestlady.com/audrey/article1.html.

247   *a thin layer:* Ibid.

247   *Having at last:* Ibid.

250   *I have drawn:* AH (in St. Tropez) to George Cukor, May 18, 1966, George Cukor Collection, Herrick Library / AMPAS.

251   *My private life:* Steven M. Silverman, *Dancing on the Ceiling: Stanley Donen and His Movies* (New York: Knopf, 1996), p. 298.

251   *I longed to get closer:* Ibid.

251   *Audrey was very:* Jacqueline Bisset to DS, May 16, 2005.

252 *I didn't even know:* Michael Pearse, "Does Audrey Hepburn Still Love Her Husband?" *Modern Screen*, Dec. 1967.

252 *She and Albie:* "A Tribute to Audrey Hepburn," *People Extra*, Winter 1993, p. 43; see also *Motion Picture*, Dec. 1967.

252 *one of the closest:* "Tribute to Hepburn," n.p.

252 *I really love Albie:* Quoted many times—e.g., Sheridan Morley, *Audrey Hepburn: A Celebration* (New York: Simon & Schuster / London: Century Hutchinson, 1988), p. 142.

253 *Mel splits his time:* AH to Joseph Ruston, Aug. 11, 1966, in Warren, "Daily News."

253 *I remember there was:* Sean Hepburn Ferrer, in *The Age* (Australia), Nov. 29, 2003.

254 *The role required:* Silverman, *Dancing*, p. 305.

254 *We are both here:* AH (in Beverly Hills) to Joseph Ruston, Feb. 6, 1967, in Warren, "Daily News."

256 *superior:* Variety, Oct. 25, 1967.

256 *beautifully modulated:* Frank Thompson, "Audrey Hepburn," *American Film* 15, no. 8 (May 1990), p. 56.

256 *It will be a long time:* Pearse, "Does Audrey Hepburn."

256 *I really quit:* Stephanie Mansfield, "Audrey Hepburn, Will of the Wisp," *Washington Post*, Aug. 5, 1985, p. B1.

256 *I could not bear to be separated:* AH, on her application to become a goodwill ambassador for UNICEF, March 1, 1988.

258 *She liked things:* J. D. Podolsky, "Life with Audrey," *People* 42, no. 18 (Oct. 31, 1994).

258 *The breakup:* Pamela Fiori, "Audrey Hepburn, A Loving Look," *Town and Country*, May 2003.

258 *My parents never argued:* Lina Das, "Another Audrey," *Mail on Sunday* (London), Nov. 7, 1999.

258 *I still don't know:* Ibid. All the quotations attributed to Mel Ferrer at this point are from this article.

259 *I am completely recovered:* Quoted by Dorothy Manners in *Modern Screen*, Oct. 1968.

259 *She never spoke badly:* Joseph Barry, "Audrey Hepburn at 40," *McCall's*, July 1969, p. 125.

259 *and the underlying feeling:* Sean Ferrer, in Fisheye Films, *My Best Friend . . . Audrey Hepburn*, BBC Television (2005).

259 *He wasn't an easy man:* Sean Ferrer, on *Larry King Live* (CNN), Dec. 24, 2003.

259 *But she stayed too long:* Ferrer, in *My Best Friend . . . Audrey Hepburn*.

259 *They were both responsible:* Ibid.

259 *Success isn't so:* Barry, "Hepburn at 40."

261 *miserable:* Ibid.

262 *My parents didn't talk:* Sean H. Ferrer, in *The Age* (Australia), Nov. 29, 2003.

262 *She maintained a warm:* Richard Corliss, "Serene Majesty," *Film Comment* 29, no. 2 (1993), p. 4.

263 *I'm in love:* Barry, "Hepburn at 40."

263 *After she met:* Ibid.

263 *Somewhere between:* Ibid.

265 *Of course we will all:* Julia Kay, "Audrey Hepburn," *Photoplay*, Apr. 1969, p. 76.

265 *She is a great:* Ibid.

265 *I worked nonstop:* Barry, "Hepburn at 40."

266 *You shouldn't tempt:* People 42, no. 18 (Oct. 31, 1994).

CHAPTER FIFTEEN: 1971–1986

271 *I'm afraid I:* Gene Ringgold, "Audrey Hepburn," *Films in Review* 22, no. 10 (Dec. 1971), p. 601.

272 *She did all the things:* Pamela Fiori, "Audrey Hepburn: A Loving Look," *Town and Country*, May 2003.

272 *She used to surprise my friends:* J. D. Podolsky, "Life with Audrey," *People* 42, no. 18 (Oct. 31, 1994).

273 *a grande dame:* Ibid.

273 *I am incredibly busy:* Bob Thomas, "Audrey Hepburn Back at Work," Associated Press, May 1975.

273 *I think you need:* "Why I Made My Comeback" [no byline], *Photoplay* 27, no. 6 (June 1976), p. 60.

274 *It's not that she was destitute:* Quoted in Podolsky, "Life."

275 *Because my husband encouraged:* Eric Gerber, "Hepburn Is Back!" *Houston Post*, Mar. 21, 1976.

275 *stomach aches:* "Champions: Robin and Marian," *Time* 107, no. 78 (Mar. 22, 1976), p. 78.

275 *I never said:* Thomas, "Back at Work."

276 *It was actually very frightening:* Gerber, "Hepburn Is Back!"

276 *Down to the smallest:* Andrew Yule, *The Man Who "Framed" the Beatles: A Biography of Richard Leske* (New York: Donald I. Fine, 1994), p. 262.

276 *Audrey could get along:* "Champions," p. 79.

276 *I've never made:* Ibid.

277 *petrified the first day:* Gerber, "Hepburn Is Back!"

277 *I hung on to both:* Lesley Salisbury, "Audrey Is the World's Fair Lady Now," *TV Times* (UK) 147, no. 44 (Oct. 31, 1992), p. 16.

277 *I think she knew:* Sean Ferrer, on *Larry King Live* (CNN), Dec. 24, 2003.

277 *Dotti was not much:* Lynn Barber, "Hepburn's Relief," *Sunday Express* (London), May 1, 1988, p. 21.

277 *What she didn't do:* Sean Hepburn Ferrer, *Audrey Hepburn—An Elegant Spirit* (New York: Atria Books, 2003), p. 13.

277 *My stepfather:* Sean H. Ferrer, in *The Age* (Australia), Nov. 29, 2003.

277 *humiliated:* Quoted in Podolsky, "Life."

278 *I was no angel:* Ibid.

278 *There's not one drop:* Jim Watters, "The Voice, the Neck, the Charm . . ." *People,* Apr. 12, 1976, p. 58.

278 *She must have matters:* Ibid., p. 63.

278 *On camera:* Ibid., p. 59.

278 *I'm not trying to be coy:* Michiko Kakutani, "Why Has She Done So Few Films in Recent Years?" *New York Times,* Jun. 4, 1980, p. C23.

279 *and regarded it:* Quoted in Fiori, "Audrey Hepburn: A Loving Look."

279 *In her mind:* Robert Wolders, in *Audrey Hepburn Remembered*, written by Suzette Winter, produced by Gene Feldman (1993).

280 *There was Irene:* Sheridan Morley, *James Mason: Odd Man Out* (London: Weidenfeld & Nicolson, 1989), p. 164.

280 *something was already happening:* Ben Gazzara, *In the Moment: My Life as an Actor* (New York: Carroll & Graf, 2004), pp. 188ff.

281 *When it happens:* Ibid.

281 *no movie kiss:* Ibid., p. 189.

281 *No promises:* Ibid., p. 191.

281 *a night filled:* Ibid.

281 *Faceless chic:* Derek Elley, in *Films and Filming* 25, no. 11 (Aug. 1979), p. 37.

281 *bloodless, ludicrous: Variety,* Jul. 4, 1979.

282 *I want to see you:* Gazzara, *Moment,* p. 205.

282 *Obviously I wasn't:* Ben Gazzara, interview by Edward Guthmann, *San Francisco Chronicle,* Nov. 18, 2004.

282 *I took note of it all:* Peter Bogdanovich, *Who the Hell's in It: Portraits and Conversations* (New York: Knopf, 2004), p. 430.

282 *Her real life:* Ibid., p. 441.

282 *to play out:* Ibid., p. 193.

283 *Audrey showed a lot:* Ibid., p. 217.

283 *Ageing doesn't bother:* George Haddad-Garcia, "Audrey Hepburn—privacy is precious to me," *Photoplay* 30, no. 10 (Oct. 1979), p. 58.

284 *I was charmed with him:* Glenn Plaskin, *Turning Point: Pivotal Moments in the Lives of America's Celebrities* (New York: BirchLane Press, 1992), p. 108.

284 *I got a kick:* Fiori, "Audrey Hepburn: A Loving Look."

284 *great collection of jewels:* Sheilah Graham, *Hollywood Revisited: A Fiftieth Anniversary Celebration* (New York: St. Martin's Press, 1985), p. 36.

285 *That's it:* Fiori, "Audrey Hepburn: A Loving Look."

285 *Mr. Bogdanovich treats:* Vincent Canby, review of *They All Laughed*, in *New York Times,* Nov. 20, 1981, p. C6.

286 *I have just brought her back: New York Times,* Aug. 22, 2003.

286 *There was some tension:* Pamela Clarke Keogh, *Audrey Style* (New York: HarperCollins, 1999), p. 188.

287 *It's the only time:* AH to Roger Young, thence to DS, May 17, 2005.

288 *Well, I'm having:* The account of *Love Among Thieves* comes from Roger Young to DS, May 17, 2005.

289 *She was not merely:* Robert Wagner to DS, May 18, 2005.

CHAPTER SIXTEEN: 1987–1990

290 *Due to my early:* AH also wrote these words in her formal application to be a goodwill ambassador for UNICEF, Mar. 1, 1988.

291 *She was so natural:* Christa Roth to DS, June 14, 2005.

291 *I guess everyone:* Bob Thomas, "Audrey Hepburn Is Back at Work," Associated Press, May 1975.

292 *I've been given:* Stuart Wavell, "Ambassador for Aid," *Guardian* (London), Mar. 29, 1988, p. 2.

293 *I have always accepted:* AH, application to UNICEF.

295 *It is a menacing emergency: Time,* Apr. 4, 1988.

295 *You can't just get up and say:* Dominick Dunne, "Hepburn Heart," *Vanity Fair* 54, no. 5 (May 1991), pp. 199–200.

297 *Never in a million:* Natalie Gittelson, "Personalities: Audrey Hepburn," *McCall's* 116, no. 11 (Aug. 1989), p. 31.

297 *No, . . . it's just the sort:* Ibid.

298 *Miss Hepburn was fully:* George Kassis, internal memo, UNICEF, Mar. 28, 1988.

298 *I was a little cynical:* Lynn Barber, "Hepburn's Relief," *Sunday Express* (London), May 1, 1988.

299 *to coordinate/facilitate:* Contract between Robert Wolders and UNICEF for work from Apr. 6 to Dec. 6, 1989.

299 *Each time [we traveled]:* Pamela Fiori, "Audrey Hepburn: A Loving Look," *Town and Country,* May 2003.

300 *It's not a sacrifice:* Barber, "Relief."

300 *The whole thing terrified me:* Dunne, "Hepburn Heart."

302 *He had acute anemia:* Lesley Garner, in *Sunday Telegraph* (London), May 26, 1991.

303   *I was exactly the same age:* Ibid.

303   *We both reread:* Michael Tilson Thomas to DS, Nov. 11, 2004.

304   *She is certainly:* Garner, in *Sunday Telegraph*.

305   *You know, I was thinking:* Pamela Clarke Keogh, *Audrey Style* (New York: HarperCollins, 1999), p. 207.

305   *She was always on time:* Ibid.

306   *How would you like:* Frederica von Stade to DS, Jul. 10, 2005.

306   *Giving is living:* AH to Harry Smith, on *CBS This Morning*, Jun. 3, 1991.

CHAPTER SEVENTEEN: 1991–1993

307   *I never thought:* Lesley Salisbury, "Audrey Is the World's Fair Lady Now," *TV Times* (UK) 147, no. 44 (Oct. 31, 1992), p. 16.

309   *The country is in:* AH's remarks on Somalia and Kenya are drawn from a UNICEF film made during the trip; from UNICEF reports; from her press conference in London, reported in *Independent on Sunday* (Oct. 4, 1992); and from a lengthy article in *Christian Science Monitor* (Oct. 5, 1992).

311   *She generated hope:* Martha Hyer Wallis to DS, Nov. 2, 2004.

311   *on Hepburn's final illness:* Many of the details may be read in Sean Hepburn Ferrer, *Audrey Hepburn—An Elegant Spirit* (New York: Atria Books, 2003), pp. 145ff.

312   *irritated:* Ibid., p. 151.

312   *Neither the boys nor I: Intimate Portrait: Audrey Hepburn,* written by Suzie Galler and Roy McDonald, directed by Suzie Galler (1996).

313   *My one wish:* "Christmas Wishes," *Harper's Bazaar*, Dec. 1990.

313   *Take the blue one:* Hubert de Givenchy, in *Newsweek* (South American ed.), Jul. 19, 1999.

314   *Mmmm:* J. D. Podolsky, "Life with Audrey," *People* 42, no. 18 (Oct. 31, 1994).

314   *They are expecting me:* Ibid.

314   *I'm sorry:* Ibid.

314   *My life has been:* Michiko Kakutani, "Why Has She Done So Few Films in Recent Years?" *New York Times*, Jun. 4, 1980, p. 623.

Bibliography

ANDERSON, LINDSAY, ED. *Making a Film: The Story of "Secret People."* London: Allen & Unwin, 1952.

ANDERSON, ROBERT. *After.* New York: Random House, 1973.

ARCE, HECTOR. *Gary Cooper: An Intimate Biography.* New York: William Morrow, 1979.

ASTAIRE, FRED. *Steps in Time.* New York: Harper, 1959.

BEATON, CECIL. *Cecil Beaton's Fair Lady.* New York: Henry Holt, 1964.

BERGMAN, INGRID, AND ALAN BURGESS. *My Story.* New York: Delacorte, 1980.

BOGDANOVICH, PETER. *Who the Hell's in It: Portraits and Conversations.* New York: Knopf, 2004.

BOOLEN, J. J., AND J. C. VAN DER DOES. *Five Years of Occupation: The Resistance of the Dutch Against Hitler-Terrorism and Nazi-Robbery.* Amsterdam: De Algemeene Vrije Illegale Drukkerji, 1946.

BOWYER, JUSTIN. *Conversations with Jack Cardiff: Art, Light and Direction in Cinema.* London: Batsford, 2003.

British Overseas, The: A Guide to Records of Their Births, Baptisms, Marriages, Deaths and Burials, 3rd ed. London: Guildhall Library, 1994.

BROWN, JARED. *The Fabulous Lunts: A Biography of Alfred Lunt and Lynn Fontanne.* New York: Atheneum, 1986.

BUCKLE, RICHARD, ED. *Self-Portrait with Friends: The Selected Diaries of Cecil Beaton, 1926–1974.* London: Weidenfeld & Nicolson, 1979.

CAPOTE, TRUMAN. *Breakfast at Tiffany's.* New York: Vintage/Random House, 1986.

CARDIFF, JACK. *Magic Hour.* London: Faber, 1996.

CASPER, JOSEPH ANDREW. *Stanley Donen*. Metuchen, N.J., and London: Scarecrow Press, 1983.

CHANDLER, CHARLOTTE. *Nobody's Perfect: Billy Wilder, A Personal Biography*. New York: Simon & Schuster, 2002.

CHESHIRE, ELLEN. *The Pocket Essential Audrey Hepburn*. Harpenden, UK: Pocket Essentials, 2004.

CLARK, G. N. *Holland and the War*. Oxford: Clarendon Press, 1941.

CROWE, CAMERON. *Conversations with Wilder*. New York: Knopf, 1999.

DEAR, IAN, AND M.R.D. FOOT, EDS. *The Oxford Companion to the Second World War*. London: Oxford University Press, 2001.

DICK, BERNARD F. *Hellman in Hollywood*. Madison and Rutherford, N.J.: Fairleigh Dickinson University Press, 1982.

EPSTEIN, NORRIE. *The Friendly Shakespeare*. New York: Viking, 1993.

FARRAR-HOCKLEY, ANTHONY. *Airborne Carpet: Operation Market Garden*. London: Macdonald, 1970.

FERRER, SEAN HEPBURN. *Audrey Hepburn—An Elegant Spirit*. New York: Atria Books, 2003.

FISHGALL, GARY. *Against Type: The Biography of Burt Lancaster*. New York: Scribner's, 1995.

———. *Gregory Peck: A Biography*. New York: Scribner's, 2002.

GAZZARA, BEN. *In the Moment: My Life as an Actor*. New York: Carroll & Graf, 2004.

GRAHAM, SHEILAH. *Hollywood Revisited: A Fiftieth Anniversary Celebration*. New York: St. Martin's Press, 1985.

GROBEL, LAWRENCE. *The Hustons: The Life and Times of a Hollywood Dynasty*, rev. ed. New York: Cooper Square Press, 2000.

HARRIS, RADIE. *Radie's World: The Memoirs of Radie Harris*. London: W. H. Allen, 1975.

HARRIS, WARREN G. *Audrey Hepburn: A Biography*. New York: Simon & Schuster, 1994.

HARVEY, A. D. *Arnhem*. London: Cassell, 2001.

HEAD, EDITH, AND JANE KESNER ARDMORE. *The Dress Doctor*. Boston: Little, Brown, 1959.

HEAD, EDITH, AND PADDY CALISTRO. *Edith Head's Hollywood*. New York: Dutton, 1983.

HIGHAM, CHARLES, AND JOEL GREENBERG. *The Celluloid Muse: Hollywood Directors Speak*. London: Angus & Robertson, 1969.

HOFSTEDE, DAVID. *Audrey Hepburn, A Bio-Bibliography*. Westport, Conn.: Greenwood Press, 1994.

HOLLOWAY, STANLEY. *Wiv a Little Bit o' Luck*. London: Leslie Frewin, 1967.

HULME, KATHRYN. *The Nun's Story*. Boston: Atlantic Monthly Press/Little, Brown, 1956.

————. *Undiscovered Country: A Spiritual Adventure.* Boston: Atlantic Monthly Press/Little Brown, 1966.

HUSTON, JOHN. *An Open Book.* New York: Knopf, 1980.

INGE, M. THOMAS, ED. *Truman Capote: Conversations.* Jackson: University Press of Mississippi, 1987.

KARNEY, ROBYN. *Audrey Hepburn: A Star Danced.* New York: Arcade, 1995.

KAUFFMANN, STANLEY. *A World on Film: Criticism and Comment.* New York: Harper & Row, 1966.

KEOGH, PAMELA CLARKE. *Audrey Style.* New York: HarperCollins, 1999.

LEROY, MERVYN (as told to Dick Kleiner). *Take One.* New York: Hawthorn Books, 1974.

LOGAN, JOSHUA. *Movie Stars, Real People, and Me.* New York: Delacorte, 1978.

LOOS, ANITA. *A Cast of Thousands.* New York: Grosset & Dunlap, 1977.

LORD, GRAHAM. *Niv: The Authorised Biography of David Niven.* London: Orion, 2003.

MACLAINE, SHIRLEY. *My Lucky Stars: A Hollywood Memoir.* New York: Bantam, 1995.

MADSEN, AXEL. *William Wyler.* New York: Thomas Y. Crowell Co., 1973.

MANGAN, RICHARD, ED. *Sir John Gielgud—A Life in Letters.* New York: Arcade Publishing, 2004.

MAYCHICK, DIANA. *Audrey Hepburn: An Intimate Portrait.* New York: Birch Lane, 1993.

MEYERS, JEFFREY. *Bogart: A Life in Hollywood.* Boston: Houghton Mifflin, 1997.

MILLER, GABRIEL, ED. *Fred Zinnemann: Interviews.* Jackson: University Press of Mississippi, 2005.

MORLEY, SHERIDAN. *James Mason: Odd Man Out.* London: Weidenfeld & Nicolson, 1989.

————. *Audrey Hepburn: A Celebration.* London: Pavilion, 1993.

NEAL, PATRICIA, WITH RICHARD DENEUT. *As I Am: An Autobiography.* New York: Simon & Schuster/London: Century Hutchinson, 1988.

NELSON, NANCY. *Evenings with Cary Grant: Recollections in His Own Words and by Those Who Knew Him Best.* New York: Morrow, 1991.

PARIS, BARRY. *Audrey Hepburn.* New York: G. P. Putnam's, 1996.

PAYN, GRAHAM, AND SHERIDAN MORLEY, EDS. *The Noël Coward Diaries.* London: Weidenfeld & Nicolson, 1982.

PETERS, MARGOT. *Design for Living: Alfred Lunt and Lynn Fontanne—A Biography.* New York: Knopf, 2003.

PLASKIN, GLENN. *Turning Point: Pivotal Moments in the Lives of America's Celebrities.* New York: Birch Lane Press, 1992.

POWELL, MICHAEL. *Million-Dollar Movie.* London: Heinemann, 1992.

PREVIN, ANDRÉ. *No Minor Chords: My Days in Hollywood.* New York: Doubleday, 1991.

PRYCE-JONES, DAVID. *Unity Mitford: A Quest*. London: Weidenfeld & Nicolson, 1976.

RICCI, STEFANIA, ED. *Audrey Hepburn: Una donna, lo stile*. Milan: Mondadori, 1999.

ROGERS, HENRY C. *Walking the Tightrope: The Private Confessions of a Public Relations Man*. New York: William Morrow, 1980.

RYAN, CORNELIUS. *A Bridge Too Far*. London: Hamish Hamilton, 1974.

SELDES, MARIAN. *The Bright Lights*. Boston: Houghton Mifflin, 1978.

SEMBACH, KLAUS-JÜRGEN. *Audrey Hepburn*. Munich: Schirmer/Mosel, 2000.

SHIPLEY, JOSEPH T. *The Crown Guide to the World's Great Plays from Ancient Greece to Modern Times*. New York: Crown, 1984.

SILVERMAN, STEVEN M. *Dancing on the Ceiling: Stanley Donen and His Movies*. New York: Knopf, 1996.

SPECK, GREGORY. *Hollywood Royalty: Hepburn, David, Stewart and Friends at the Dinner Party of the Century*. New York: Birch Lane, 1992.

SPERBER, A. M., AND ERIC LAX. *Bogart*. New York: William Morrow, 1997.

SPOTO, DONALD. *The Dark Side of Genius: The Life of Alfred Hitchcock*. Boston: Little, Brown & Co., 1983.

————. *Notorious: The Life of Ingrid Bergman*. New York: HarperCollins, 1997.

THOMAS, BOB. *Golden Boy: The Untold Story of William Holden*. New York: St. Martin's Press, 1983.

VAN KLEFFENS, E. N. *The Rape of the Netherlands*. London: Hodder & Stoughton, 1940.

VERMILYE, JERRY. *The Complete Films of Audrey Hepburn*. New York: Citadel/Carol, 1998.

VIDOR, KING. *King Vidor on Filmmaking*. New York: David McKay Co., 1972.

WALKER, ALEXANDER. *Audrey: Her Real Story*. London: Weidenfeld & Nicolson, 1994.

WALLIS, MARTHA HYER. *Finding My Way: A Hollywood Memoir*. HarperSanFrancisco, 1990.

WARMBRUNN, WERNER. *The Dutch under German Occupation*. London: Oxford University Press, 1963.

WILLOUGHBY, BOB. *Audrey: An Intimate Collection*. London: Vision On, 2002.

WOODWARD, IAN. *Audrey Hepburn, Fair Lady of the Screen*. London: W. H. Allen, 1984.

YULE, ANDREW. *The Man Who "Framed" the Beatles: A Biography of Richard Lester*. New York: Donald I. Fine, 1994.

ZINNEMANN, FRED. *Fred Zinnemann: An Autobiography*. London: Bloomsbury, 1992.

ZOLOTOW, MAURICE. *Billy Wilder in Hollywood*. New York: G. P. Putnam's Sons, 1977.

Index